1001 All-Natural Secrets To A Pest-Free Property

BY
DR. MYLES H. BADER

IF THEY ARE

FLYING, CRAWLING, BURROWING OR SNEAKING IN

THIS BOOK HAS THE SOLUTION

1001 All-Natural Secrets
To A Pest-Free Property

By

Dr. Myles H. Bader

Illustrations by Jason Herbert

Printed in the United States of America
First Printing September 2003

A WORD ABOUT THE AUTHOR

Known as the *"Wizard of Food"* as well as *"The Buggy Professor"* Dr. Bader has been a guest on over 5,000 radio and television shows in the United States and Canada and is internationally recognized as a leader in the Preventive Care and Wellness fields. Recent appearances on television shows include Help at Home, The Food Channel, The Oprah Winfrey Show, The Discovery Channel, Crook and Chase, America's Talking, Trinity Broadcasting, QVC, Smart Solutions, Help at Home, NBC, HGTV, etc.

Dr. Bader has studied extensively in the field of zoology (bugs and critters) before receiving his Doctoral Degree from Loma Linda University in Preventive Care. Dr. Bader was also a professor at a California University teaching health services. He has counseled in areas of weight control, exercise physiology, stress management, all areas of nutrition and has lectured extensively on anti-aging for 26 years. He has also established prevention and executive health programs for numerous safety departments, city governments, and Fortune 500 companies.

His interests have always been in the field of food and cooking and many of his books are related to helping the chef or cook with cooking and kitchen secrets that may gave been forgotten over the years. This has lead him to include household hints and other related subjects in his books.

Current books Dr. Bader has authored include 20,001 Food Facts, Chef's Secrets & Household Hints, Grandma's Kitchen Wisdom Library, Cookbook's Companion, 21st Century Reference Guide to Cooking Secrets & Helpful Household Hints, 1,001 Secret Money Saving Formulas, 10,001 Food Facts, Chef's Secrets & Household Hints, 5,001 Mysteries of Liquids & Cooking Secrets, 250 Future Food Facts & Predictions for the Millennium, To Supplement or Not to Supplement, Weighting to Die, and The Wellness Desk Reference.

At present, Dr. Bader's books have sold over 2 million copies through Reader's Digest, Doubleday, Book of the Month Club, 5,000 radio talk shows, QVC, HSN and Barnes & Noble.

DEDICATION

TO MY DAUGHTER SHERYL

AND HER SPEEDY RECOVERY

MEOW

TABLE OF CONTENTS

6

8

INTRODUCTION

Controlling insects and pets without the use of pesticides is the safest method in protecting the health of you and your family from the harmful chemicals they are composed of. These chemicals can pollute underground water supplies and the bugs that they are supposed to kill will eventually develop immunity to that particular chemical. Breathing commercial insecticides and pesticides can cause damage to the lungs of susceptible individuals as well as polluting the air in your home.

The public needs to become more aware of the dangers involved from using these chemicals and start using a more natural approach to getting rid of insect and critter pests. While many of the methods mentioned in this book provides ways of ridding your property of the pest without killing them, a number of the methods, even though they are all-natural will kill certain insects and small critters that burrow underground.

There are methods of dealing with almost any type of insect and critter but the information has been difficult to obtain until now. The information in this book is accurate and very effective. Hundreds of the facts have been handed down for hundreds of years; long before pest control services became popular with all their harmful chemical cures.

There are over 2 billion pounds of insecticides manufactured in the United States ever year. These are a major threat to groundwater in every state and the problem keeps growing worse. Our grandparents didn't have the luxury of a magic spray that killed off all the pests and had to use ingenuity and natural methods, which did work but did take a bit more effort.

In 2002 more than 3.2 million people suffered medically related side effects from the use of pesticides. Some of the immediate effects included dizziness, nausea, headaches and loss of energy. Cancer may be caused by over 65% of all current pesticides in use through animal laboratory studies.

The book has been designed to make it easy to find the information you need and the answers to your questions are very precise. The substances that are recommended are easy to locate and easy to assemble into a usable controlled substance.

Always try the simplest method first before going to a stronger one. Some of the stronger methods may harm many of the beneficial insects and even some animals.

The author assumes no responsibility for any damage to plants, animals or people from the use of any solution or formulas given in this book. Care should be taken when spraying or using any harmful chemicals. Even though almost all the formulas are prepared from natural ingredients they may still be poisonous or cause illness and should be kept away from pets and children.

IDENTIFYING YOUR PROBLEM

Before trying to remove the pests and critters from your garden or yard, you must first identify the problem pest. This may not be easy since there are many pests that will do similar damage to your plants making it hard to find out which pest is guilty.

It is first necessary to study the damage and solve the mystery. If the plants leaves are full of holes, the type of hole and its shape may give you a clue. The plant may be cut off at the base and pulled underground. The leaves may be chewed around the edges or there may be a small hole in the stem. Was the damage done during the day or during the night?

A careful study of the surroundings and the underneath side of the leaf is important to see if the culprit has left behind a clue to its identity. Many insects lay their eggs on the underneath sides of leaves and the color of the eggs can be a clue. Dropping from insects and critters are an excellent clue to follow up on. You must narrow the possibilities down so that you can attack the pest with the most efficient means available.

If the ground is moist you may be able to find tracks, which are an excellent method of identification. If you do find out that it is a night intruder than check the garden after dark with a flashlight. Many insects can be caught in the act after dark, which makes identifying them much easier.

The damage may not be done by insects and may be caused by animals in which case you will have to approach the problem from a totally different angle. There are many methods of eliminating the problem such as trapping, spraying, use of pathogens, placing barriers, glue strips, baiting or parasites may be used. Initially trapping is one of the best methods of identifying the pest or pests.

This book provides many methods of solving the pest and critter problem and you can pick the best method for your yard that will cause the least amount of damage to your healthy plants. Identification may include bringing a sample of the problem to your local garden or agricultural supply store. In some case you may have to bring the sample to a local college or university entomologist.

CHAPTER 1

ANTS & THEIR RELATIVES

ANTS & THEIR RELATIVES

There are literally thousands of methods of controlling and killing ants. However, there are only a handful of methods that are really effective. Ants can be viewed as a well-organized military unit that is trained to find food and water at all costs. They are tenacious and if there is any food or water to be located they will find it. There are over 12,000 species of ants in the world with California having over 200 species.

The average life expectancy of an ant is only 45-60 days. An ant brain has about 250,000 brain cells. The human brain has 10,000 million brain cells, however, a colony of 40,000 ants has the same brain capacity as a human.

There are fewer ants running around when there is a lot of rain. When there is a dry weather period they multiply very quickly.

GIVING THE QUEEN HEARTBURN
Mix the following ingredients together in a small bowl:

3 ½	Ounces of Strawberry jam (any sweet jam will do)
1 ½	Tablespoons of wet, canned cat food (cheap brand)
1	Tablespoon of boric acid

This concoction is a treat for ants and the workers will bring the treat to their queen. The queen gets excited and quickly gobbles up the goody and within a few hours dies of heartburn. Make sure this treat is out of reach of children and animals that you wish to have around for a while. If they do ingest it, it will make them very sick. However, it doesn't take very much to do the job and eliminate the queen.

FEED THEM MELON
If you have a bad ant problem and can't get rid of them, just leave a slice of watermelon or cantaloupe in your yard far from the house. They would prefer melon to anything you have in the house most of the time (unless you spilled honey on the floor).

WINDOW BOX PROTECTOR
If you have window boxes and have an insect problem in them, just clean them out and whitewash them. This will stop the insects and reduce the risk of dry rot.

THE ANT TRAPPER
The following ingredients will be needed:

6	Tablespoons of granulated sugar
6	Tablespoons of active dry yeast (fresh)
½	Cup standard grade molasses or honey
10	Small plastic lids or bottle caps

Place all the ingredients in a small bowl and mix thoroughly until it is smooth. Place the mixture into the lids or caps and place near an ant trail or near their mound. The mixture can also be spread on a piece of cardboard or small stick and placed in their pathway or in a crevice.

ANTS BY THE POUND

It takes 500,000 sugar ants to equal 1 pound. If you weigh all the ants on earth, they will weigh more than all humans on earth.

BIG NEWS! ANT KILLS ELEPHANT

In Africa a hungry ant can enter an elephants ear and eat them from the inside out. A number of elephants every year fall prey to ants.

GETTING RID OF ANT HILLS

The following ingredients will be needed:

¼	Cup of liquid hand soap
1	Gallon of cool tap water

Place the ingredients into a bucket and mix well, then pour 1-2 cups on the anthill and repeat after 1 hour to be sure that the mixture penetrates deep into the chambers.

ANT DUST

The following ingredients will be needed:

¼	Pound of dried peppermint (from health food store)
¼	Pound rock dust (from nursery)
¼	Pound seaweed powder (from garden supply)
¼	Pound alfalfa meal (organic, from health food store)
¼	Pound cayenne pepper

Place all ingredients in a well-sealed jar or plastic container and shake well to mix. Avoid getting any of the powder on your hands and possibly into your eyes. Use a small amount of the powder where the ants frequent. This will keep them away but not kill them. **Keep away from children and pets.**

FOLLOW THAT ANT

All ants leave a scent trail, which you need to follow by observing the ant's behavior. If you can find the nest, you can eliminate the entire nest thus solving the problem.

BEAN THEM!
Soyabean® (glycine max) is an excellent ant repellant and has been used for many years in Africa. Just prepare the spray by soaking the plant stems in water for 24 hours then using the water as a spray. This also works for aphids and codling moths.

ANT SPRAY FOR THE GARDEN
The following ingredients will be needed:

2	Tablespoons of flaked Ivory soap
1	Tablespoon of Tabasco Sauce™
5	Drops of sesame seed oil (from health food store)
5	Drops of Jungle Rain™ (from garden supply)
1	Gallon spray bottle

Place all ingredients in the gallon bottle and shake to mix well. This can be sprayed directly on the ants or on their pathways. **Keep away from children and pets.**

POWDER THEIR NOSES
Place diatomaceous earth (DE), powdered charcoal, powdered pyrethrum-silica dust or bone meal around the base of the plants in an area; in which the ants are bothering the plants.

REPEL THEM WITH TANSY
If you sprinkle some fresh tansy leaves in the corners of your kitchen counter and in the windowsills it will repel ants 100%.

ARGENTINE ANTS

This is one of the more common house ants that come in when it rains or gets too hot outside. They are a little bigger than the sugar ant and are usually brown to black in color. You need to locate where they are coming in to stop them. The remedies are the same for the sugar ants.

These are hard colonies to get rid of since they usually have more than one queen. Best to give them a bait to take back to the queen instead of trying to spray killer on them.

GET OUT THE MAGNIFYING GLASS

If you think you know where the ants are entering the house and need to be sure, just place some strips of masking tape glue-side up and put some sugar or honey on it. Check it in the morning and see how many ants you trapped.

SLIPPERY SUGGESTION

To keep ants from getting on your plants, just place some lard, Vaseline®, Crisco®, butter, etc. around the base of the plant.

CARPENTER ANTS

Identification:

Carpenter ants come in five sizes from about ¼ inch to ¾ inches and are about ½ inch longer than most other ants. It has a pinched wasp waist and elbowed antennae. The colony consists of a queen, male, minor workers, intermediate workers and the major workers. One nest may contain ants of all five sizes and they are easily confused with termites, but will usually not have wings. The termites also tend to remain at home while the carpenter ants travel about.

General Information:

These are normally beneficial insects that chew up mountains of dead wood and turn it into sawdust. However, when they get into a wood structure the damage can be horrendous. Their initial nest is established in decayed wood, however, after they get established they tend to head for healthy wood and end up doing extensive damage.

If the ant colony becomes too large they tend to form satellite colonies in a nearby structure. There is usually only one queen and she remains in the parent colony. The ants will go back and forth from satellites to parent colonies. Peak traffic hours on their trails are usually at night starting at sunset. They are attracted by sweets but can survive on insects and other animal remains.

Queens can live up to 15 years and lay over 70,000 eggs. Best to eliminate the queen if you have a problem with carpenter ants. A pest control service is best if you have a large infestation.

TYPE OF HOUSE TO BE ATTACKED

- Wood frame
- Crawl spaces
- Houses with cedar or plywood siding
- Slightly slopping roof
- Houses more than 7 years old
- Houses with vegetation next to the house
- Houses near a forest

PUT A TAIL ON THEM

If you spot a carpenter ant, it is best to follow them to their nest. They come out late at night and you will need to place some honey out for them on a piece of cardboard or any other object that you can easily clean up. They will take the honey back to the nest. When you find their entrance, drill small holes and blow boric acid in to fill their living spaces. Boric acid will kill them! They may not be in the house and you may have to follow them outside to find the nest. It is critical to find the parent nest if you plan on getting rid of the ants.

ELIMINATE THE PROBLEM

- Correct any water leaks on your property.
- Eliminate any wood to ground contact points, especially where soil has been pushed up to the side of the house.
- Make sure that there are no tree limbs or bushes touching the house.
- Firewood should be a good distance from the house and elevated off the ground since this is their favorite location for a nest.

MAKE THEM SNEEZE

Mix together 1 teaspoon of table salt and ½ teaspoon of fine white pepper in 1-quart of water and mix well, then strain and spray the ants. This will work great to repel them and will kill the workers but not the queen.

NESTING LOCATIONS

- The outside walls...................35%
- Attic...21%
- Ceilings & crawl spaces.........20%
- Stacked lumber, firewood, etc.

LOVE CERTAIN TREES BEST
Carpenter ants prefer evergreen, cedar and Douglas fir trees best and will look for the for satellite locations as the original nest fills up and gets over-crowded.

LONG LIVE THE QUEEN
Carpenter ants are very resourceful and if you kill the queen the workers can produce special eggs that will produce a new queen. Most of the ants remain in the nest and only about 2% are out foraging for food. If the food supply is low the queen will eat her own eggs and the smaller larvae.

NESTING LOCATIONS OUTSIDE STRUCTURES
- Forest, if within 100 yards of house.............25%
- Live trees...18%
- Dead stumps, buried wood...........................16%
- Landscape wood... 7%
- Stacked lumber/woodpile............................ 3%

THE GOURMET ANT FEAST
Carpenter ants eat aphid's honeydew or tree sap. They also feast on grasshoppers, crickets, craneflies, aphids, spiders, moth larvae, earthworms, bees and flies. They really like our food as well when they can get it and prefer soda pop, candy, syrup, honey, raisins and pet food. They are smart enough to take more solid foods over to water and allow the food to soak and get soft before they eat it. They are very good at eating insect parts and extracting nutrients and liquid from them.

YOU MUST FIND ALL NESTS
Since carpenter ants have satellites as well as a home nest, it is necessary to locate all satellites as well as the home nest if you ever plan on eradicating them. You can find the nest in your home and destroy it but the workers will find a new nest in the home in very short order. Once you find the nest in your home you can spray the entire perimeter to stop a new housing development.

FIRE ANTS

Identification:
Colors may vary from red to brown to black depending on the area of the country they are found. They have a very narrow junction between their thorax and abdomen. You may find more than one queen per colony since they are continually raising queens.

General Information:
Fire ants tend to nest in a mound of sand or dirt and will defend their colony when disturbed. They have a painful sting and their venom will leave a white sore and a permanent scar in the area. Allergic reactions are possible. The imported Fire ants moved to the United States in 1930 and entered through the port of Mobile, Alabama. They are more aggressive than their American relatives and tend to build bigger and better colonies and mounds. Once they get into the area they throw their American relative out and take over.

Their garden preferences are okra, potatoes, strawberry, citrus, and seed corn. They also dine on almost any other insect they can find as well as compost piles.

GIVE THEM A STEAM BATH
If you locate a fire ant mound you may want to try a hot water bath to kill the colony off. Just prepare 2-3 gallons of really hot water (doesn't have to be boiling) at 170^0 F. and pour the water down the mound around noon to 2PM on a warm day. The queen is more active at this time of day and your chances of getting her are very good. Be real sneaky and stay away from the mound until you are ready to pour the water in or the workers will hide the queen. It may take more than one treatment (usually three) to get rid of the colony.

FIRE ANT REMEDY
The following ingredients will be needed:

1	Quart of cold tap water
¼	Ounce of peppermint powder
5	Tablespoons of Jungle Rain™ (from a nursery)
2	Ounces of powdered Ivory Soap®
1	Ounce of Citra Solve™ (from health food store)
1	Spray bottle

Place all ingredients in a plastic bottle with a lid and shake to mix. Spray the solution anywhere ants have been seen and in their nest if you can find it.

THE BAND OF GOO
If the fire ants are chewing up your plants, just place a small band of a sticky substance a few inches up the base of the plant or tree. Tangle-Trap™ and Stickem™ work very well to keep them at bay.

THE DE MOAT

If you lay a 3-inch wide band of DE around your home and garden the fire ants will not cross it and the ones that do will die. Wear a mask when you do this since the dust may irritate your lungs and eyes. However, DE is harmless to humans and pets.

JAMMING UP THE QUEEN

Getting to the queen to kill her is the number one way to end a colony. One of the best methods is to mix up 1 tablespoon of grape jelly with ¼ teaspoon of boric acid and ½ teaspoon of wet cat food. Roll it up in a small ball and leave some balls where they frequent. This is too big a treat for the workers so they bring it back to the queen as a treat.

WORM THEM OUT

Nc nematodes are being used very effectively against fire ant infestations around the Southeastern United States. Check with your garden or agricultural supply houses for these beneficial worms. If you do decide to use Nc nematodes make sure you order the special strain of the worm called "Nc nematode." Place 1-2 million of these in water and spray into the colony nest, then add an additional 2 quarts of water to the nest to help them hatch. You can also mix 1 million of the Nc nematodes in 3 gallons of soapy water and pour that down the nest.

LOVE THEM GRITS

Leave a small pile of instant grits in their pathway or near their colony mound. The ants will eat the grits and take some back for their friends. This will cause them to bloat up and die. Southern ants really go for the grits. If you leave some potato chips or tuna fish with the grits they will really go for it since they are attracted to oils.

CALL FOR A PRO

A very effective method of removing ants is to use a bait trap. One of the most popular ones is called the AntPro™.

USE THE BULB-BASTER

Fill a bulb-baster with talcum powder or medicated body powder and puff it into the nest. Try not to breathe in the powder. This will eliminate the nest completely but will probably not kill the queen.

A NATURAL ENEMY
A fly from South America may soon be imported into the United States to kill the fire ants. The fly is the Phorid fly, which is a natural enemy of the fire ant and the fly's favorite food source.

GIVE THEM A LIMING
This killer works really well! All you have to do is to mix 16 tablespoons of Ivory Liquid Soap® and 1-cup of lime into 4 gallons of warm water, then pour the solution down the nest. This will eliminate most colonies in short order. If you spray this solution directly on the ants it will kill them.

LATHER 'EM UP GOOD
Two soap sprays will work great for keeping them away from your home. Make up a solution using either Jungle Rain™ or Dr. Bronner's Peppermint Soap® and spray anywhere you have a problem.

DEATH TO THEM ALL
One of the best baits to kill fire ants is called "Fire Ant Bait™." It contains the chemical "avermectin," which is a naturally occurring soil organism. Place some of the bait out and the workers will bring it to the queen and will kill off the entire colony within three months or less.

SMELLS GREAT TOO
A sure killer of fire ants is pine oil; however, make sure you purchase only pure pine oil without any other added chemicals. Use only 1 drop in 1 quart of water to be effective.

ONE OF THE BEST ORGANICS
The product is called "Sevin™" and contains a combination of pyrethrums and DE. It is safe to use in vegetable gardens, which most other pesticides are not.

CALL IN "SUPER STRAW MITE"
The fire ant has a naturally occurring predator called the "straw mite (*Pyemotes tritici*)." They can be purchased in most garden or agricultural supply stores. They also kill a number of beetle and caterpillar larvae as well as many true bugs.

THE STEAM PROBE
Tests are underway to eliminate the nests with probes that go into the nest and inject steam. You may contact your pest control in your area to see if this method is available in your area.

THEIR FAVORITE BAIT
Peanut butter with a dab of sugar on it is a real treat for a fire ant and they will hurry it back to the nest. This makes them very easy to follow and locate the nest. Another favorite if you find an ant in the house is mint-apple jelly mixed with a small amount of boric acid. **Keep pets and children away from this one.**

MANURE TEA FOR THE BUGS
If you mix horse manure and hot water, allow it to cool then spray the areas where a problem exists you will never see these bugs again (or your neighbors).

DOODLE BUGS TO THE RESCUE

The larval stage of brown lacewings (doodle bugs), are called "ant lions." Check with your garden supply house to see if these are available in your area. They are not available everywhere but are very effective in eliminating the ant colony.

PHARAOH ANT (sugar ant)

Identification:
Very small light yellow ant

General Information:
This is the tiny common household ant that is found everywhere and needs to be eliminated when they appear. They are capable of carrying pathogens such as salmonella, staphylococcus, and even streptococcus. They like to build their nest near sources of food and water. Spraying and killing visible ants will not eliminate the problem, however, spraying pesticides in possible locations where their nest may do the job.

SUDS 'EM UP

Place 1 tablespoon of Ivory Liquid Soap® into 1 quart of water and mix well. Place the mixture into a spray bottle and squirt the little devils. Ants don't like to wash and this will get rid of them and wash away their scent pathway.

SERVE THEM A SALAD

However, only serve them cucumber peelings. Most ants have a natural aversion to cucumber peelings and will avoid them like the plague. The best location to place them is on the windowsills.

SCRUB-A-DUB-DUB

Clean your counters once a week with a solution of ½ vinegar and ½ water. A mild solution of Clorox™ can be used but vinegar and water is safer.

CIGARETTES FOR ANTS

To make an all around insect spray, just place one cigarette in 1 quart of water and allow it to stand overnight. The nicotine that is released is a deadly poison. Place the mixture in a spray to kill ants, etc.

HERBS TO THE RESCUE

There are a number of herbs that will repel ants:

- **Bay Leaves** – Place these in all the drawers in the kitchen or cupboards where a problem exists. They can be placed in a cookie jar, flour container or sugar jar. Be sure and only use fresh whole leaves.
- **Cloves** – Place them anywhere a problem exists.
- **Mint Leaves** – Crushed mint leaves have been used for thousands of years to repel ants.
- **Cinnamon** – Place some powdered cinnamon to block their path back to their home colony.
- **Garlic** – If you place a few small pieces of garlic in cracks where you have a problem, it will deter the ants.

I DARE YOU TO CROSS THE LINE

Ants will not cross a line of certain food items such as cayenne pepper, baby powder, citrus oil soaked into a piece of string or coffee grounds.

KILLING OFF THE COLONY

Mix up a batch of sweet stuff consisting of honey and boric acid, about ½ teaspoon of each should do. Place the mixture into very small bottle with the lids off. The ants will carry the mixture back to the colony and **ZAPPO**, no colony. This is a danger to pets and children so use with caution.

20 MULE TEAM TO THE RESCUE

A good organic recipe to get rid of ants is to mix ¼ cup of granulated sugar and 1 teaspoon of borax into 1 cup of water. Place some of the mixture into small caps and place in areas where the problem exists. Make sure you change the sugar source every month since the ants are smarter than you think. **Do not use around pets or children.**

FEED THEM PEANUT BRITTLE

Leave a large piece of peanut brittle out for the ants and it will be covered with trapped ants. The peanut brittle can be washed off and re-used over and over again.

THEY MAY USE SUNGLASSES

Ants like to work at night as well as the daytime. However, if you leave a small light on at night in areas that they frequent, it will discourage their foraging for food and water. Ants do not like changes in light patterns.

ANTS LOVE AFFAIR WITH APHIDS

Aphids are one of the ant's favorites. They will find an aphid and stroke the aphid with their antennae until the aphid releases a drop of honeydew, which they bring back to their nursery to feed their young.

POWDER THEM UP

An excellent ant deterrent is talcum powder or any medicated body powder. These work excellent and will repel many insects, especially ants. Talcum powder would be the safest choice since the powder dries the ant out and kills it.

THE DOCTORS PERSONAL SOAP

To make your own spray for ants, just purchase a bar of Dr. Bronner's Peppermint Soap™ at a health food store. Mix 1 tablespoon in 1 quart of cool tap water and place the mixture into a sprayer. Spray all the baseboards and wherever you are having a problem. If you add a small amount of the soap to your mop water it will act as a deterrent on the floors. The spray works well on the outside as well as inside the house.

CLEANER THAT DETERS ANTS
You can purchase a natural cleaner called Citra Solve™. It is a natural citrus based cleaner that is not soap but is very effective in repelling ants. It does have a pleasant citrus aroma, so smell it before you purchase it to be sure that the smell will not be offensive to you or anyone in your family. This product will actually dissolve most insect bodies and is safe around the house. Use ½ tablespoon per 1 quart of water.

PROTEIN IN PLACE OF SWEETS
You can replace sweets in all recipes with a protein source such as peanut butter or any type of moist pet food for excellent results mixing it with either boric acid or borax. Keep away from pets and children. If you place the mixture in a shallow dish, be sure and leave a small glob of honey in front of the dish to attract them.

INSTANT KILLS
The use of instant grains has been popular to kill most ants in recent years. The grains tend to expand in the stomachs and cause the stomachs to burst killing the ant. The best grains to use are instant rice and instant grits.

OUTSIDE KILLER
Pyrethrum is a natural substance that can be purchased in any garden shop. The powder does not blend well with water, but if you add a few drops of liquid soap to 1 cup of water and add 1 tablespoon of pyrethrum it will make a great paste that can be used outside and can be used in a sprayer if strained well.

IT'S TEA TIME FOR ANTS
If you prepare a tea using molasses and Jungle Rain™, which is a natural, organic soap based product it will act as a great ant deterrent when used in a sprayer.

GERMANS PROTECT ANTS
Since ants have a vital role in the health of a forest, the German government protects ants from being eliminated by natural or artificial means. However, since they are not welcome in homes, you will find lavender blossoms near the doors and windows in German households to repel the ants.

SKIP THE EXPENSIVE SPRAYS
Window cleaner will kill all ants, so keep that in mind the next time you are going to purchase the expensive bug spray.

CAUSING STATIC
The essential oil called Tea Tree Oil interferes with the ant's antennae signals and they are unable to transmit or receive information. This oil is safe to be used inside or outside the home. Ants will never frequent an area where they cannot communicate with the other ants.

CITRUS PEEL WORKS GREAT
Place orange and lemon peels in very hot water and allow it to remain overnight. Strain and pour the liquid around any plants that the ants are bothering.

"T" IS FOR TURMERIC
If you can locate the tunnel entrance to an anthill, just place a small powdering of turmeric powder around the opening. Ants hate the herb turmeric and will never come back to that location.

IT WILL TAKE <u>SENSE</u> TO FIND THE <u>SCENTS</u>

Trail Locations Outside the House

- Edges of the foundation or sidewalk
- Edge of the driveway
- Fence stringers
- Edge of the lawn or border of flower beds
- Separation grooves in the sidewalk
- Next to cement blocks or wood steps

Trail Locations inside Homes

- Next to wiring or plumbing that has been cut through studs
- Trails through insulation in wall spaces
- Edges of cabinets and close to furniture
- Tree branches or bushes that touch the house
- Old stump root channels that may go underneath the house

PUT OUT THE STOP SIGNS

Ant activity in the home tends to increase 5-10 minutes before sundown and is at its busiest between 10PM and 2AM; however, some species prefer to be active from 8PM to 4AM in some parts of the country. The temperature and rainfall does not affect the ant's activity.

FOLLOW THE FAT ANT

If you can get a good look at the ant, check out their abdomen. If the abdomen is distended it means that they have had a great dinner and are heading back to the nest to watch some TV. This is the ant you want to follow, not the skinny one looking for a meal. Most of the full ants will usually be carrying a doggie bag back to their friends.

PROTECT YOUR GARBAGE

Planting tansy and peppermint around your garbage can area will eliminate ants and flies from taking up residence there.

SAVE YOUR OLD COFFEE GROUNDS
If you spread coffee grounds around your windows and doors the ants will not come near them. Coffee grounds are a natural ant repellent.

NOT JUST FOR A TOOTHACHE
If you place some oil of clove or camphor on a cloth and wipe down any areas that are a real problem it will stop the ants from using that entrance. Be sure and wipe the door and windowsills.

RED ANTS

The common red ant can be found looking for food in the house and is an unwanted guest since they do have a nasty bite and can be somewhat aggresive.

NATURAL HERBAL REMEDY
These ants can easily be driven away by scattering the herb "sweet fern" (*Comptonia asplenifolia)* around where they are frequenting. This is not really a true fern but a small shrub. Check with your local garden store for more information.

SULFUR WORKS GREAT
If your place small bags of sulfur in areas that the red ants frequent; you will never see them again. **Be careful around animals and children.**

WHITE-FOOTED ANTS

These are harmless to humans and don't bite or sting. They seem to love the weather in Florida and are only found in that state at present. The colonies can have over 2 million members and their favorite meal is sweets. They will protect aphids, mealy bugs and scales since they produce honeydew. The workers tend to eliminate pesticides from the food before the queen gets any, which makes it hard to eradicate the ants.

BAIT THEM OR LIVE WITH THEM
The only method found to date that will eliminate the colony is to bait them into a trap. The AntPro™ is one of the only recommended traps; that seems to work.

VITAMIN C BAIT
Mix together 1 part of baking soda with 1 part of powdered sugar and 1 teaspoon of powdered vitamin C. Place the mixture into a mixture of ½ teaspoon of DE and honey, mix well and make into small balls. This should eliminate the queen and get rid of the colony. **Keep away from pets and children.**

CHAPTER 2

TERMITES

TERMITES

Termites change areas and homes by colonization flights from one colony to set up a new one. This usually takes place in the fall or early in the spring or summer and depends of the species of termite. Even if your home has been protected you may still be at risk of the colony setting up housekeeping. When the termite lands both the male and female break off their wings, run around in circles and then hide under a rock for protection and seal themselves in and mate for life.

Colonies have to grow very slow at first so that they can develop their workers. Termites cannot digest wood with the support of microscopic, one-celled protozoa, which are responsible for breaking down the cellulose in the wood so that they can digest and utilize it. The termite develops the protozoa by consuming each other's fecal material.

Termites must have moisture and have contact with the soil so if you find a nest and open it they will die.

NATURAL METHODS OF ELIMINATION

DOWN WITH THE QUEEN
Termites; are really not a bad insect. They are the best wood recycler around and will turn a dead log into food for many other insects. Unfortunately, they are not fussy where they find wood and your home is a handy source of food. The queen is the key to the termite "swarm."

There are over 300 varieties of termites in the world; however, only four varieties can be found in the United States. The problem termite is the "subterranean termite," which is responsible for 95% of all damage. Termites cannot be attracted to bait unless you place wooden stakes in the ground to see where they are. Once you can determine where they are foraging you can replace the wood with a bait to kill them. If you do identify a termite infestation the best thing to do is to call a professional.

GIMME A "D", GIMME AND "E"
Diatomacious earth (DE) is one of the safest and most effective termite controlling natural substances. Best to paint it on the exposed wood surfaces by using 1 part DE to ¼ part boric acid. Add the mixture to just enough water to make a paint consistency and paint it on all wood surfaces.

SPRAY THE CRAWL SPACES
The attic and all crawl spaces should be sprayed with the same DE, boric acid mixture. Just make the mixture very watery so that it will be easy to spray.

CALL FOR SHERLOCK HOLMES

If you can locate their colony in the infected wood, just remove the wood and replace it with new wood that has been treated. Make sure all tube pathways are located and removed or sprayed to make them unusable.

CALL FOR TEAM BORAX

A good method of eliminating the termites is to use 20 Mule Team Borax™. Just dust their tunnels and it will eliminate the problem (providing you find all the tunnels). Try not to breathe in the dust particles (wear a mask). Borax can also be sprayed into their home and made into a paste and painted on the wood. Treating the wood with borax will provide you with a long-term solution.

BUILD A SAND MOAT

If you dig down 3 feet deep and 3 feet away from the house around your entire home, then place a layer of construction sand (90%) mixed with DE (10%) you will never have a termite problem. This is easier if you are building a new home since garden and trees tend to get in the way.

RING THE DINNER BELL

Nc nematodes (microscopic worms) have been used for hundreds of years to control and eliminate termites. They can be ordered through a company called Arbico and are placed into the subterranean tubes to eat the termites.

HIRE SOME CARPENTER ANTS

Carpenter ants are sworn enemies of termites and will kill them every chance they get. Actually almost any ant will fight termites. As far as using carpenter ants it is a toss up, which is worse, the termites or the carpenter ants. Almost any other ant, however, would be beneficial to have around the house to control the termites. To identify the termites, remember that they have very thick waists, while ants have very thin waists (they probably exercise more).

ESSENTIALLY YOURS

Two essential oils that can be purchased in a health food store are vetiver oil and clove bud oil. Vetiver oil has the ability to repel the termites and keep them away from your property, while the clove bud oil will kill the termites within two days of exposure. Both of these remedies are natural and safe.

TERMITE EATING PLANT
There is one plant in the world that is carnivorous and only eats termites. The pitcher plant (Nepenthes albomarginata) tends to entice the termites with white hairs that are all around the top of the plant. Termites find the hairs irresistible and fall prey to the plants sticky and slippery trap. Usually when the plant attracts one termite the rest of the nest follows. Unfortunately the plant only lives in the rain forest.

CLEAN OUT THE SANDBOX
A layer of sand that has uniform particles will stop termite movement through the soil. This would be best if it were done pre-construction, especially for slab construction. Sand is a physical barrier through which termites avoid and cannot build tunnels in, since the tunnels would collapse easily.

PASS THE FUNGUS AMONGST US
A recently developed fungal strain (Metarhizium anisopliae) has been produced by the EcoScience Corporation and is an effective termiticide. It is odorless, has no vapors and will not stain. The termites can pass the fungus to other termites, which in turn spread it throughout the colony eliminating it.

CALL IN THE SPECIALISTS
There is one Nc nematode (termask) that is very effective of getting rid of termites. You need to purchase them through an agricultural supply house and use injection equipment to apply them. Depending on how well the colony has sealed certain compartments will determine the effectiveness of this method.

TERMITE PROOF A NEW HOME
Check with pest control companies regarding the type of foundation that will deter termites from entering the house. Brick and concrete foundations are among the best but there are no guarantees.

THE TERMITE DOG

Some termite companies now employ specially trained dogs to locate the termite colonies in and around your home. These dogs are called "Tadd" dogs and for additional information call (800) 354-TADD.

ALOE THE TERMITES
Crush all the plant parts of an aloe plant in water and use 1 part aloe to 5 parts of water to be used as a spray. Allow it to stand for 1 hour before use and strain before placing into the sprayer. This spray works very well on termites

POPPY OIL DOES THE TRICK
The oil of the Mexican poppy is very effective in repelling termites from your property. It can be mixed with water as a spray or you can use the powder.

ALOHA TO THESE TERMITES
The Formosa termite is mainly in Hawaii and parts of the southwestern United States. These are very aggressive termites unlike most others. They will work faster and do more damage as well as being more resistant to pesticides. A colony may consist of 2 million termites and cover an acre of land. To identify their soldiers, look for their oval-shaped heads instead of the typical square head.

BIOLOGICAL CONTROL
If you place a piece of wood where the workers will find it and place the chemical "methoprene" on it, it will prevent the termite nymphs from maturing into adults, which are capable of reproducing. The workers will take the infected wood back to the colony for food.

GIVE THEM A HOTFOOT
A relatively new method employs heat to kill the colony. A portable propane heater blows hot air into a tented home. The temperature reaches 150^0F, which is needed to acquire the minimum kill temperature of 120^0F. The termites can only survive for about 20 minutes at this temperature.

However, this does kill a number of the beneficial insects that might be living in the home as well as the bad insects. Computers, chocolates, some plastics and certain pharmaceutical medications must be removed from the house. This is usually completed in one day.

ZAP, ZAP, ZAP

You can also use Electro-Gun™ to electrocute them and hot air treatments for the entire house. This is manufactured by the Etex Company and can be leased to zap the termites. It is used against drywood termites and can also be used to kill powderpost beetles.

It literally zaps them with and electrical charge but can only be used in parts of the home that you can get to. The arc of electrical current is shot directly into the burrow and then travels along the moist tunnels killing the termites. This pulsed high frequency current does not damage the wood in any way.

TERMITE-PROOFING YOUR HOME

- Never allow the paint on the outside of the home to deteriorate and expose the wood.
- Never allow any wood to come into contact with the soil or a bush.
- Never leave any tools or other objects leaning against the house for any length of time. This includes planter boxes.
- Never have any wooden trellises attached to the house and touching the ground.
- Be sure that all firewood is stacked on a cement base with adequate room around it. If you do find termites burn the wood as soon as possible or pour soapy water on it to kill them.
- Check stumps that are near the house regularly.
- If you have a crawl space under your home, be sure that it is kept as dry as possible.
- Shrubbery next to a home is one of the most common entry points for termites.
- Repair all cracks in concrete or masonry.
- Check any separation in wood joints; they should be inspected on a regular basis.
- Trees that overhang your roof are a great entry point for termites.

PUT OUT THE STOP SIGNS

Ant activity in the home tends to increase 5-10 minutes before sundown and is at its busiest between 10PM and 2AM; however, some species prefer to be active from 8PM to 4AM in some parts of the country. The temperature and rainfall does not affect the ant's activity.

GIVE THEM A DOSE OF CASTOR OIL

Use the castor oil plant and soak the green seeds, leaves and the roots in 2 quarts of water for 24 hours, then strain and use in a sprayer or use as a drench if you know where their nest is. The seeds and leaves can be dried and used as a powder.

CHAPTER 3

COCKROACHES

COCKROACHES

A ROACH BY ANY OTHER NAME, IS STILL A ROACH

Roaches do not mind living outside, but if you give them a chance, they will move in with their whole family. Roaches are known by a number of different names, such as water bugs, palmetto bugs and cockroaches. They are bugs of the night and will go looking for any drop of water or food that may be within their grasp, since they are not fussy eaters. Outside they will take up residence almost anywhere, such as a tree, woodpile, planter, under rocks, etc. In many instances roaches will find a warm, damp location, which is where they prefer to breed.

Cleanliness will reduce or eliminate most roach problems, but frequent professional spraying if a problem exists by an expert or placing out bait also works well. Roaches will not come back to an area where they are frequently poisoned.

Cockroaches can be found all over the world and are going strong. They can be controlled or eradicated but it will take some effort. The best method of controlling cockroaches is to have a clean kitchen. Any small piece of food or readily accessible water source will be located. Americans spend about 1.5 billion dollars annually trying to get rid of cockroaches, but to no avail. The roaches are now becoming resistant to most pesticides and chemicals.

There are over 3800 species of cockroaches worldwide and they have been around for 360 million years. People who are allergic to house dust will be allergic to cockroaches, since parts of their bodies when they die become mixed with house dust. Asthma can be induced from cockroach dust particles in susceptible individuals.

The roach can identify poisons with their fine sensory hairs and will avoid areas that have been baited with poisons. In the late 1800's people would place a mirror in front of a cockroach and felt that its reflection would scare it away.

The most common roach's in the United States are:

American Cockroach
Has also been called a water bug or Palmetto bug. It is reddish-brown and about 1½-inches long. It has wings but rarely flies. They will eat anything including the backing off wallpaper. The American cockroach is the largest cockroach found in dwellings, especially in restaurants or food preparation areas. They are reddish-brown to brown in color.

Smoky Brown Cockroach
Somewhat small than the American cockroach and is dark brown almost black in color. Has well-developed wings that will stretch to the tip of the abdomen. Their preferred diet is plants but they will eat anything. Normally found in greenhouses and is more common in the Southern United States.

Oriental Cockroach
May also be called a "waterbug" or "black beetle." It is about 1¼-inches long and has wings but is unable to fly. Usually found around garbage cans and does not need a water source. It is a glossy dark brown to black in color. Prefers decaying organic matter and is the filthiest of all cockroaches. They will invade a building when the weather turns cold, and is more commonly found in the eastern states.

German Cockroach
This roach prefers apartments, restaurants and motels (even the better ones). Their eggs are usually transported on peoples clothing, which is how they get into the locations. The adults are only ½ to ¾ inches long and they will eat anything! This is the most common cockroach in the Pacific Northwest. It can be identified by the two brown lengthwise stripes on its shield behind the head.

The German cockroach can produce more eggs and has more cycles per year (3-4) than any other cockroach. They hide during the day and only forage for food at night.

Brown Banded Cockroaches
These are a light brown and are usually found in warmer climates especially in the Southern States. They are only about ½ inches long and have two light, irregular bands along their wings. They are often confused with the German roach, which has two dark bands behind their head. They prefer starches, but will eat anything.

Woods Roach
Very similar to the American roach and is light brown in color. They are attracted to light, which is their major difference and can usually be found under a log or in a woodpile.

NATURAL METHODS OF ELIMINATION

THE ROACH EXTERMINATOR
The following ingredients will be needed:

½	Pound of borax
30	Ounces of powdered sugar
½	Ounce cocoa powder
1	Ounce of sodium chloride

Place all the ingredients into a medium plastic container and mix thoroughly. This bug poison should be sprinkled around wherever the problem exists. **This is harmful to pets and children and should be used with caution.**

HERB TO THE RESCUE
There are a number of herbs that will repel cockroaches. They are bay leaves, cucumber and cayenne. Cucumber peelings work very effectively to deter them. Place them wherever a problem exists and the cockroaches will not frequent that area.

THE CATS MEOW

A natural repellant to cockroaches is catnip. The chemical in catnip is called nepetactone, which is harmless to humans and pets. If you leave small sachets of catnip in locations that the cockroaches frequent, you will never see a cockroach. If you make a tea from catnip, allow it to cool and then place it in a spray bottle it will eliminate your ever seeing a cockroach again.

A CLEAN ROACH IS NOT A HEALTHY ROACH

A method of killing cockroaches is to place 1 tablespoon of Ivory Liquid Soap™ into 1 quart of water then place the mixture into a spray bottle and spray the cockroach. This is an instant kill since they hate to be clean.

ONE OF THE MANY USES FOR BAKING SODA

If you place a small shallow bowl where you are having a roach problem with equal parts of baking soda and powdered sugar it will kill the roaches. **Make sure this is kept away from pets and small children.**

BOTTOMS UP, LITERALLY!

Take a 1 pound coffee can and place 2 slices of bread in it that have been soaked with beer. Place the can anywhere a roach problem exists. Save the lid and dispose of the canned roaches.

A LITTLE HERE, A LITTLE THERE

Sprinkle boric acid down any cracks or crevices in non-food areas. **This is toxic so keep it away from children or pets.** This is usually the treatment of choice in hard to reach areas only. This is also one of the items that roaches have not developed a resistance to. Boric acid is a poison.

THE SWEET ROACH EXTERMINATOR

The following ingredients will be needed:

½	Pound of borax
2	Pounds of powdered sugar (10X)
½	Ounce of cocoa powder
1	Ounce of sodium fluoride (from pharmacy)

Place all the ingredients in a small bucket and mix thoroughly. Sprinkle in areas where the roaches frequent. **Keep out of reach of children and pets.**

DOING THE BACKSTROKE

The reason you see roaches lying on their back when they die is that they are killed by an inhibition of cholinesterase, which is an enzyme that transmits nerve impulses to the muscles. When they die there is a loss of muscular control resulting in violent twitching that forces them to end up on their back. The violent twitching causes their center of gravity to become higher than their center of balance.

THIS APPLE WAS PROBABLY USED BY THE WICKED WITCH

Hedgeapples have been used for hundreds of years to repel cockroaches. They are the fruit of the Osage orange tree and contain a natural chemical that repels roaches. It only takes one small apple in a room to eliminate the roaches. Hedgeapples will last about 2 months before needing replacement. Hedgeapples can be obtained through the Internet at www.hedgeapple.com.

WALKING THE PLANK
Place Vaseline® around the inside rim of a medium size jar, then place half a banana in the jar and put a piece of wood or tongue depressor on the outside of the jar to be used as a ramp so that they can easily walk into the jar to get the banana. The Vaseline® will make it too slippery for them to get out and they die.

HERE YE, HERE YE DOCTOR DOES IT AGAIN
One of the best all-natural methods of pest control, especially cockroaches is to place 1 capful of Dr. Bronner's Peppermint Soap™ in 1 quart of warm water and spray the areas where you have a problem.

THE LARD ROACH EXTERMINATOR
The following ingredients will be needed:

½	Cup of all-purpose flour
1/8	Cup of granulated sugar (any sugar will do)
¼	Cup of lard
8	Ounces of boric acid
	Cool tap water

Place all the ingredients into a small bowl and blend thoroughly making the solution into small balls of dough. Place 1-3 dough balls into an open small plastic bag and place in areas where the roach problem exists. **This is toxic and needs to be kept out of reach of children and animals.**

SPICE 'EM UP

For a really hot roach, just place 2 tablespoons of Tabasco Sauce™ or other very hot sauce in 1 quart of water then mix well and spray the areas where a problem exists. You will never see another roach!

BAITING THE GERMAN ROACH

If you are going to use bait on a German cockroach there are certain foods they prefer over others. They are very fond of flour, brown sugar and light Karo® syrup. They prefer carbohydrates to proteins as well. Being German they love their beer but it has to be stale since they don't like the carbon dioxide. If you lace any of these foods with 5% food-grade DE or borax it will do the trick. **Be careful of pets and children around the baits.**

THE KILLER VACUUM

If you are sure that you have roaches, wait until at least 1 hour after dark and go into the room you suspect with a red light (don't turn on the room lights) and a vacuum, then vacuum up all the roaches. If you are going to use a dry vacuum, place 1 teaspoon of cornstarch in the vacuum bag to kill the roaches.

THE ROACH MOTEL

Use a 2-liter plastic soda bottle and cut off the top about 3-4 inches down. Place some Vaseline® around the inside of the top and the bottom that is left, then place the top you cut off inverted (like a funnel) back into the bottle. Then duct tape the top back on and place masking tape around the bottle to make it easy for them to climb up. Then place a few pieces of bread soaked in beer inside. They will enter and not be able to leave because of the Vaseline® is too slippery.

THE ROACH TRAP

There are a number of roach traps on the market, which have a one-way door. The bait is placed inside and they can't get out. These are very effective if placed in the right areas where they frequent.

BAKING 101 FOR ROACHES

To prepare roach dough, just combine ¼ cup of Crisco® with ½ cup of 10X powdered sugar, ¼ red onion, ½ cup of all-purpose flour and 8 ounces of baking soda (very fresh). Add water as needed to prepare a dough-like consistency. Make the dough into small balls and leave out for the roaches to find.

ROACH & ANT REPELLER
The following ingredients will be needed:

1	Cup of borax
¼	Cup of crushed fresh black pepper
¼	Cup of crushed bay leaves

Place the ingredients in jar with a well-sealed lid and shake well. Sprinkle a small amount of the mixture in the corners of the cupboards and drawers. You should never see another cockroach or ant again.

ROACH SPRAY
To 1 quart of tap water add 1 crushed clove of garlic, 1 tablespoon of cayenne pepper and 1 small crushed white onion. Place the mixture on the range and allow it to come to a simmer. Remove from the heat and allow it to steep for 1 hour before placing it in a sprayer and spraying the locations that the roaches frequent.

DUST THEM OFF
As a last resort insecticidal powder will need to be forced into all cracks and crevices. Check with a pest control company and ask them to use a safe powder that can be used around pets and children. **Remove all pets such as birds, cats, fish and dogs from the premises when dusting is being done.**

WORKS ON VAMIPRES BUT NOT COCKROACHES
Some species of cockroach are actually attracted to garlic, so best not to try and use garlic to get rid of roaches.

WHY DID THE CHICKEN CROSS THE ROAD?
Probably to get to a cockroach! Chickens love to chase and eat cockroaches and in some countries the chickens are allowed to go in and out of the house freely to control the cockroach population.

CHEMICAL KILLER

Silica gel (aluminum silicate) can be used to dust areas where the roaches frequent. It has the ability to scratch their protective coating away and kill them. Caution should be used, when dusting and a mask and gloves should be worn even though the dust is considered non-toxic. The names of commercial silica gel product are Dri-Die™ and Drione™ and can be purchased in your local garden or agricultural supply stores.

PREVENTION IS STILL THE ANSWER

Best to prevent the problem by following a few rules:

- Clean out the back of the refrigerator and any food that has been pushed underneath by children.
- Vacuum regularly.
- Make sure the kitchen floor is always clean.
- Wipe off counters daily.
- Clean out pet food dishes and don't leave them out at night.
- Your garbage can should have a tight lid.
- Seal all cracks and crevices.
- Fix any leaky pipes since they love a cool drink.
- Repair loose wallpaper since they will eat paste.
- Eliminate any stacks of lumber near the house.
- Remove any foliage that is too close to the house.
- Eliminate stacks of magazines or newspaper. These make great places for them to reside.

HIRE A TALKING GECKO

Gecko's love cockroaches and will chase and consume them when they can find them. They hunt them at night and they are one of their favorite meals. If you let just one gecko loose in an apartment building it will eliminate all the roaches and their relatives in about 7-10 days. However, remember that they don't like cats and the cat will eat the gecko for dinner.

CHAPTER 4

SPIDERS

SPIDERS

There are 40,000 species of spiders worldwide and they are all carnivorous. Spiders are beneficial insects and are welcome in most homes. There are only four spiders that are poisonous in the United States, the black widow, the hobo, the yellow sac and the brown recluse. Spiders consume about 100 bugs every year and you are never more than 12 feet away from a spider at any time. An orb web spider will eat their web daily and spin a new one. Spiders can regenerate their lost limbs. The only thing a spider does is hunt for food and make new spiders.

Spiders kill more bugs than birds do and the total weight of bugs that spiders consumes in one day will be more than the weight of all the humans on earth. In China spiders are so revered that farmers even build them small teepee-like homes to hibernate in during the winter months. Spider's silk is stronger than tensile steel of the same diameter and is so fine it has been used as cross hairs in gun sites.

Spiders only live for about one year. Their hairy legs contain their organs for hearing, touch and smell. All spiders inject a chemical that liquefies their host and then they suck up the goodies.

99% OF ALL SPIDERS ARE HARMLESS

A FEW OF THE MORE COMMON SPIDERS

- *ARIZONA BROWN SPIDER*
Best to wear gloves and use a soapy spray directly on the spiders to kill them.
- *BLACK WIDOW*
Spray with a strong soapy solution. Spray all cracks and areas where they are located. Best to spray the areas once a month. Black widows will only bite you if you provoke them. They prefer to run away rather than confront you in any way.
- *BROWN RECLUSE*
Usually found in wooded area, attics or woodpiles. Best to wear gloves when working in these areas. A soapy spray will get rid of them.
- *CRAB SPIDER*
They are white or yellow and just wait to ambush their prey. They are capable of changing colors depending on their environment.
- *JUMPING SPIDER*
They have excellent vision, which helps them hunt and destroy their prey. They are very bright colored.
- *LYNZ SPIDER*
They are more common in the southern United States. They use their green camouflage to sneak up on their victims in the daylight.
- *RED SPIDERS*
Usually found on plants that have poor air circulation and suffer from malnutrition or lack adequate water. Spray the plant with a mild soapy water solution to get rid of the spiders, then feed and water the plant well.

- *TARANTULAS*

These cute hairy spiders will usually not harm a human and just want to be left alone. They live in burrows and go out hunting after dark.

- *WOLF SPIDER*

These can either be a hairy gray or brown color with eight eyes. These are excellent hunters and will chase down their prey. However, wasps kill 99% of all wolf spiders.

NATURAL METHODS OF ELIMINATION

AN APPLE A DAY KEEPS THE SPIDERS AWAY

If you want to repel all types of spiders without killing them, just place a hedgeapple or two in the room where the problem exists. These are the fruit of the Osage orange tree and have been used for hundreds of years as a crawling insect repellant. For more information see www.hedgeapple.com.

GOOD USE FOR OLD PANTYHOSE

If you place cedar chips in the toe of some old pantyhose and hang it where you have a problem, the spiders will avoid the area. However, so will your friends and neighbors when they see the pantyhose hanging all over your home.

AN HERBAL SOLUTION

If you sprinkle the herb pennyroyal in areas that spiders frequent they will never come back. Pennyroyal can be purchased in any health food store.

CHESTNUTS ROASTING ON AN OPEN FIRE

Fresh chestnuts have been used for centuries as a spider deterrent. You can't use packaged shelled or roasted, only fresh, shelled chestnuts. If they are placed across any entry point it will stop them dead in their tracks.

WHAT IS A COBWEB?

Cobwebs are actually "draglines" laid down by spiders wherever they go. This is their lifeline that can be used to drop from one place to another or to help them get out of danger. When they get coated with dust they are called cobwebs.

SOLVING CORNER PROBLEMS

To prevent cobwebs from returning to the corners, just spray the area with a solution of 5% white vinegar with a teaspoon of coconut oil added. The spiders will leave the area alone.

SPIDER SPECIFICS

It is best to purchase an all-natural soap that contains pyrethrum and no other chemical substance to use on spiders. Jungle Rain™ is excellent as well as Dr. Bronner's Peppermint Soap™.

SALT KILLS

To eliminate spiders just mix 1 ounce of table salt in 1 gallon of warm tap water. This will kill them within a short period of time. Best for use outside and keep away from plants.

SMOKE 'EM IF YOU GOT 'EM

Place a whole package of chewing tobacco in 1 gallon of boiling water, remove it from the heat and allow it to cool. Strain the solution into a container, then place 1 cup of the solution and ½ cup of lemon-scented liquid soap into a hose-end sprayer and spray your yard and around the outside of the house. This will eliminate all spiders even the good guys for some time to come. Never use nicotine on roses or they will turn black. It is poison to humans, animals and fish. Cigarette smoke will also kill spiders, but we do not recommend taking up smoking to kill them.

KILLER OILS

Only one drop of the following oils in 1 quart of water will kill spiders. Use citronella oil, lavender oil, cinnamon oil, peppermint oil, citrus oil and tea tree oil. It will also kill a number of other insects as well. When mixing citrus oil in a quart of water add 5 tablespoons of Dr. Bronner's Peppermint Soap™ to give it some extra kick.

RED SPIDER MITE

These adult and nymph spiders will suck the juices from your plants and turn the leaves yellow, silver or even speckled. They lay their eggs on the plants and are closely related to the horseshoe crab than to insects. They are so small that you should check your plants with a magnifying glass to locate them. They make tiny tents that look like cobwebs on the underneath sides of leaves. They like it dry and too much moisture will drive them away.

SALT THEM

Red spider mites can be eliminated from an area by spraying with a solution of 1 ounce of table salt mixed into 1 gallon of water. Seawater will work great but be sure that the plant will tolerate being salted.

DUST THEM WITH POISON

Spider mites: can easily be eliminated by using tobacco! If you dry and powder the tobacco leaves and then dust the plants it will eliminate the mites in short order. Never use nicotine on roses or they will turn black. **Nicotine is a poison to humans, fish and animals.** High concentrations will also kill plants.

BUTTER THEM UP

To prepare a plant dip for houseplants that have become infested with spider mites, just place 2 cups of buttermilk in 1 gallon of water. Dip the plant in the solution and allow it to remain overnight before rinsing it off.

PREDATORS WORK GREAT

There are two predators that really work great in eliminating the red spider mite. They are the lacewing and the ladybug beetles.

LIME THEM

You can spray them with an insecticidal soap or a combination of soap and lime. Dusting them with a lime dust will also eliminate the problem.

GET THEM DRUNK!

Red spiders; can be eliminated by mixing 1 cup of rubbing alcohol with 1 quart of cool tap water. Place the mixture into a spray bottle and be sure and test a leaf first before spraying to be sure you won't damage the plant. If the mixture is too strong reduce the alcohol to ½ cup. Best to wait one day after the leaf test to be sure no damage will occur. Never use this spray in the hot part of the day for the best results.

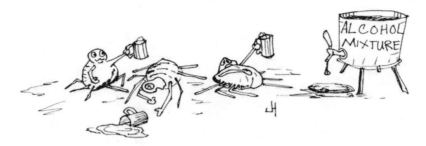

GREAT SPRAY FOR SPIDER MITES

1	Cup of all-purpose flour
4	Tablespoons of buttermilk
1	Gallon of cool tap water

Prepare a paste from the flour and water before adding the balance of the liquid. If the mite infestation is mild, then just paint the mixture on the leaves instead of using a sprayer. Best to do the underneath, sides of the leaves as well.

SPEARMINT SPRAY

1	Cup of chives
1	Cup of crushed spearmint leaves
½	Cup of hot peppers or ¼ cup Tabasco Sauce™
1	Small horseradish plant (ground)
1	Quart tap water
¼	Cup Ivory liquid soap

Grind all the ingredients in a blender or food processor and add just enough water to liquefy. Add the quart of water and the liquid soap and refrigerate. To use mix ½ cup of the base to 1 quart of water then strain into a spray bottle. Works great for mites, cabbage loopers and most caterpillars.

GREAT KILLER

The United States Department of Agriculture (USDA) reports that coriander oil will repel the red spider mite. Prepare an emulsion of 2% coriander oil and spray the areas where the spider mite condition exists.

CHAPTER 5

MISCELLANEOUS

GARDEN & PLANT BUGS

MISCELLANEOUS

GARDEN & PLANT BUGS

GENERAL BUGGY INFORMATION

There are many natural and chemical remedies to eliminate insect pests. Some work better than others, however, I am providing the ones that tend to work the best. Most of these concoctions can be made with readily available products that will easily be found around the home or purchased from a supermarket or garden supply store. It is always best to only spray the plants that are infested, since many sprays will damage healthy plants that are not infested.

DIPPER

Dipping houseplants upside down in a bucket of water is a popular method of getting rid of most bugs. A soapy water bath cleans the leaves as well as getting rid of the pests. Do not use this method on African violets, cactus or plants that have hairy leaves and stems. This method works especially well to eliminate aphids and spider mites. Make sure that the soil is very secure before you do the dipping. Make sure the container is big enough so that it will not break off the stems.

DE-BUGGING A DELICATE PLANT

African violets and other types of delicate plants that will not tolerate a severe water spray to dislodge the bugs need to be placed into a plastic bag that has been sprayed with hair spray. The plant needs to be quickly inserted into the bag after the spray, then tied with a tie and left to stand overnight. This will kill all bugs on the houseplant.

A SPOT OF TEA WITH A DASH OF AMMONIA

If you want to keep bugs off your indoor plants, try spraying them with a solution of 10-parts weak tea mixed with 1 part household ammonia. **Keep the ammonia away from pets and children.**

HOUSE PLANT PROTECTOR

When you clean your plants leaves, try adding a few drops of liquid detergent to the water and it will keep the bugs off the leaves.

WASH 'EM DOWN THE DRAIN
If you get pests on your houseplants one of the easiest methods of removing them without chemicals is to just place the plant under running water in the sink. The force of the running water will wash off aphids, mites, whiteflies, etc.

INDOOR PLANT PROTECTOR
Sprinkle diatomaceous earth (DE) in the saucer under houseplants to eliminate all insects from setting up housekeeping.

ODOR DETERRENT
If you place one peeled garlic clove, narrow end up, just under the soil of a houseplant it will keep most bugs away from the plant.

BORROW YOUR CHILDS SQUIRT GUN
If you think that you have a pest problem on a houseplant, take the plant outside and give it a few squirts with a strong stream of water. However, be careful not to damage a delicate plant.

DON'T BECOME A BUG MAGNET
A variety of different bugs are attracted to different colored clothing. If you wear blue the thrips will follow you around and whiteflies love yellow. Best to wear basic brown or green since these colors don't seem to attract bugs.

POISON GAS??????????
If you have a plant that is already infested, place the plant into a plastic bag and blow a good quantity of cigarette smoke into the bag then seal it up with a tie. This will kill any bug that is in the plant. Allow it to remain overnight and hopefully the plant will survive the smoke.

APHIDS

Identification:
These pear-shaped 1/10th to ½ inch long insects are also called plant lice and are not fussy as to which plants they infest. They can be green, yellow or black. They are usually found on the underneath side of leaves with over 4,000 species identified at present.

General Information:
You can find aphids on shrubs, potted plants, all garden plants and even trees. They will cause plant stunting, wilting, yellowing and will eventually kill the plant.
They insert their piercing mouth into the plant stem or leaves and proceed to suck out the sap from the plant and deposit honeydew, which attracts other insects. Aphids usually appear in the fall.

They tend to transmit a number of diseases and are a serious threat to most gardens. If you use a high nitrogen fertilizer you will attract even more aphids.

Beneficial insects that will kill aphids can be used in a greenhouse and raised by placing some aphid-infested leaves in a plastic bag, making sure that the aphids are still on the leaves. In a few days the beneficial larvae will emerge and can be harvested with the tip of a small paintbrush while they are crawling about inside the bag. They can then be released inside the greenhouse to eliminate the aphid problem.

OIL THEM UP
Mix 1 tablespoon of canola oil and add 3-4 drops of Ivory soap, then add to 1 quart of water and mix well. Place the contents into a spray bottle and spray the plants from the top down and then from the bottom up making sure the underneath sides of the leaves are saturated.

ICKY STICKY MESSY
Flypaper is very effective in your garden to trap aphids. If you want to make your own, just use a heavy paper stock and spread Tanglefoot™ on it. Tanglefoot™ can be purchased at most garden supply houses.

THEY SMELL NICE AND DIE
Mix together:

¼	Teaspoon of eucalyptus oil
½	Teaspoon of Ivory Liquid Soap™
½	Teaspoon of canola oil
½	Gallons of water

Place all the ingredients into a bucket and mix well. Place the mixture into a spray and spray the affected areas.

SIC THE ANT LION ON THEM
There are a number of natural predators that will eliminate aphids. One of the most effective is the aphid lion, which are also known as Dobson fly, green lacewings or antlions. They can be purchased in most garden stores, especially on the east coast of the United States or can be purchased by mail order through an agricultural supply house. They also feast on mealybugs, scales and love to munch on thrips for dessert. Most garden supply stores will sell 1,000 eggs for about $10.00.

A GOOD USE FOR TOBACCO

Aphids love roses and will do a lot of damage if not discouraged from getting to them. A good natural method of deterring aphids is to bury a mixture of 1 cup of tobacco (cigarettes are a good source, organic tobacco would be better) mixed with ½ cup of powdered garlic and 1 cup of compost mixed into the soil around the base of the bushes.

THE KILLER LEMON

Bring 1 pint of tap water to a boil, remove from the range and add the grated rind of 1 lemon. This mixture needs to steep overnight to release all the citrus oil. Strain the mixture and either, spray it on the aphids or use it on a soft bristle brush and paint the plant with the solution. Any citrus rind can be used, but lemon and lime seem to be more somewhat more effective. The two active ingredients are limonene and linalool.

PEPPER SPRAY WORKS GREAT

1	Tablespoon of Tabasco Sauce™
6	Cloves of garlic
1	Quart of warm tap water

Chop the garlic up very fine, then add the Tabasco Sauce™ and the water. Allow it to stand for 1 hour before you strain and place in a sprayer. One teaspoon of cayenne pepper may be substituted for the Tabasco Sauce™.

NO LADY WHEN APHIDS ARE AROUND

Ladybug beetles love to eat aphids and will assist you in controlling them very effectively.

SMOTHER THEM WITH OIL

A relatively new agricultural product that was developed for aphid infestations is called "Sunspray™." This is horticultural oil that will smother aphids and their eggs.

ARE APHIDS DOING THE BACKSTROKE?

THANK You FOR THE TREAT.

Water garden plants, can be attacked by aphids and get their juices sucked out just like any other plant. One of the easiest methods of removing them is to hold the plant under water until they release and get drowned. If you have fish they will really love you for the treat, which they rarely get. If you plant fennel or butterfly weed in your water garden it will attract aphid eaters.

SPRAY THEM WITH COOKING OIL

Aphids will suffocate if sprayed with cooking oil. You can make a cooking oil spray by adding 1 teaspoon of insecticidal soap and ½ teaspoon of cooking oil to 1 quart of water. You can also use a commercial spray, such as Pam™.

GETTING TO THE ROOT OF THE PROBLEM

Cassava root is a very effective root when it comes to controlling aphids. You will need to crush the root to obtain the juice then dilute it with equal parts of juice to equal parts of water. Spray the area, affected by the aphids immediately and wait 15-20 days before planting.

PLOW UP YOUR GARDEN

If you plow up your garden in the fall it should eliminate the aphid eggs. Then if you plant some mint plants that will end their cycle.

LIME DOES MAGIC

Use ¼ cup of lime in 1 gallon of warm tap water, add 4 drops of liquid soap and place the mixture in a sprayer. A soap that works really well is *Ringer Aphid-Mite Attack Insecticidal Soap™*.

MARIGOLD SOLUTION

To get rid of aphids, just soak 15 mature diced-up marigold plants in 5 pints of boiled water and allow the mixture to cool before adding 3 drops of liquid soap. Strain and spray on the affected areas and be sure to spray the underneath sides of the leaves.

SWEET POTATO WATER

Next time you boil sweet potatoes be sure and save all the water to use in a spray to get rid of aphids. This works really well on small insects such as aphids and ants. The leaves of the sweet potato plant can also be soaked in water and the water used as a very effective spray.

WOOLLY MAMMOTH NO RELATION TO WOOLLY APHID

Tea (cammelia sinensis) can be very effectively used to combat woolly aphids. The leaves are high in caffeine and can be used to prepare a spray. Make a tea from the leaves and allow it to cool then place the tea in a sprayer and spray the aphids. The crushed tea, leaves can also be placed around plants as a deterrent.

TOMATO JUICE SPRAY

2   Cups tomato leaves and stems
1   Quart of tap water

Grind-up the tomato parts them process them in a food processor with 2 cups of water. Allow the mixture to stand overnight, then strain it and add 2 more cups of water. Use as a spray to get rid of aphids.

DON'T BE SCARED OF THIS MUMMY

If you are aphid hunting and spot an aphid that is swollen and looks metallic, brown or blackened, you have found a "mummy." This is an aphid that has been parasitized by a wasp. Don't kill it or you will kill the wasp larva.

A PLANT REPELLENT

If you plant nasturtiums around plants that are susceptible to aphid attacks it will keep the aphids away. Garlic and onion plants are almost as good but nasturtiums seem to be more effective.

FOILED AGAIN

Placing aluminum foil around plants that aphids like seems to work very well, in fact, it tends to keep a number of insects away due to the reflection from the aluminum foil, which confuses the insect. This also aids in reducing weeds and helps the soil retain moisture.

THE CLAY KILLER

A dilute solution of soft wet clay will kill the soft-bodied aphids.

RUB-A-DUB-DUB

Be gently and rub the affected leaves between your fingers to remove the aphids. This method has been the preferred method for hundreds of years.

BORERS

There are two main types of borers; they are the caterpillars that eat plants and the grubs of beetles that attack trees. They can bore into the plant or tree and proceed to feast on the insides, usually in an upward direction. They are difficult to find before they do a great deal of damage. Tree diseases in many trees can usually be traced to borers, especially if you have plants or trees that are weak and undernourished. These weak trees or plants are prime targets for borers.

Woodpeckers love to go after borers and find them a tempting meal. If the trees are wrapped, however, it usually stops most borers from getting up the tree and getting a foothold. If you can spot the gum and sawdust mixture that they leave behind when they are boring into the tree, it is best to locate and go after them right away.

ASH BORER

These bugs tunnel into the trunk of ash trees usually at ground level or below ground. They can cause extensive damage to the tree and even kill the tree. To reduce the infestation it is sometimes necessary to remove the section or limb of the tree where the infestation is taking place. All methods of control for any borer will be viable for these ash borers.

CLEAR THE WAY

If you keep the ground around the trees clear of any grass or weeds the birds will be able to spot the bugs.

EUROPEAN CORN BORER

Identification:
They are about 1 inch long, gray-pink in color with brown spots. They bore holes in corn and a variety of grasses. Check the underneath side of leaves for their egg masses.

GETTING CONTROL

The eggs can be attacked by ladybugs, lacewings and trichogramma. If there is a bad infestation and the holes are in the corn, it would be best to spray the corn with Nc nematodes or they will enter the stalk and kill the entire corn stalk. As a preventive measure if you feel that the problem is going to occur, spray the corn with Bt. You can also cut a hole and physically remove the borer.

LESSER CORN STALK BORERS

These are green, brown or blue-banded caterpillars that will tunnel into corn stems. The caterpillar will exit the stalk through a silken web that resembles a tunnel and pupates in the soil. Tends to prefer the southern United States cornfields.

GET OUT THE SYRINGE

Many farmers prefer to inject Nc nematodes into the boreholes. However, a number of farmers will make a small cut near the borehole and physically remove the pest screaming and kicking. Keep a bucket of soapy water with you if you decide to remove them.

BEFORE THEY SET UP HOUSEKEEPING
Prevention is always the best method of control. Spraying the field with a solution of Bt or NVP will solve the problem.

POUND THEM ROOTS
Crush up 2 pounds of French marigold roots and place them in 2 quarts of water. Allow to soak for 1 hour, strain and place in sprayer and spray on infested soil.

LIMA BEAN POD BORER

Identification:
This is green or reddish caterpillar with a light yellow head that prefers the southern United States. It grows to about one inch long and will wriggle violently when bothered.

General Information:
This bug will pierce through the Lima bean pod and eat the seeds. It has the tendency to pass from one bean to another and has the tendency to destroy beans even if it is not hungry. When it does finish eating it will enter the ground to pupate.

PICK'EM UP
The best method to eradicate these pests is to handpick them from the plants before they do too much damage. If the crop is planted late they will do more damage than they will to an early, planted crop. If you do plant early you may avoid the pest all together.

PACIFIC FLATHEAD BORER

Attacks fruit and nut trees above the ground and usually attack trees that already have some form of damage, usually a sunburned area, making it easier for them to bore into. Their tunnels cause sap to be released from their holes. The beetle has a dark mottled appearance with a bronze colored shell.

PAINT WITH LATEX
Paint the tree trunk with an indoor white latex paint or use whitewash. You will need to paint the area of the trunk at least 2 feet from the soil line and about 1 inch under the soil to be effective.

RASPBERRY CANE BORER

Identification:
This is a thin beetle that has black wing covers and a yellow body.

General Information:
The female lays her eggs on a young shoot and the grub that hatches eats the pith inside the cane. The top of the cane will then wilt and die. The best control is to cut off the wilted shoot well below the point of injury and be sure to burn them.

SQUASH VINE BORER

Identification:
This is a red and black moth that has clear wings and is about 1½-inches long. Larvae are wrinkled, white with brown heads.

General Information:
These are wasp-like moths that lay a single egg usually near the base of the plant stalk. When the caterpillar hatches it bores into the stalk or a leaf stem and then tunnels along the inner tissue, pushing brown garbage out of their tunnel entrance. They usually attack squash, pumpkins and cucumbers. If you see a sudden wilting of a leaf check for borers and remove the leaf or plant part and destroy the borer. The Baby Blue and Butternut varieties of squash are fairly resistant to these bugs.

TRICH THEM
Releasing trichogramma will attack the borer eggs and kill them. Use Nc nematode infested mulch around the base of the vegetables for excellent control. If you find a borehole, just inject Nc nematodes into the borehole with a medicine dropper.

SAVE THOSE RUNNERS
Use a weekly spray of Bt as soon as you start to see the vine runners to keep the borers away.

PASTE 'EM UP
Prepare a thick paste made from water and wood ash and paint it on the trunk of the tree to stop the borers from climbing up.

SMELLY ONES WORK GREAT

These borers hate the smell of garlic and onions. If you intersperse these plants among your vine plants it will keep the borers at bay. Planting radishes is said to work well to keep the borers away.

PUT DOWN A CARPET

Fabric row covers (from garden supply stores) are a great way to stop moths from laying their eggs since they are looking for moist soil.

ALUMINUM WRAP

Try wrapping the base of the plant with a layer of aluminum foil to stop the moths from laying their eggs on the stem of the plant.

ITS RAINING SOAP SUDS

There are two good methods to deter these bugs. You can hang bars of soap on the tree and when it rains the soap will run down the tree or you can squirt a liquid hand soap on the limbs and the soap will run down the tree when you water the tree.

STRAWBERRY CROWN BORER

The grub does the major damage by boring into the main root of the plant and weakening or killing it. The adult is a brownish beetle with red patches on its wings and feeds on stems and leaves. Strawberry plants can usually defend against the beetle if they are good strong plants.

KEEP NEW BEDS AWAY

Since the beetles cannot fly, planting a new bed 300 yards away from an old bed where a problem exists usually eliminates the problem.

BOX ELDER BUGS

LEMON TREE VERY PRETTY
If you have a problem with box elder bugs on your plants, just spray the plants with a solution of diluted Lemon Joy® or any dishwasher detergent (use 1 ounce per 1 quart of tap water). Spray a few leaves first to be sure you will not damage the plant before spraying. To make the Lemon Joy® even more effective add 1 drop of essential peppermint oil to the mixture.

MILLIPEDE

These creepers can grow up to 200 pairs of legs and usually help to eliminate decaying material. However, they are also pests and may attack roots and stems of healthy plants, especially if they need water during a dry spell. When they get a taste of sweet sap they will keep feeding. They have been known to do a lot of damage to seedlings.

FLOODING DOES THE TRICK
If you can bring them to the surface you can catch them and kill them off. Drench the area with a solution of a nicotine preparation to bring them to the surface.

FUNGUS/MOLDS

THERE'S A FUNGUS AMONG US
Mix 2 tablespoons of baking soda in 1 quart of water and mix well. Place the mixture into a spray bottle and spray directly on fungus every 2-3 days as needed.

PASS THE SALAD DRESSING
Over 85% of all molds can be killed with white vinegar. Make sure that the vinegar is at least 5% to be effective.

MOLD KILLERS
Borax, sodium borate, table salt and lime are all commonly use mold killers. Baking soda and food-grade diatomaceous earth (DE) can also be used very effectively.

MILD LOVES HUMIDITY
Dehumidifiers, fans and air conditioners will reduce the amount of mold by reducing the level of humidity in the home.

BLEACH 'EM OUT
To control mold place 1 cup of household bleach into 1 gallon of water and mix well and sponge or spray on to control the mold spores.

SURGICAL REMOVAL
If you are having a problem with black spot fungus, you will need to remove and destroy the affected limb. Best to find all the areas where it is hiding and remove it before winter sets in. The fungus is able to survive the winter on fallen leaves and even the stems of roses.

AMARANTH FIGHTS FUNGI

Use about 2 pounds of amaranth leaves or fresh grain and extract the juices. Mix the juice with 2 quarts of water and use as a spray. Strain if necessary and allow the mixture to sit for 1 hour before using. This will combat the following fungi: Alternaria, cercospora, colletotrichum, curvularia, helminthosporium and pestalotia. Bring a leaf with fungus on it to your local gardening supply house for identification.

FUNGI AND GINGER

A number of fungi can be killed using ginger. These include leaf mold, early blight, frogeye and leaf spot. The rhizome needs to be crushed and the juice used in a spray. Test and area first to avoid any plant damage and allow it to remain overnight.

GRASSHOPPERS

Grasshoppers; are a real pest in the family garden because of their big appetites. They prefer grasses, clover and weeds, but when these are not available will go for the veggies. Their powerful hind legs allow them to jump up to 30 inches and they can fly long distances. Their powerful jaws can make short work of plants.

If you dig up the soil in the fall you can kill most of their eggs, however, you will need to go down about six inches to reach all of them. Heavy mulch also makes it difficult for them to get out of the ground.

Grasshoppers are more of a serious threat to crops in areas that receive between 10-30 inches of rainfall. The areas of more concern are the Midwestern United States and Canada and sometimes in the Mountain States. They spend 6-8 months in the egg stage and if fields are plowed in late fall it will help to reduce the possible infestation in the spring or early summer.

BEGONE LITTLE HOPPERS

You can purchase products made from naturally occurring protozoans called Semaspore™ or Nosema Locustae™ in many garden or agricultural supply houses. Grasshoppers eat the protozoan, become infected and die as well as spreading the disease to newly hatched grasshoppers.

ALTERNATIVE METHODS

Praying mantis' love to feast on grasshoppers. Spray them with Nc nematode and soap spray in the late evening or at night.

PLANT TOMATOES

To keep grasshoppers away from your plants, just plant tomato plants around the garden instead of just one area. Tomato plants are a natural insect repellent and really works great.

HUNT THEM DOWN

Grasshoppers sleep at night on plant leaves and can easily be found if you hunt for them with as flashlight. They can easily be picked off and drowned in a bucket of soapy water with a little cayenne pepper added. They are not early risers and if you get up early you can still pick them off the plants.

HOT PEPPER SPRAY WORKS
Prepare a spray using onions, garlic and hot peppers or Tabasco Sauce™. Blend the onions, peppers and the garlic in a food processor with 2 cups of water and allow it to stand for 1hour. Strain and use ½ cup in 1 quart of water to stop grasshoppers from attacking your plants. Best to test a few leaves first to be sure that the spray is not too potent. If it is add more water to dilute it.

ELIMINATE ROADSIDE WEEDS
Roadside weed areas are the home for many grasshoppers. If you clear these areas and plant a perennial grass such as crested wheatgrass it will reduce the problem.

MULCH THEM
If you place a good layer of mulch or compost down it will stop the grasshoppers from surfacing in the spring.

HIRE A GUINEA HEN
Guinea hens are one of the best grasshopper catchers around. They will patrol your garden and eliminate the hopper problem. When they have cleared the area, cage them!

IMPORTED CABBAGEWORM

One of the more common cabbageworms is the Imported Cabbageworm. They are about 1 inch long, green with a yellow stripe down their back and loves to eat leaves. Those common white butterflies come from this caterpillar.

STANDARD CATERPILLAR CONTROL
Very effective control can be achieved if you release trichogramma and lacewings, or spray or dust with Bt or NPV. You can also handpick the larvae off plants and then use a butterfly net to catch the moths. If you plant rosemary, thyme or sage in your garden they will stay away. A Bt spray is also very effective.

LEAFROLLERS

These caterpillars spin their web in leaves and then roll them up. They will infest large numbers of leaves and can do a lot of damage. They are not too fussy and will use plant leaves if a tree is not handy.

BEST TO SPRAY
One of the best methods for these caterpillars is to spray them with Bt, then use a mixture of NVP or soap and lime spray. An alternative method would be to release lacewings and trichogramma to destroy the eggs.

OBLIQUEBANDED LEAFROLLER

The greenish larvae roll the leaves and actually tie them together to form their home. This leafroller attacks most vegetables, flowers, shrubs and fruit trees. If there are only a few, just pinch off the leaves and destroy them. If you have a serious infestation you will need to spray with a mixture of tobacco dust and pyrethrum powder. If you are unable to find the tobacco dust: substitute rotenone for the tobacco.

MITES

CHEESE MITE
The cheese mite will cause dermatitis (skin irritation) and is larger than the grain or mold mite. It needs an ideal temperature of 73^0 and humidity of 83% to thrive.

CONTROLLING CHEESE MITES
- Make sure you inspect cheeses that are not wrapped.
- Inspect pet food that is purchased in bulk.
- Store foods in a clean, dry area.
- Never place new grains on top of old grains in storage bins.
- Store foods in well-sealed containers.
- Vacuum up spills and never leave them around.

FREEZE THEM
If you think that you have mite-infested foods, just place the foods in the freezer at 0^0F for seven days or in a shallow pan at 140^0F for 30 minutes in the oven. If you wish to use a microwave place the foods in there for 5 minutes on high.

THEY MAY WEAR SUNGLASSES

Dust mites will be killed by direct sunlight. If you place upholstered furniture in the sun for a few hours it will kill any mites that may reside there. Bedding should be wash and changed weekly and washed in water that is at least 120°F.

THERE GOES THE TEDDY BEAR

Plush animals are usually loaded with dust mites and need to be placed in a plastic bag in the freezer for 24 hours once per week. If they are washable they should be washed once per week.

NOW I LAY ME DOWN

Pillows are one of the most common items that contain dust mites. Almost 25% of all pillows are contaminated and should at least be replaced every 4-6 months. If you ever had your bed evaluated for the dust mites you would probably never sleep in it again or buy a new one.

DUST MITES

These microscopic insects can be found anywhere in your home. They can be found in our beds, clothing, upholstered furniture, bookcases and even stuffed animals. They thrive on dead skin cells and may be a hazard to people with allergies or asthma. Best to reduce their numbers as best you can. There are 35 million people who have allergies to dust mites. **Every home collects about 40 pounds of dust per year, which contains 15 species of dust mite.** One ounce of dust can contain 42,000 dust mites. In England 33% of all cereals inspected was contaminated with dust mites.

- Vacuuming works great on mattresses and pillows.
- Bedding should be washed in very hot water. Detergents and soaps will not kill the mites unless the water temperature is very hot.
- The bedroom should be kept clear of stuffed animals, clothes hampers and throw rugs.
- Stuffed animals should be periodically washed in very hot water.

- Problem areas should be dusted with tannic acid powder since this neutralizes the allergens. This is available at most health food stores.
- All mattresses and pillows should be covered with laminated covers so that the mites cannot penetrate them.
- Fabric-covered headboards are a perfect place for mites.
- Heating ducts should be covered with a special filter that can trap dust particles smaller than 10 microns.
- Mites love humidifiers and thrive on the warmth and moisture.

EAR MITES

OIL THEM
Place a few drops of olive oil on a cotton ball and place it in the ear for a minute or two, then be sure and remove all traces of the oil.

GRAIN MITES

THE GROCER'S ITCH
Since there are so many mites around, especially in foods, there are two, mite infestations that have been related to people that work with grains. The grocer's itch and the baker's itch are commonly found in markets and bakeries. Best to keep humidity out of your grains.

HOT CHILI TO THE RESCUE
If you place a very hot chili pepper in the grain you will not have any insects residing there. The hotter the better but be sure that it is a whole pepper with no externally visible damage or you will ruin the taste of the grain.

MOLD MITE

LOVES HUMIDITY
The mold mites will invade almost any food, especially grains and breads if the humidity is relatively high. The drier the products are kept the better. If you have this problem in your area it would be wise to store grain and grain-related products in the refrigerator or freezer.

STINKBUG

These are flat green, shield-shaped bug that will cause tomato plants to develop white spots as they suck out the juices. If they are not causing a problem these may be beneficial since they will act as a parasite and kill pest caterpillars and beetles. They will lay a cluster of brown or green eggs on the underneath side of leaves.

68

PARASITE TO KILL A PARASITE
The parasite that will eliminate the stinkbug is called *Trissolcus basilis*. You can also hand pick the stinkbugs and their eggs off your plants.

SPRAYS WORK WELL
A soap spray using 4 drops of liquid soap and ¼ cup of lime in 1 gallon of water will take care of the problem.

THRIPS

Identification:
These are very small (almost invisible) yellow or black insects that attack plants and flowers and suck out their juices as well as spreading many plant diseases. Under a magnifying glass they will look like long, elongated bugs that have a double wing with fancy fringe. They can range in color from yellow to almost black.

General Information:
When you disturb thrips they will fly or hop for a very short distance and have the tendency to flip their abdomen over their head like a scorpion to try and scare you away. They will lay their eggs on leaves and plants and look like a walking spot that is only about 1/16th of an inch long. They may be yellow to black in color and there are over 600 species in North America.

They prefer to feed on beans, tomatoes, potatoes, carrots, cucumber and squash. They also like gladioli and roses. If you see a silvery spot or streak it may very well be thrips that have settled in.

CALL IN THE MITES
There are two predatory mites that can be purchased to control thrips. They are *Amblyseiulus mackenseii* and *Euseius tularensis*. Dragonflies also like to feast on thrips. Using Nc nematode mulch around the base of plants may also do some good.

SPECIAL SPRAY
Check with your garden supply store for a spray that contains sabadilla dust, which is usually combined with sugar. Soap sprays early in the morning are also very effective as well as yellow sticky traps.

OLD 1800'S FORMULA
Prepare a nicotine spray by using 10 cigarettes and placing them into 3 pints of very hot tap water for 24 hours then strain and dilute it with 12 pints of water and use as a spray. Do not harvest plants within 3 days of using the spray since the poison needs to be diluted. Never use tobacco on roses and the nicotine is poisonous to fishes, earthworms and many beneficial insects.

YELLOW AND BLUE TRAPS
Thrips are attracted to the colors yellow and blue. If you use some construction paper and place a sticky substance on it they will go over for a look see and get all stuck up. If you place the sticky substance on the plant stems it will stop them from climbing up the plant. Tanglefoot™ is excellent to use as the sticky substance.

FOILED AGAIN
Foil collars work great for low-lying plants. Make sure that they extend at least 12 inches around the plant on all sides to be effective. If the plants are over 2 feet tall, you will need to place stakes around the plants and extend the foil from the stakes.

GENERAL METHODS OF INSECT CONTROL

CLOCHE ME
This resembles a miniature greenhouse and is used for seedbeds and very young plants as well as acting as a barrier against insects and pests. The cloche must be opened every day to allow watering, especially on hot days. However, this is a negative since when it is opened it may allow insects and pests to enter. It is, however, an excellent method of allowing plants to get a good start.
The healthier the plant the less likely insects stand a chance of damaging them. Check with your garden supple house about building plans or purchasing a ready-made cloche.

ALL-PURPOSE SPRAY PESTICIDES
The following formulations will be effective against most pest insects. Place the formula in a spray bottle and either spray on the insect or into its home.

- Water to fill the bottle ¾ full then add 4 drops of Ivory liquid soap, ¼ teaspoon of hot pepper sauce and ½ crushed garlic. This formula will need to be strained before you place it into the spray bottle.
- Finely crush 2-3 habanero peppers, 2 large yellow onions and 1-large garlic clove. Place the mixture into 1 quart of very hot water and allow it to steep overnight before straining and using in a sprayer.
- Mix together 1 tablespoon of Ivory liquid soap and 1 teaspoon of canola oil in 1 quart of tap water.
- Finely crush 15 garlic cloves and allow them to soak in 16 ounces of mineral oil and 4 drops of Ivory liquid soap for 12 hours, then strain and add 3 pints of water. Best to test on a leaf or two before using this formulation on the whole plant.
- Finely crush ½ cup of Serrano peppers in 2 cups of warm water, strain well and spray.
- Place 2 cups of rubbing alcohol in 1 quart of water and spray the plants that are infected. Best to allow the mixture to remain on 1-2 leaves overnight and then check for damage.

- Crush up some rhubarb or oleander leaves and place them into 1 quart of warm water. Allow it to stand overnight then strain before using. **This is very toxic so keep it away from pets and children.**

FLOATING ROW COVERS

This method uses lightweight opaque materials, which are draped over the entire garden bed. The material allows sunlight and water to pass through, but will keep insects and birds from damaging your plants. Since the material is so light, the plants will push it up as it grows. The edges are anchored with a heavy object such as a rock to avoid being pushed up by the wind. The material will break down after a few years and is sold in rolls and is fairly inexpensive.

PHEREMONES

These are biological mating hormone scents given off to attract other insects of a particular species. Pheremones are sold by garden supply stores and can be placed on flypaper or in traps to attract insects. This method is a very effective method of ridding your garden of insects.

CHAPTER 6

CATERPILLARS

CATERPILLARS

ONE CATERPILLAR, TWO CATERPILLAR
One of the best methods of getting rid of caterpillars is to just pick them off and drive them at least 10 miles away from your garden and release them.

KILLS THE YOUNG ONES
This naturally occurring bacteria, is used to kill the young ones of the gypsy moth. Just spray them with *Bacillus thuringiensis (Bt)*, a good natural biological caterpillar control weapon that you can purchase in a garden supply house.

HIT THEM WITH A BLACKJACK
Blackjack is an annual weed that has flowers with white and yellow centers. The seeds are small, black and thin with tiny claws on one end. They usually stick to people's clothes or pets fur. A spray can be made; by using the mature seeds if you just take a cupful in water and allow it to boil for about 8-10 minutes or allow them to soak for 24 hours. If you boil them allow them to cool then add 1 quart of water and 1 teaspoon of liquid soap and spray immediately. This will also eliminate aphids, beetles, cabbage root flies and whiteflies.

ELIMINATE THEM WITH PAWPAW
To prepare a spray using pawpaw (carica papaya) use 2 pounds of shredded leaves and add them to 4 cups of water and mix well. Strain and add the juice to 2 pints of water then add 2 teaspoons of paraffin and 3 drop of liquid soap. Spray into the soil to get rid of caterpillars and cutworms.

SMELLY SOLUTION
Jimson weed (purple stink weed) can be used to combat aphids by just drying and then powdering the stems and leaves, then using the powder to dust the plants. This plant has also been called thorn apple. **This plant is poisonous to humans and animals so handle it with caution.**

BAGWORM

This caterpillar lives in a silk cocoon that looks like a bag. It has small pieces of leaves attached to the outside as camouflage and carries the bag with it when it is feeding. The bag is about 2 inches long when it is fully matured. They lay their eggs in the fall and they hatch in May or early June.

HERE-A BAG, THERE A BAG
One of the best methods of getting rid of the bugs is to hand pick them from the trees or plants and burn them.

BURP 'EM
The Burpee Company, Inc. sells a pheromone trap that is prepared specifically for your bagworms.

HERBAL SPRAY

1	Pound of quassia chips
1	Gallon of water

Place the quassia chips in the water and allow it to stand overnight then strain and dilute with water in a ratio of 1:10. Add a small amount of liquid soap and spray. The quassia chips are available at most garden supply stores.

CABBAGE LOOPER

Identification:
These little white-striped green caterpillar critters just love broccoli, kale, kohlrabi, radishes, turnips, peas, cabbage and cauliflower plants. Their body forms a loop as they travel along. You can easily identify the looper by its *"humpback"* appearance. The moth is brown with silver markings on the center of each wing.

General Information:
They tend to feed on the underneath sides of the leaves. They lay their greenish-white eggs singly on the upper surface of the leaves. To stop them from laying their eggs on your plants, just plant onion sets around the area totally surrounding your plants. The loopers will not come near a garden that has an onion fence around it. Space the onion sets about 4 inches apart for the best results.

BEGONE CABBAGE LOOPERS
For natural control of cabbage loopers it is best to release trichogramma and lacewings. If you want to get rid of them in a hurry then dust or spray with Bt or NPV from your garden supply or agricultural store. Best to begin spraying once a week after the moths or butterflies start appearing.

A SOUR SOLUTION
If your cabbage has been infested, just make some sour milk by adding 4 teaspoons of white vinegar per cup of milk to turn it sour. Spray or sprinkle the mixture over the heads of cabbage to get rid of the bugs.

HERE A LITTLE, THERE A LITTLE
This is an oldie but a goody! Prepare a mixture of ¼ cup of table salt with ½ cup of all-purpose flour then place the mixture into a large saltshaker and sprinkle the cabbage during the growing season. Best to do this a few times and not depend on just once to do the trick.

ASHES WORK GREAT

Wood ashes can be sprinkled on the leaves to repel the cabbage loopers as well as the imported cabbageworms. This is an excellent method and won't hurt the plant.

TIDES IN

Ocean saltwater; is used very effectively by many farmers to kill the cabbage loopers and their eggs as well as stopping the caterpillars from eating the leaves. Cabbage plants can tolerate the salt from a spray of saltwater.

THIS REALLY ISN'T CORNY

If you sprinkle cornmeal or rye flour on cabbage plants the caterpillars will eat it and soon die. This is a very safe method of controlling these pests.

A CANOPY OF LEAVES

If you place geranium leaves over the cabbage plants it will deter a number of pests including the cabbage looper.

GIVE THEM A LAXATIVE

Try placing a small squirt of mineral oil into the tip of each ear of corn to smother the worm. This should be done after the silks are starting to wilt and turn brown. You can also add a small amount of cayenne pepper to the oil for an extra charge.

TIGHT HEADS KEEP THEM AWAY

There are a few varieties of cabbage that have very tight heads, which the bugs do not like. These are Mammoth Red Rock, Savoy Chieftain and Savoy Perfection Drumhead cabbage.

PLANTS THAT REPEL

If you plant any of these plants near your cabbage you will not have a problem with loopers. They are onion, garlic, celery, tansy, hyssop, mint, sage, rosemary, tomato or thyme.

CABBAGEWORMS

PUT SALT ON THEIR TAIL

One of the best methods to stop cabbageworms is to spray them with a solution of 1 ounce of table salt in 2 gallons of water. The salt may damage your plants, so be careful where you spray. Salt will also stop plant growth.

CABBAGE WORM CURE

The following ingredients will be needed:

½	Cup of table salt
1	Cup of all-purpose flour

Place the ingredients in a small dish and mix well. Sprinkle the powder on the plants early in the morning when the plants still have some dew on them.

CORN ARMYWORM

Identification:
These are around 2 inches long and light tan or dark brown in color. They also have either; orange, yellow or dark brown contrasting stripes.

General Information:
The damage to the corn may appear in the form of chewed leaves and the damage usually appears on the edges of the leaves. They will eventually bore into the ear of corn and set up housekeeping until there is no more to eat before they move to a new ear.

SPRAY THOSE NEMATODES
Spraying Nc nematodes early in the season will help reduce the number of bugs. If you see a borehole it would be best to inject the nematodes directly into the hole. You can also hand pick them by making a slit next to the borehole.

KILL THEM WITH GRAPEFRUIT

1	Whole grapefruit
2	Cups of boiling water
2	Cups cool tap water

Grind up the grapefruit in a food processor and add the mixture to the boiling water. Allow it to remain overnight then strain and add the cool water before you spray. When sprayed on the plants it will stop caterpillars and most beetle larvae from chomping on your plants.

CORN EARWORM

Identification:
This worm is about 2 inches long and may be found in shades of green, brown or yellow. Its sides will be darker than the bodies. The adults are light brown or gray moths with black spots and about a 1½-inch wingspan.

General Information:
These worms are also known as tomato fruitworms or cotton bollworms. Their garden food consists of corn, tomatoes, cotton, peppers, eggplant, okra, potatoes, squash, beans and peas. They will attack the tender shoots as soon as they break the surface. They love to chew on the corn silk and disrupt the germination process. They chew holes in green tomatoes and may move on and not even finish their meal. If you have flower buds that have become damaged it would be best to remove them.

CLOTHESPINS TO THE RESCUE
If you clip a clothespin to the tip of each ear of corn to keep the husk tight you will not have a worm problem. You will, however, have the funniest-looking cornfield in your vicinity.

PLANT RESISTANT VARIETIES
There are a number of varieties that can be planted that the worms will not bother with. These include ones with tight husks such as Try Country Gentleman or Silver Cross Bantam corn.

PLANT REPELLANTS
There a few plants will repel these worms very efficiently. These need to be planted within the rows and include smartweed or sunflowers.

BIOLOGICAL CONTROL
Bt sprayed on the plants works great. Tachinid flies and wasp parasites will also do the trick. The commercially available virus Elcar™ can also be used as well as NPV very effectively.

SCREEN THEM IN
If you have a number of valuable plants the best thing to do is to screen them in with a piece of cheesecloth.

CUTWORM

Identification:
There are many species of cutworms and their color varies from green to white, brown and even black. They may also have stripes or be banded. They are plump, soft-bodied larvae covered with coarse hair.

General Information:
They seem to like vegetables the best and head for corn, beans and cabbage first if they are available. They will eat almost anything. One of their favorite foods, are tender seedlings. They don't eat a lot but can cause a lot of damage by cutting off the plants by the stems and killing them. Some cutworms will climb up the plant and eat the leaves. They will be on the soil surface at night, which leaves them vulnerable.

ATTACK THE EGGS FOR CONTROL
Use trichogramma and lacewings to attack and eat the eggs. They love cutworm egg omelets. Applying Nc nematodes around plants will also solve the problem.

FOILED AGAIN
You can wrap aluminum foil around the stems of plants that you may be worried about to stop cutworms from eating the stems. Rub a little garlic juice on the foil to make it more effective.

COLLARS FOR THE BUGS
If you are having a problem with cutworms, try placing small cardboard collars around the stem of the plant and place it just under the ground at least 1-2 inches. You can use old toilet paper or paper towel tubes. Just cut them; place them on and then staple them closed. You can also use tarpaper rolled up and aluminum foil will also do the trick wrapped around the stem.

LEAVES AS WRAPS
Hundreds of years ago cutworm infestations; were solved by placing hickory or walnut leaves around the stems of the plants. Cutworms shy away from these leaves.

MUMMIFY THEM
Prepare a mixture composed of molasses, hardwood sawdust and wheat bran. If the cutworm even crawls into this mixture it will dry them up and make sweet little wooden mummies out of them.

SANDPAPER TO THE RESCUE
If you place a collar of sandpaper or roofing shingle around the base of the plant as a collar it will stop the cutworms from doing their thing.

AH CHOO
Cutworms can be eliminated with black pepper spray. Just crush up 1 tablespoon of the seeds into a powder, add water and spray any stored grains where you have a problem. The powder can also be used and spread around the affected area.

GRAIN KILLS CUTWORMS
Soak 2 handfuls of finger millet (grain with grass-like leaves) in 1 quart of water, strain and spray.

CRUSH THOSE SEEDS

The castor oil plant can be used to eliminate cutworms by placing 4 cups of the crushed, shelled seeds into 2 quarts of water and boiling for about 10 minutes then adding 2 teaspoons of paraffin and ½ teaspoon of liquid soap to the mixture. Add 7 more quarts of water to dilute and spray into the soil in the affected areas. **Castor bean seeds are poisonous to some animals and humans.**

THEY HATE TO COMMUTE

You can go out at night and find these pest with a flashlight and look for them chomping on the plant leaves. In the daylight they tend to rest just next to the base of the plant so that they will not have far to go for their next meal.

PAWPAW SEEDS WORK

Crush 1 cup of pawpaw seeds and place them in 2 cups of water and allow it to stand for 24 hours. Strain and spray the areas. Test a leaf or two to be sure that there will be no plant damage. If there is damage add more water and dilute the spray.

LE PEW

Garlic spray for cutworms:

3	Cups of warm tap water
3	Tablespoons of mineral oil
3	Whole garlic bulbs
1	Tablespoon of Ivory Liquid Soap™

First separate the cloves of garlic and chop in a food processor. Place the cloves in a jar with the mineral oil and allow it to stand for 24 hours before adding the water and soap. Best to store the mixture in the refrigerator with a tight cover. To use as a spray dilute ½ cup in 1 quart of water. Spray directly on the plants for an instant kill.

OUCH THAT HURTS MY FEET

If you sprinkle oak leaf mulch or use crushed eggshells around the plants it will stop the cutworms from attacking the plants. The sharp edges hurt their tender footsies. You can also sprinkle DE or wood ashes around to irritate them.

BLOATING UP A CATERPILLAR
If you want to kill them just sprinkle some cornmeal around the plants and they will eat it, bloat up and die.

EASTERN TENT CATERPILLAR

Identification:
The Eastern Tent Caterpillar have white stripes down their back as well as yellow and brown lines and blue spots on their sides. They spin tent-like waterproof webs, which is their distinct characteristic.

General Information:
They will eat fruit and leaves but will not touch an evergreen tree. They lay their eggs in masses that will encircle twigs and they will hatch in the spring. There can be up to 300 caterpillars in a single web and they can remove all the leaves on a tree in a very short period of time.

SPRAY THE LEAVES
There are a number of ways to eliminate this pest. You can spray the leaves with Bt or a solution of lime and soap directly on the caterpillars. Lacewings, Bt and trichogramma wasps will also do the job.

SEAWEED TO THE RESCUE
Go down to the beach and collect seaweed and place the seaweed in all the crotches of the tree. This needs to be done in the spring to repel the caterpillars. As the seaweed disintegrates it also makes excellent mulch, full of trace minerals.

GET OUT THE MAGNIFYING GLASS AND YOUR OVERCOAT
Check the tree in the winter months for egg masses and remove them and place them into a bucket of soapy water.

TAKE DOWN THE TENT
Remove all the tents that you can locate and place them in a bucket of soapy water to kill them.

GARDEN WEBWORM
This worm attacks beets, beans, corn, strawberries and peas primarily. They make webs from leaves and consume them. They may be found in a variety of colors but most have three dark spots on each side of each segment with one to three bristle-like hairs growing from each segment. All webbed leaves must be clipped off and destroyed.

GREEN FRUITWORM
These worms attack apple fruit trees and strawberries and feed on the leaves, tying them together with silk. They will do damage to fruit and begin their attack at petal fall. They are a large green caterpillar and are sometimes speckled. The mature ones have a cream-colored line down their backs. The best control is to use Bt.

GYPSEY MOTH LARVAE

Identification:
These are 2 inch long gray caterpillars that little brown tufts of brown and yellow hairs extending from their sides. They also have 10 blue spots followed by 12 red spots on their back. If you find one there will be plenty more where they came from.

General Information:
They will totally defoliate a tree and kill it. After they kill the tree they will leave and look for another tree or work on your plants for dessert. They are usually only found from New England to West Virginia and are now being seen in other states. They leave large brown egg masses on trees.

CHASE THEM DOWN WITH PARASITES
Control can be effective with a number of parasites such as the lacewing, *Glyptapanteles flavicoxis* and *Cotesia melanoscelus*. The eggs contain a scale that the trichogramma cannot seem to break. Spray Nc nematodes around the base of trees to kill migrating caterpillars. The foliage should be sprayed with Bt or NPV at the first sign of an impending attack. You can also spray the Nc around the tree trunk.

PICK ME A CATERPILLAR
If you tie a rope around the tree and place a burlap bag on the rope the caterpillars will rest there for some time to chat about their daily activities. This will give you plenty of time to interrupt them and drive them 10 miles from your property and release them, or just snuff them out where they stand.

MOUNTAIN ASH SAWFLY

This tiny green caterpillar is only about ½ inches long and is covered with spines. They will strip the leaves and skeletonize them, leaving only the ribs and veins. They prefer the leaves at the top of the plant or tree. They will appear around the middle of May and are usually found only in the northeastern United States.

LOOKING UP
The bug lays eggs in clusters on the underneath sides of leaves. You can spot them by the white spots on top of the leaves.

NAVAL ORANGEWORM

These caterpillars attack walnut, almond and pistachios and enter the nut after the hulls split, then feed on the nutmeats contaminating the nuts with their excrements. The caterpillar has a white to pinkish body with a reddish-brown head.

It has a crescent-shaped mark on the second segment behind the head, which makes it easy to identify from a codling moth. They will weave their home around a nut making it into a *"mummy nut."* These nuts should be removed and destroyed.

WATCH FOR NUT-SPLIT
You need to harvest the nuts as soon as nut-split occurs so that the worm will not have a chance to set up housekeeping.

PARASITES ARE AVAILABLE
There are two parasites that are commercially available that will combat the naval orangeworm problem. They are *Copidosommopsis plethorica* and *Goniozus legneri*.

ORANGE TORTRIX CATERPILLAR

This is a brownish-colored caterpillar that has a larva that rolls up in a leaf with a web and will feed inside it. If you find that you have a number of oranges falling before their time it is probably due to this pest boring into the rinds.

It will lay their eggs on the surface of the leaves or underneath the leaf looking like cream-colored discs. The eggs will destroy the leaves. If you see one of these caterpillars with white eggs on its back it would be best to leave it alone. The eggs are from a parasitic wasp and will be beneficial to your garden.

TWO GOOD KILLERS
There are two good methods of getting rid of these pests; either use Bt or dust or spray with pyrethrum.

EXOCHUS TO THE RESCUE
The parasite wasp species *Exochus* attacks the larvae of the orange tortrix caterpillar and has been found to be very effective. Other parasites that are also effective in control are *Apanteles aristolilae* and a tachinid fly called *Nemorilla pyste*.

POTATO TUBERWORM

Attacks tomatoes, potatoes, eggplant and peppers at their terminal end and burrow in killing the fruit or vegetable. They are somewhat pinkish with dark heads. Be sure and check potatoes before storing or they will kill most of the potatoes. If you have a problem with potatoes and this bug, be sure and do not plant tomatoes or eggplant near the field.

SALTMARSH CATERPILLAR

These caterpillars attack beans, lettuce, tomatoes and love grapes. They will skeletonize leaves in short order and are not a very welcome visitor to your garden. They have very long hairs with orange, white and black tufts. They usually lay their eggs in a weedy area and then go to the garden for their meals. The best method of stopping them has been with a barrier of aluminum foil or Bt.

TOMATO HORNWORMS

These are 4-inch long caterpillars that are green with white bars and feed on tomatoes, potatoes, sweet peppers and eggplants. They have a horn but do not sting. A similar horned worm called the tobacco hornworm prefers tobacco plants. Handpicking is one of the best methods of eradicating these bugs.

BUGS VS WORMS

There are a few bugs that will keep these worms in line; they are the lacewing, trichogramma and the ladybug. Spraying Bt on the leaves will also help as well as planting strong-smelling herbs.

A PLANT BARRIER

Planting herbs or flowers that they do not wish to be around is an excellent method of controlling these pests. If you plant basil, borage or marigolds around your garden you will never have a problem with the tomato hornworm.

SPARYING WORKS

Using a hot pepper or limonoid spray will keep this pest from eating you plants. Either crush citrus fruit peels in water overnight or mix Tabasco Sauce™ and water to make the sprays and be sure to strain before using. Always test a few leaves and allow it to stand overnight to be sure that you do not have too strong a formula for that particular plant.

PREDATORS TO THE RESCUE

Predators that will eliminate these bugs include ladybugs, trichograma wasps and lacewings. Also if you plant some dill they will head right for it making it easier to catch them.

TOMATO PINWORM

These small caterpillars attack tomatoes and are usually found in coastal areas around Southern California and the San Joaquin Valley. They bore into the tomatoes at the stem end and make narrow blackened tunnels, which then expose the tomato to bacterial infestation and decay. The caterpillars are gray to a yellowish color with red or purple around each segment. If you are having a problem with this worm it is best not to grow tomatoes in the area for about 3 months and there should be no tomatoes grown within 4 miles of the area. Pheromone traps also work well.

WHITEMARKED TUSSOCK MOTH

This is a weird-looking caterpillar that has a red head from which will sprout two hornlike tufts of long black hair with another tuft appearing from the tail. It has a black and yellow stripe down its back. It will skeletonize leaves of a variety of plants including geranium, German ivy, rose and many fruit trees as well as a number of deciduous shade trees.

REMOVING THE PROBLEM
Look for the egg masses and remove them, then paint the areas with creosote. If you have birds around they will give you a hand and the scary looks of the caterpillar will not affect them at all.

LITTLE BEETLE SAVES THE DAY
The tiny dermastid beetle called *Trogoderma sternale* will feed on the eggs and are used as a natural control in Southern California.

COMMON CATERPILLARS FOR WHICH PHEROMONES ARE COMMERCIALLY AVAILABLE

CATERPILLAR PEST	CROP
Black Cutworm	Vegetable Gardens
Codling Moth	Apple, Pear & Walnut Trees
Leafroller	Orchard Crops, Grapes
Orange Tortrix	Citrus Trees, Grapes, Berries
Oriental Fruit Moth	Orchard Crops
Peach Twig Borer	Stone Fruits, Almond
Redbanded Leafroller	Orchard Crops
Tomato Pinworm	Tomatoes
Beet Armyworm	Vegetable Gardens
Cabbage Looper	Vegetable Gardens
Diamondback Moth	Cole Crops

Fruit Tree leafroller	Orchards
Tentiform Leafminer	Apple Trees
Apple Pandemis	Apple Trees
Variegated Cutworm	Vegetable Gardens
Artichoke Plume Moth	Artichokes
Sunflower Moth	Sunflowers
Carpenter Worm	Fruit Trees
Potato Tuberworm	Potatoes, Tomatoes
Peachtree Borer	Stone Fruit

CHAPTER 7

TREE PESTS

TREE PESTS

CRAWLEES ON FRUIT TREES

To get rid of most crawling insect pests on fruit trees, just purchase a solution of lime sulfur and dormant oil at a garden supply house and spray it on the trunk and branches of dormant trees. This will suffocate the insect eggs. A pump sprayer will be needed for this type of application (best to rent one). If you want to make your own concoction, which will be less toxic and without kerosene, mix 1 cup of canola oil and 2 tablespoons of Ivory Liquid Soap™ in a 1-gallon container of water. The oil and soap should be mixed first and then add the water.

STOPPING SNAILS AND SLUGS

To stop snails and slugs from climbing your fruit trees, just protect the tree by placing a 3-inch wide strip of thin copper sheeting completely around the trunk about 1-2 feet from the ground.

GROUND APPLES ARE BAD

When apples fall on the ground they are perfect locations for a number of insects to start housekeeping in. Remove any apple or other fruit when it falls to the ground. This will reduce the bug population that may cause damage to your fruit trees.

KILLING THE WINTERING INSECTS

Many insects spend their winter in trees waiting for the warmer weather of spring. It would be wise to eliminate these insects before they become active again. Special winter or dormant oils should be used when the trees are dormant. These are heavy oils that are slow to evaporate and should be used before new growth starts to appear in the spring. The oils will not harm the tree but will kill the vacationing insects. Be sure that the tree is well watered before spraying any oil.

SCALE REMOVER

To remove scales on trees, just use mustard seed flour. The scales will suffocate if the flour is sprinkled or sprayed on them. To prepare a spray solution, just mix 1 pound of mustard seed flour with 1 gallon of water and use in a sprayer.

ALL AROUND OIL

The summer or superior oils are lightweight and can be used all year round. These oils have the ability to smother the pests and their eggs by clogging them up. Be sure that any tree that is to be oiled is well watered before spraying the oil. If the plant or tree is under, lack of moisture stress, it can damage the plant or tree.

SPECIAL OIL SPRAY

2	Quarts of tap water
1	Teaspoon of horticultural oil
2	Cups of isopropyl alcohol

The alcohol mixed with the oil will kill bugs on contact. The oil helps the mixture stick around long enough to really do some good.

MAKING TREE PASTE

This is only practical if you have a few trees that are bothered by aphids. Make a paste of:

1/3	Sticky clay
1/3	Cow manure
1/3	Sand

Mix with water into a paste and paint it on the tree trunk and large branches.

NEVER USE ANY OILS IF THE OUTSIDE TEMPERATURE IS OVER 90ºF

ALMONDS

ALMOND PEST PROBLEM SOLVER

THE PROBLEM	CAUSED BY
Nut meat with worms, webbing with brownish fecal matter	Navel orangeworm
Young shoots die back to several inches from tip in spring	Peach twig borers, oriental fruit moth
Leaves tied together with webbing, young fruit eaten	Leafrollers

APRICOTS

APRICOT PEST PROBLEM SOLVER

THE PROBLEM	CAUSED BY
Young shoots die back one to several inches from tip in spring,, small worms in shoots	Peach twig borer, oriental moth
Leaves and fruit webbed together and eaten in spring, sunken brown scars	Leafrollers, tussock moth, green fruitworm
Fruit may have whitish worm inside and fall off tree prematurely	Codling moth
Foliage infested with green bugs in spring, leaves and twigs have honeydew on them, Irregular holes in leaves with no webbing, holes	Mealy plum aphid, earwig
Tiny holes in ripening fruit, green beetle with black spots hanging around	Cucumber beetle
Fruit partially eaten	Birds and squirrels

APPLE TREES

APPLE MAGGOT

These are yellow-white legless larvae that will bore into an apple after they hatch from an egg. The eggs: are laid by the adults in small punctures in the apple. The punctures are so small that they are hardly noticeable. The problem may not become evident until you bite into the apple and find the worm. The telltale hole will appear in the apple when the worm leaves. After they become mature the maggots leave the apple and just fall to the ground, enter a pupate stage and remain for the winter. They are common everywhere apple trees are grown. These are also known as the apple tree fly or railroad worm.

GET THEM DRUNK

It is best to catch the pest when it is in the fly stage before you have a problem. Set a baited trap by mixing 1 part of molasses to 9 parts of tap water, add yeast so that it will ferment, then pour the liquid into a wide-mouthed jar. After the fermentation relaxes, hang the jars in the trees.

YUK, PLASTIC FRUIT AGAIN!

This will really irritate and kill them at the same time. Hang plastic fruit from the trees and paint Tanglefoot™ or Stickem™ on the fruit. They will land and be stuck for the rest of their lives.

WORMS TO THE RESCUE

One of the best ways to eliminate maggots is to apply Nc nematodes to the topsoil around the apple trees in the late summer to early fall. This will kill all the maggots as soon as they fall to the ground.

PASS THE FAUX APPLE PLEASE

If you string some fake apples that are yellow and red in the apple trees and place Tanglefoot™ or any other sticky substance on them it will trap the females that are going to lay their eggs. This should be done in the spring or early summer for the best results. You can also purchase some traps that can hang in the trees.

APPLE RED BUG

These bugs are normally found in the north central and northeastern United States. The bark crevices hold the eggs until they hatch and they become mature about June. They feed on the fruit and leave small russet scars or slight dimples. If you do a delayed spraying of dormant oil it should eliminate the pests.

APPLE SEED CHALCID

This is a tiny wasp that is found in the northeastern United States and lay their eggs in apples and other fruit. The apple will have a dimpled appearance since the larvae feed on the seeds. Check the fruit for signs of dimpling and destroy the infested fruit to get rid of the problem.

BUFFALO TREEHOPPERS

These bugs are triangular in shape and have a short snout and horns at each shoulder. They do their damage by puncturing the bark of the trees to lay their eggs. The young trees are more susceptible to damage than the older trees. The eggs are laid in September and October. If you have this problem don't plant alfalfa, legumes or clover as a cover crop. Their favorite plant is bindweed, which must be kept out of orchards. Spraying with a dormant oil spray should kill the majority of the wintering eggs.

CANKER WORM

These worm spin a silken thread and you can see them descending from branches on apple trees. If you cultivate the soil under the apple tree during the first week of June, chances are you will eliminate most of these worms since this is when the larvae tend to descend and enter the ground.

THE ELIMINATOR

Spraying with Bt is the recommended method of controlling these bugs. Spray in April or May for the best results.

APPLE PEST PROBLEM SOLVER	
THE PROBLEM	CAUSED BY
Brown granular material around core that may leak out holes	Codling moth
Leaves and blossoms tied up and eaten, bronze-colored scars	Leafrollers
Leaves eaten in spring, small gouges	Western tussock moth
Irregular spots on upper side of leaves, looks like blisters	Tentiform leafminer
White cottony masses on woody areas of the tree, warty growths on limbs and roots, honeydew and black sooty mold	Woolly apple aphid
New leaves distorted and curled, honeydew	Rosy apple aphid
New growth stunted, honeydew present and black sooty mold on leaves and fruit	Green apple aphid
Pieces of apples missing	Birds and squirrels

CODLING MOTH

This caterpillar will bore into the core of the apple and is one of the more significant apple bugs that do crop damage. There are a number of methods of controlling the bug naturally.

WE NEED A GOOD BAND

One of the best controls is to band the tree. In the spring use strips of corrugated cardboard to tempt the larvae looking for a place spin their cocoon. Wrap the bands in several thicknesses; then tie them on firmly. The exposed ridges should be facing toward the tree, if not, the larvae will not spin a cocoon. In warm weather you should remove the bands every 2 weeks and in cool weather about every 3 weeks, then remove and kill the larvae.

EUROPEAN APPLE SAWFLY

This is a brown and yellow bug with many transverse lines. It is somewhat larger than a common housefly and is active in the northeastern United States. The larvae live just under the skin of the fruit until they are about one-third grown and then bore into the fruit and do extensive damage.

FLATHEAD APPLE BORER

This is a pest with a big appetite and will infest the following trees: apricot, cherry, boxelder, elm, hickory, chestnut, linden, oak, peach, plum, sycamore and willow. Their feeding tunnels will actually show through the bark in sunken areas. The larvae spend the winter in these tunnels.

The tunnels will eventually fill with a dry powder known as "frass," which is composed of droppings and sawdust produced by the boring. The adults are dark bronze beetles that have a metallic sheen. The beetles come out in May and June and will relax on the sunny sides of the trees and lay their eggs in the crevices of the tree.

GET OUT THE BURLAP BAGS
Trees that have been transplanted and seedlings need to be protected with a wrapping of burlap or cardboard from the soil up to the lower branches.

PAINT THE TREES
You can apply a generous coating of white exterior latex paint to the tree trunk, protecting them from the bug.

ROUNDHEADED APPLE TREE BORER

This borer likes to tunnel deep into the trunk of the apple tree near the ground. Infestations will weaken a tree and can kill young trees. They will also eat both the leaves and the fruit. If you find brown castings above or just below the ground you know that they are active. If you do see the holes, snake a wire into the hole to kill them.

SUDS-A-WAY
If you use a thick wash of soap applied to the lower trunk of the tree it will discourage the beetles from laying their eggs.

WHITE APPLE LEAFHOPPERS

When feeding, these leafhoppers remove large amounts of chlorophyll and leave the foliage with white spots. The nymphs are pale yellow and will feed on the underneath sides of the leaves. They will leave dark spots of excrement behind. Spraying with rotenone will solve the problem.

CATCH THE DROPPINGS
One of the best methods of reducing the problem with these bugs is to remove any fruit that has dropped on the ground. Most of the time when fruit drops prematurely it is due to an infestation.

HIRE A HOG
Many farmers allow a hog to run free in the orchard eating all the dropped fruit. This solves the problem of having to pick up all the fruit that has dropped.

SPRAYING WORKS

Spraying does work to control most pests that will attack your fruit trees. Spray Rotenone or Ryania at pink and petal fall for the best results.

CHERRY TREES

CHERRY FRUITWORM

This worm hatches out toward the end of May in the northeastern United States. The pinkish worm larvae bore into the cherries and feeds for about 2 weeks. The adult fruitworm is actually a gray moth with black spots. It will lay its eggs on the fruit in mid-July and they hatch as small green caterpillars, which proceed to eat the cherries near the stem and build their web around a cluster of cherries.

PARASITES TO THE RESCUE

There are two parasites that are used to control these bugs. The first is a parasitic fungus called *Beauvaria bassiana*, which is also used against the cranberry fruitworm and the second is a parasitic wasp called *Trichogramma minutum*.

OPEN THE FLOODGATES

Large commercial orchards sometimes flood the orchard to get rid of these bugs and others. In smaller operations handpicking works well.

CUCULIO BUGS

These tiny bugs feed on the tender foliage, buds and blossoms of different fruit trees as soon as they have finished blooming. They will drill circular hole in the newly set fruit. The females lay their eggs and the grub proceeds to eat the fruit for about 15 days, then bores out and enters the soil. It then proceeds to form a hard shell and turns into pupae.

SHAKE THEM UP

When these bugs are in the tree and the tree is shaken they tend to curl up in a ball and play dead. They will easily fall from the tree in a large tarp placed under the tree. When the tree is shaken they all fall out into the tarp for disposal.

CHERRY TREE PEST PROBLEM SOLVER

THE PROBLEM	CAUSED BY
Leaves curled in spring, cluster of black insects	Black cherry aphids
Leaves tied together with webbing and eaten in spring	Leafroller
Leaves have brownish patches, skeletonized leaves	Pear slug

GUARD HENS TO THE RESCUE

If you allow hens to roam around the fruit trees they will handle the problem by eating the grubs as they descend. This will end their life cycle very efficiently.

CITRUS TREES

CITRUS TREE PEST PROBLEM SOLVER

THE PROBLEM	CAUSED BY
Reddish-brown round scales on leaves and twigs, leaves may yellow and drop	California red scale
Fruit and leaves have honeydew and black sooty mold	Soft scales
Leaves curled and may have honeydew and mold	Aphids

Honeydew on fruit and leaves, flies fly away when disturbed	Whiteflies
Honeydew on fruit and leaves, cottony secretion on leaves and twigs	Cottony cushion scale
Fruit and leaves with honeydew and black mold	Mealybugs
Ring or partial ring of scarred tissue on stem and fruit skin, young leaves may be deformed	Citrus thrips
Fruit scarred but no ring around stem	Wind abrasion
Holes in blossoms, leaves or new fruit	Citrus cutworm
New leaves with holes, webbed together	Leaffrollers
Leaves and green fruit have yellow stippling	Citrus red mite

ELM TREES

MISCELANEOUS PESTS

EUROPEAN ELM SCALE

These pests can easily be spotted on the bark of the trees during the early summer, which is when the scales reach their maturity. The scales are oval, reddish-purple and have a white, waxy secretion. If you crush them with your fingers they will cause a red stain. They cause the leaves of the tree to become prematurely yellow, especially on the lower branches. If you have a bad infestation the leaves will turn a gray-green and wilt.

WHOOOOSH
One of the easiest ways to eliminate the scales is to use a forceful stream of water using a garden hose. If that doesn't work use a spray of dormant oil in the early spring.

EUROPEAN RED MITE

This mite attacks fruit trees. The adult is very small and the female is dark red with a few white spots. The most serious infestation usually occurs in the hottest part of the summer around July and August. They feed on chlorophyll and cause the foliage to become bronzed and the fruit may then drop prematurely as well as being small and low in sugar content. If the infestation is early in the season, the bud set for the following year may be reduced.

EGG KILLER

Apply a superior dormant-oil spray in early spring to kill the over-wintering eggs. This is one of the best methods of eliminating the problem. Most of the time natural predators will take care of the problem since the mites are at the bottom of the food chain.

FRUIT TREE LEAFROLLER

The leafroller prefers citrus trees, apple trees and most stonefruit trees. The caterpillar likes to feed on the young leaves, buds and developing fruit. The majority of damage occurs in the spring and early summer months. About mid-summer the pest will be inactive in the egg stage until the spring when it goes back into action. The caterpillar is green and has a shiny black head and it will feed inside of rolled up leaves or blossoms. When disturbed it will fall on a spun thread.

OIL THEM IN THE WINTER

One of the best methods of controlling these pests is to spray oil in January or February before any of the buds begin to open to kill the egg masses on the twigs.

ORIENTAL FRUIT MOTH

The larval stage tunnels into tender peach shoots and other fruits very early in the season and later enters the fruit. If you get a wormy peach it is usually this pest that is at fault. The mature larvae are pinkish and about ½ inches long. The first indication of a problem is the wilting of the terminal of growing shoots. It is not easy to identify the problem with the worms eating the peach around the pit. You may sometimes notice a gummy residue on the outside of the peach. If they enter through a tiny hole in the stem you may never notice them until its too late. Dormant oil sprays do not work on these pests.

PARASITE SAVES THE DAY

There is one parasite that is very useful and will save the crop. The wasp *Macrocentrus ancylivorus* has been used very effectively when this pest is identified.

STOP THE MATING

A relatively new pheromone product called Isomate-M™ will disrupt their mating and reproduction process. It is being used successfully in commercial orchards only.

96

FIG TREE

FIG TREE PEST PROBLEM SOLVER

THE PROBLEM	CAUSED BY
Premature fruit drop, loss of leaves, stunted growth, tiny knots on roots	Nematodes
Yellow stippled leaves with webbing	Spider mites
Small black beetles on ripe fruit	Sap beetle
Fruit has warty appearance, oyster shell-shaped scale on leaves, twigs and fruit	Fig scale
Surface of fruit scarred	Green fruit beetle
Sap and sawdust coming out of branches	Carpenter worm

PEACH TREE

PEACH & NECTARINE PEST PROBLEM SOLVER

THE PROBLEM	CAUSED BY
Young shoots die several inches from tip, worms living in shoots, ripening fruit infested	Peach twig borer, oriental fruit moth
Leaves become curled, tiny green insects visible	Green peach aphid
New leaves become yellow to reddish and curl	Leaf curl fungus
Leaves yellow, roots have galls	Root knot nematode

PEACH TREE BORERS

These are a relative of the squash vine borers and are prevalent all over North America. They will do damage to peach trees around the bottom 10 inches of the trunk and will get started at the soil line. The larvae, feeds below the surface of the soil or beneath the bark and may completely girdle the tree. This is also a major pest of stone fruit trees.

They are capable of killing young trees and will cause the trees to be too weak to withstand adverse weather conditions as well as reduce productivity.

It is common to bring this borer home from a nursery and you should pay careful attention to any trees before you purchase them. If you find one better start looking for more. Most of the controls mentioned for squash vine borers will work for these borers as well.

POWDER THEM
Placing a layer of diatomaceous earth around the base of the tree in the early spring will stop the borers from getting to the tree. **Tobacco dust works great too but may harm pets and other animals.**

CRYSTALS WILL HELP
If you spread moth crystals (poison) around the base of the trees in late summer then cover them with 3-4 inches of soil, mounding it around the trunk of the trees it will eliminate the problem. Be sure and remove the mounded soil before winter rains come or you irrigate the trees. **Harmful: to animals and humans.**

CALL FOR THE TIN MAN
To stop these borers, just force a piece of tin into the ground all around the tree trunk. Leave a space of about two inches between the tin shield and the tree bark. About mid-May fill the space with tobacco dust and when it rains it will become a potent barrier. This treatment should be done every May.

PEAR TREES

PEAR PSYLLA

The nymphs are small yellow bugs that will feed on the tops of leaves and skeletonize them. The adults are dark orange with transparent wings and look like miniature cicadas. They will hibernate under the edges of rough bark on tree trunk branches and come out during the first warm days of April. They will then deposit their eggs in old leaf scars, cracks and crevices. If the infestation is not caught in time by mid-summer, a badly infested tree will have blackening on the leaves, which will fall off prematurely.

PREVENTION IS BEST
Dusting with limestone will work, however, a good spraying with dormant oil in the spring is even better. Apply a 2% oil solution just as the buds begin to swell and the psylla are beginning to lay their yellow eggs on the twigs and buds. If they are already established then you will need to spray the tree with soapy water with as hard a spray as possible that will not cause damage to the buds.

NATURAL ENEMIES
There is a chalcid wasp that will eradicate these pests called *Trechnites insidiosus*. Just one of the parasitic wasps will parasitize up to 90% of the nymphs during July and August in unsprayed orchards.

SAN JOSE SCALE

This little sapsucker will suck the sap from fruit trees such as pear or peach and just about any other they can get to. Serious infestations will damage the tree and kill off a number of branches. The mature female is yellow and the size of a pinhead. When the young are hatched they are so light that the wind will carry them to other trees. The Osage orange trees will support these pests even though the fruit from this tree (hedgeapples) will repel most other insects.

SQUIRT, SQUIRT
In order to control the scale you will need to spray the new buds in the early spring with an oil emulsion. This treatment should be repeated about one week later to assure good results.

PARASITE TO THE RESCUE
The parasite *Aphytis melinus* has been used very effectively against the scale. They are available commercially through you garden or agricultural supply stores.

SHOTHOLE BORER

This small dark brown beetle lives and breeds under the bark of pear and peach trees. The holes that the beetles emerge from: look like small buckshot holes. They are usually found in the northern states and loves weak trees.

PEAR TREE PEST PROBLEM SOLVER	
THE PROBLEM	**CAUSED BY**
Worms in fruit, brown granules in holes	Codling moth
Leaves and blossoms eaten and neatly tied together then webbed, young fruit gouged	Leafrollers
Leaves have brown or pink spots, skeletonization	Pearslug
Irregular spots on upper side of leaves, small blisters on underneath side of leaf	Tentiform leafminer
Fruit and foliage have honeydew and yellow insects on leaves, tree defoliated	Pear psylla
Fruit has clear honeydew and black sooty mold	Mealybugs
Leaves distorted, new foliage stunted, green insects on new shoots	Aphids
Fruit is brownish and rough, foliage has dry, rusty look	Pear rust mite

Reddish blisters on flowers and buds turning brown or black	Blister mites
Round holes along leaf margins in spring	California pear sawfly

PLUMS & PRUNES

PLUMS & PRUNES PEST PROBLEM SOLVER

THE PROBLEM	CAUSED BY
Young shoots die back 1-7 inches from tip in spring, caterpillar inside the shoots	Peach twig borer
Leaves tied together with webbing in spring	Leafrollers, orange tortrix
Leaves attached to fruit with webbing in summer	Eyespotted bud moth
Brownish patches on leaves and skeletonization	Pearslug
New growth with green insects, leaves curled, fruit split, white mealy substance	Mealy plum aphid

WALNUTS TREES

WALNUT TREE PEST PROBLEM SOLVER

THE PROBLEM	CAUSED BY
Green nuts fall off or dry up on tree, webbing on nut, older nuts worm infested	Codling moth
Nuts are worm infested at harvest time, covered with webbing and brown material	Navel orangeworm
Leaves tied with webbing and eaten in spring	Leafroller
Tiny black spots on husks turning into black areas that are soft, nut meat still OK	Walnut husk fly
Leaves covered with honeydew and black sooty mold, nuts become sunburned	Walnut aphid

CHAPTER 8

BEETLES

BEETLES

Many, many, many years ago farmers used to hang toads in the doorway of their grain storage facility to keep the bugs out. The toad had a string around its leg and would eat the bugs that tried to get in to get the grain. I am sure if we tried this now we would have animal rights people all over us, so best to forget this type of bug repellant.

GENERAL BEETLE REPELLANT
Use one handful of lantana (tickberry) and place the leaves in 2 quarts of water and allow it to remain for 3 hours before straining and adding 4 drops of liquid soap then using as a spray. The leaves can also be crushed and powdered and used as a dusting powder. If you just pound all parts of the plant and spread around the areas where grain are stored it will repel all beetles.

IT'S RAINING BUGS
Try placing an old white umbrella upside down under your plants and then shake the plant. Bugs will fall into the umbrella for disposal in soapy water.

TRY THE OLD "SUGARING" METHOD
Farmers used a method called "sugaring" to get rid of beetles and moths that climbed up the tree trunks. To prepare the sugaring mixture, just mix up a batch of stale beer, brown sugar and add a crushed banana. Mix this into a thick consistency and smear it in a wide band around the trunk of the tree. You can also use cloth or a special plastic collar with grease or Tanglefoot™ on it. Make sure that the material used will not damage the tree trunk.

NEW FABRIC FOR PLANTS

There is a new lightweight fabric made especially to protect plants from bugs. The fabric is called spun-bonded polyester (polyethylene), which will allow water, air and sunlight in and stop insects from laying eggs on the plant. If you use the new fabric the plant must be fully covered and the fabric edges buried in the ground.

GENERAL SOAP SPRAYS

There are many products that can be used to prepare soap sprays; they are Ivory Liquid Soap™, Murphy's Oil Soap™, most soap flakes, Fels Naptha™, Dr. Bronner's Liquid Soap™ and even Basic H™. The following are a few of the formulas you can prepare at home:

SOAPY LIME SPRAY

3	Tablespoons of agricultural lime
1	Tablespoon of Ivory Liquid Soap™
2	Quarts of cool tap water

Mix all the ingredients together and use for beetles, caterpillars, aphids and tomato hornworm.

SOAPY ALCOHOL SPRAY

2	Cups of rubbing alcohol
1	Quart of tap water
2	Teaspoons of Ivory Liquid Soap™

Before spraying this mixture, try it on a few leaves to be sure it won't damage them. The alcohol will evaporate very fast. This works well on beetles, scale, mealybugs and whiteflies.

GARDEN BEETLES

ASIATIC GARDEN BEETLE

This is a small brown beetle; that are capable of doing a lot of damage. They love crisp green leaves and are a night feeder. One of the best methods of getting rid of them is with an electronic trap purchased from a garden supply house. The grubs can also be killed using Derris or Rotenone.

ASPARAGUS BEETLE

Identification:
This is a small metallic blue-black beetle that has three yellow-orange squares along each wing cover.

General Information:
It loves to munch on the asparagus stalks and is capable of doing a lot of damage. It will damage both the garden varieties as well as the wild asparagus plants. They will hibernate in trash that is left around the garden and come out in the spring looking for tender young asparagus shoots to lay their eggs on.

REMOVE THEIR HOUSING PROJECT
If you remove all the trash and the beetle cannot find a comfortable home they will pack their bags and move on. Many beetles rely on people who do not clean up before winter sets in. Most gardeners tend to leave the clean up for the spring and this is usually too late.

GIVE THEM AN ALLERGY ATTACK
These beetles do not like to be around nasturtiums and calendula (pot marigolds). They will leave your yard and look for a box of tissues.

CHICKS AND DUCK AND GEESE BETTER SCURRY
If you have a bad infestation the best method of eradication is to release some fowl into the garden. They love beetles and will round them up in short order. Then you need to get rid of the fowl, possibly fried.

HOLD THAT CONTAINER
Asparagus beetles cannot be handpicked since they drop to the ground as soon as they spot you getting too close to them. If you place a jar or can under the insect and then get close it will fall right in the container. This will take a little practice but you will get the hang of it after a while.

DON'T FENCE ME IN
If you place a fence around the asparagus plants and allow some hens to run loose they will eliminate all the beetles for you. If there is ample grass sod in the area the hens will leave the asparagus plants alone. Don't leave them there permanently just long enough to get rid of the beetles.

FEED TOMATOES TO ASPARAGUS

To prepare a spray from tomato plants, just make the spray by using the freshest leaves you can find as well as the stems and even the tomatoes. Dice up the plant and parts and mix 2 handfuls with 8 cups of water then allow it to stand for 5 hours before straining and applying as soon as possible. This mixture loses potency rather quickly. You can add 4 drops of liquid soap to beef it up a little. This spray will also stop egg laying by a number of insects. **Tomato leaves are poisonous to humans and animals.** You can also just plant tomato plants around asparagus plants and the beetles will stay away.

ASPARAGUS MINER

This bug tends to tunnel close to the base of the plant, however, some will start their tunnel as high as one foot off the ground and tunnel in, going down, then under the soil in many instances. This pest is found in the Northeast and California and is only considered a "miner" pest. If you clean up all the old asparagus stalks and remnants you will eliminate a new problem in the spring.

BEAN LEAF BEETLE

Identification:
They are about ¼ inch long, reddish with black spots and a small black head. They will lay their eggs on leaves and their larvae will enter the soil to feed on plant roots. You will only find the adult beetle feeding on leaves.

USE FRIENDLY KILLERS
The best method of controlling these pests is to employ some ladybugs and lacewings to eat their eggs. You can also mix Nc nematodes into seed furrows and into the mulch you use around plants. Handpicking them also works well.

PLANTS THAT REPEL THEM
If you plant garlic, radishes, potatoes or cloves around your bean plants the beetles will leave them alone.

BLISTER BEETLE

Identification:
Black, flying beetles that may have yellow stripes and are about ½ inches long. They have long legs and a narrow neck. They will cause a blister on your skin if handled. They will also eat leaves, fruit and stems of plants.

General Information:
If these beetles get into your garden it may be the end of the garden. If a swarm gets in the best thing to do is to physically chase them out of the garden and as far away as you can. Chickens won't even help since they get sick when they eat these beetles.

IT'S A BIRD, IT'S A PLANE, NO IT'S A FLYING BEETLE
These beetles are solid, black flying beetles. They have long legs and a narrow neck and will cause you to get skin blisters if you handle them. They prefer to eat leaves and fruit and will prey on grasshopper eggs making them somewhat beneficial. If you handpick them use gloves and wash the gloves afterwards. Nc nematodes work well since they lay their eggs in the soil.

THE SAME OLD SPRAY
Lime sprays work very well and also dusting damp plants with lime will make them leave the garden area and head for a neighbors yard. As a last resort use a soap and lime spray or use pyrethrums.

CALOSOMA BEETLE

This is a well-known beetle that looks like an Egyptian scarab. The wings are covered with a metallic blue color and are slightly ridged with a red border. They have long legs and are very speedy and release a foul smelly chemical when bothered. Their favorite meal is the tent caterpillar.

CARPET BEETLE

Carpet beetles enjoy munching on wool, feathers and even fur. These beetles actually are the ones that leave small round holes not the jagged hole that the clothes moth leaves in the clothing. Their larvae are hairy little worms that do most of the damage and they can live up to 3 years. If give the opportunity they will also dine on carpets, curtains and upholstered furniture.

DANGER! BAD BUG LIVES HERE
Carpet beetles do a lot of damage to fabrics every year, even more than clothes moths. They are difficult to get rid of once they get a foothold and love to munch on pet hair as well. One of the best methods of eradication is to vacuum frequently.

HERE LITTLE BEETLE, COME TO FISHY

Carpet beetles are attracted to fish oil and if you place some sardine oil on piece of flypaper or any sticky surface it will attract them into a trap. However, if you do this in your closet don't expect to have too many friends.

CIGARETTE BEETLES

These are very small reddish-brown beetles that are covered in a very fine hair. They prefer tobacco for their main course but if there is none around will feed on almost anything else that is available. They will even eat insecticide if you give it to them and will not die. They are usually found in spices when the tops are not on tight, so keep the tops screwed on tight.

COLORADO POTATO BEETLE

Identification:
This is a round ½ inch yellow beetle with black stripes down its back and a reddish head that loves to eat potato leaves. They lay yellow-orange eggs on the underneath side of the leaves. The grubs chew on the leaves and have black spots on their sides. Several generations can emerge every year.

General Information:
The adults hibernate in the soil over the winter. In the last few years this beetle has become more prevalent. If you find black excrement on the leaves it may be this beetle.

This beetle consumes potatoes, tomatoes, eggplant, cabbage and peppers. You may also find them munching on your petunias. If you plant Sequoia potatoes they will not eat them.

BENNIES TO THE RESCUE

Beneficial insects are one of the best methods of eradication of these pests. Use *Edovum puttleri*, ladybugs or lacewings. The ladybugs love to feast on their eggs and are the best one to eliminate the beetles. They don't like green beans and if you plant them with the potatoes they will probably leave the area alone. Bt also works very well against these insects.

KILLING THE LARVAE

Using a soap and lime spray will kill off the larvae by dehydration and a garlic and pepper juice spray will repel them and send them packing.

CRUSH THOSE EGGS

In early spring the beetles lay their eggs on the underneath side of the potato leaves. However, keep checking the underneath sides of the leaves regularly for eggs and remove them since this is one of the best methods of controlling the beetle.

NATURAL REPELLENTS

There are a number of plants that will repel these bugs if they are planted near the plants that they consume. These include marigolds, garlic, snap peas, onions, flax, catnip, coriander, nasturtiums, tansy, dead nettle and horseradish.

EXPLODING BEETLES

If you sprinkle wheat bran that has been well moistened around your plants the beetles will eat the bran before they eat your plants. They will then swell up and literally explode. The beetle's cuticle will actually give under the bloating pressure.

GIVE THEM A CUP OF TEA OR A SHOT OF SALTS

You can prepare a tea made from basil or cedar boughs and place it in a sprayer. This works very well in keeping the beetles at bay. You can also add 2 tablespoons of Epsom salts to a gallon of water and spray to protect your plants.

CUCUMBER BEETLE

Identification:
These are green and yellow beetles with either three black stripes or 12 black spots on their back.

General Information:
The biggest problem usually occurs early in the season when their larvae chew through the stalks of a member of the squash family. They prefer cucumbers, acorn squash, melons of all types and summer squash. Usually two generations appear every year. They are also known as the southern corn rootworm. They will spend their winter in garden debris, weeds or under logs. There is a chemical in cucumbers called *"curcurbitacin"* that attract these insects. It is a bitter essence that they love.

They lay their orange-brown eggs at the base of the plants and eventually tiny whitish grubs will hatch. If you use quality mulch they will not lay their eggs there.

These beetles will cause the entire plant to wilt and fall over dead since the beetles carry the bacterial wilt disease in their digestive tracts. If you feel that the plant has been infected, just slice a vine in two and squeeze the ends until the plant juices are seen. If the plant juices are a milky white substance that can be drawn out in a thread, the plant is being attacked by the bacteria and the rest of the plant is finished.

EASILY CONFUSED
Cucumber beetles are easily confused when they go in search of their favorite food cucumbers and summer squash. If you plant rattail radishes around the areas containing cucumber or cabbage plants it has the tendency to repel the beetles and they head for another yard. If you plant additional rattails between the plants it will provide additional protection.

CHECK THE DOWNSIDE
One of the best ways to control the beetles is to check the underneath sides of the leaves very early in the season. The leaves should be sprayed with a solution of insecticidal soap and water to eliminate the larvae and the eggs.

NEEM TO THE RESCUE
If you do end up with an infestation by mid-summer spray them first with Neem Oil™ to repel them from the vegetables and plants. Then you should follow-up with pyrethrums, which will kill them. These are both natural organic products, safe to use and fully biodegradable.

CALL FOR NEMA THE WORM
Nc nematodes will do the job nicely and eliminate the beetle. They don't like radishes and if you plant them with the other vegetables they will stay away from the garden. Lime and soap sprays irritate them and they won't come back or try pyrethrum and certain rotenones will eliminate them.

PEPPER SPRAY

½   Cup of hot peppers or ¼ cup Tabasco Sauce™
2   Quarts of tap water
1   Tablespoons of Ivory Liquid Soap®

Place the hot peppers or Tabasco Sauce™ with 2 cups of water in a blender, blend thoroughly then allow it to stand overnight. Strain and add the balance of the water and the liquid soap and use as a spray.

VANILLA HELPS

These beetles will not go near your plants if you spray them with a solution composed of artificial vanilla flavoring and water.

WOOD ASH/LIME SPRAY

¼   Cup of wood ashes
¼   Cup of lime juice
1   Gallon of tap water

Mix all the ingredients together and allow it to stand for 1 hour before spraying on the plants. Be sure and spray the underneath sides of the leaves.

PLANT REPELLENTS

There are a number of plants that if planted between the plants that they eat it will repel them naturally. These are tansy, catnip, marigold and radishes.

DRUGSTORE BEETLES

They are sometimes called bread beetles and are colored brown and usually found in dried up, stale bread. They got their name because they originally resided in dried medicinal plants that were once sold in the old drugstores. If you find them in your home they like to eat paprika, dried beans, grains and thrive on hot peppers. The story is that these bugs will consume anything except steel. Keep your grains in the freezer for protection.

FLEA BEETLE

Identification:
This is a jumping beetle that is only ¼ inch in length. It is usually black with pale yellow stripes. It loves to consume young leaves and makes tiny holes in them.

General Information:
Their larvae feed on seeds and some roots. They will also feed on dichondra grass, cabbage, broccoli and cauliflower. In California there is a species of flea beetle that loves arugula. If you grow tomatoes the flea beetle may be found eating the early leaves but then leave before the fruit arrives. The damage they inflict looks like the plant was hit by a shotgun blast of small buckshot. Most plants recover, the only exception is eggplant.

FLEE BEETLE
The flea beetle loves cabbage leaves and will eat hundreds of holes in them during their feast. To get rid of them use a garlic mixture. Just pulverize about 6 cloves of garlic with a hammer or run the car over them. Place the smashed garlic cloves in a glass jar and add1 tablespoon of cayenne pepper and 1 quart of warm tap water. Place a lid on and mix well, then allow the jar to stand in the sun for 2 days to steep. Spray the leaves with beetles, making sure you spray both sides of the leaves.

THESE BEETLES LOVE YELLOW
If you are having a problem with flea beetles, just purchase some yellow cards and place non-setting glue or Tanglefoot™ on them, then leave them in the areas you are having a problem. They are attracted to the yellow color and will jump on the yellow and can't escape. This will get rid of a number of other flying pests.

KEEPS THEIR BREATH FRESH
Flea beetles do not like mint. If you want to keep them away from your cabbage, just plant some mint plants among the cabbage.

WORMWOOD WILL DO THE TRICK

2	Cups of wormwood leaves
2	Quarts of tap water
2	Cups of boiling water

Place the wormwood leaves in the boiling water and allow it to steep for 1 hour. Strain the mixture and add the 2 quarts of water and place into a sprayer for immediate use. This will eliminate the flea beetles and cabbageworms.

PLANTS THAT REPEL THE FLEAS
There are a number of plants that are capable of repelling the flea beetle. These include elderberry, catnip, marigolds and mint.

CUT THE DECK

Flea beetles can be trapped using playing cards that have been smeared with a sticky substance like Tanglefoot™ or non-drying glue. You can place a small amount of beer in a shallow dish in the center of four cards placed around the dish to attract them. Flea beetles love beer, especially Coors™.

GETTING A BIT MISTY

You can dust your plants to keep the flea beetles off by using wood ashes mixed with lime, but be sure that you mist the plants first so that the dust will adhere.

FLEA RESISTANT VARIETIES

There are a number of plants that you can plant that are resistant to flea beetles. These include De Cicco, Atlantic and Italian green sprouting broccoli, Snowball cauliflower, Mammoth, Red Rock and Early Jersey Wakefield cabbage and Sequoia potatoes. Check with your local garden supply store for other varieties.

BEER TRAP

Place cheap beer in a shallow dish and bury it allowing the dish to just remain above ground making it easy for the beetle to get into the beer and drown. A number of bugs are attracted to beer. They are actually more attracted to malt liquor than they are to beer.

FLOUR BEETLE

The flour beetle was found in the tombs of ancient Egypt and will consume a variety of foods. They love grains, beans, peas, candy, nuts and dried fruit. The most common of these beetles is the red flour beetle. They do not require water to survive and lay sticky eggs that hatch and crawl to the top of grains and look like small white pupae. Discard any food if you find any sign of this beetle or its offspring. They have the ability to excrete a bad smelling chemical that contaminates the foods they inhabit.

Freezing the foods will kill them but it is already too late

GETTING TO THE ROOT OF THE PROBLEM
Rhizomes, roots of turmeric have been used for centuries to ward off these bugs and works great when left on the shelves in the pantry. Fenugreek placed out also works very well. These just repel the bugs and will not kill them.

HARLEQUIN BUG

Identification:
These bugs are either black and red or black and yellow and suck plant juices. They lay barrel-shaped eggs on the underneath side of leaves. Harlequin bugs: can be identified by the bleached areas they leave on the leaf when they feed.

General Information:
They spend the winter in old leaves and trash. Good reason to clean up the yard before the first snow. They are one of the prettiest bugs in the insect world. They love turnip seedlings and if they are not controlled you will never get a turnip. They also like to eat Brussels sprouts, cauliflower, kohlrabi, horseradish, broccoli and mustard.

ONE BUGGY, TWO BUGGY
Handpicking the bugs is one of the best methods to get rid of them. Handpick both the bugs and their eggs. If you can find a praying mantis you might ask for some assistance since they like to dine on these beetles. Insecticide soap sprays will also do the trick in short order.

PLANT BUG RESITANT VEGGIES
There are a number of vegetables that have been developed that are resistant to this bug. They are Grande, Atlantic and Coastal broccoli; Copenhagen Market 86, Headstart, Savory Perfection Drumhead, Stein's Flat Dutch and Early Jersey Wakefield cabbage; Early Snowball X and Snowball Y cauliflower; Vates, Morris Improved Heading and Green Glaze collards; Vale kale; and Red Devil, White Icicle, Globemaster, Cherry Belle, Champion and Red Prince radishes.

JAPANESE BEETLE

Identification:
This is a metallic green beetle with copper-colored wing covers. There are small tufts of short, white hairs under the wings and gray hairs on the underneath side. They are about ½ inch long and ¼ inch wide. The males are a little smaller than the females.

General Information:
The beetle is normally found in the eastern United States but is moving west. May be found almost anywhere in woods and gardens. They usually feed on only one plant and will not bother another one. They like the sunlight and will feed more in temperatures between 83^0 and 95^0F.

AN UNWELCOME VISITOR

The Japanese beetle migrated to the United States around the turn of the century, probably in the root system of a plant. The beetle spends 10 months of the year in the ground in the form of a white grub. Their white grubs feed on tender roots and grass and are the most common white grub in the eastern United States. Every species of white grub can destroy lawns and leave large brown areas. They winter in the soil until the spring and their period of greatest activity lasts from 4-6 weeks.

They are not fussy eaters and will consume almost any type of plant they come upon. Their favorites, however, are rose bushes, purple plum trees, cherry trees and myrtle. They will mass on ripening fruit and eat until nothing edible is left.

Most beetles will lay their eggs in the grass and one excellent method of reducing or eliminating the problem is to treat the grass with a killer in early spring before they hatch.

Japanese beetles are not fussy eaters and there are over 280 plants that they will dine on if given the chance. They leave the leaves of plants skeletonized.

THE ELIMINATOR
The following ingredients will be needed:

1	Pounds of hydrated lime (use with caution)
5	Ounces of alum
10	Gallons of cool tap water

Place the water in a large bucket; then add the other ingredients slowly while stirring well. Place the solution in a sprayer and spray the tops and bottoms of the leaves. This solution is poisonous and should be kept away from humans and animals. Use with caution and wear gloves.

SPRINGTIME WITH NC NEMATODES
If you spray the lawn with Nc nematode spray in the spring it will eliminate the problem of grubs munching on your grass stalks for lunch. You can also spray pyrethrums or use a garlic and onion spray.

TRAP THEM
There a number of commercial traps that work very well with Japanese beetles. Check with your local garden shop for trapping supplies. Use geraniol oil, which is a rose scent to lure them into the trap.

FEED THEM FRUIT SALAD
Place a small can of fruit salad with the top removed in a safe location where neither animals nor insects can get to it and allow it to ferment. Use a large yellow bowl and place the can in the center raised up on a block of wood. Fill the bowl with soapy water to below the top of the can and place the bowl in the garden about 20 feet from the plants that are infested with the beetle.

FEED SPORES TO GRUBS

One of the best remedies to control larvae of Japanese beetles is called "milky spores (*Bacillus popilliae*)." These spores can be purchased through a garden shop and are spread on the soil causing the grubs to contract a disease that kills them. The milky spores will not harm any beneficial organisms and only kills the grubs, thus eliminating the Japanese beetles. The milky spores will remain in the soil for many years just waiting for the grubs to appear. If you apply milky spore disease to your lawn and even fruit orchards it will eliminate the grub problem. The Japanese beetles can spend as much as 10 months every year as grubs in the soil.

MAY BEETLE

There are over 100 species of May beetle and will cause damage by eating blackberry leaves. However, in the larval or white grub stage they will eat the roots of bluegrass, timothy corn, soybeans and other crops. They deposit their eggs one to eight inches deep into the soil during the spring and hatch about 3-4 weeks later. Keep an eye out for the white grubs in the spring.

ROTATION A MUST

Rotating crops is the best method of controlling these beetles, if you have the problem. Best to use crops such as legumes, sweet clover or alfalfa, which they don't like. Legumes are your best choice.

MEXICAN BEAN BEETLE

Identification:

These are light brown round beetles, about ¼ inch long with 16 black spots on their back. They are frequently mistaken for a ladybug (these are not ladies) and are a distant relative of them. The larvae are light yellow and covered with bristle hairs that are about 1/3 inch long.

General Information:
They will eat beans, pods, leaves and stems then lay their yellow eggs on the leaf underside. Their larvae will also eat the bean leaves when they emerge. The female is capable of laying 1,500 eggs if she is in rare form but usually lays about 500 on the lower surfaces of the bean plant.

As a grub it is a yellowish color and covered with spines. It will winter in the garden area usually under a woodpile or in some rubbish or debris. They have a peculiar craving for Lima beans and will go out of their way if any are in the vicinity.

They will totally skeletinize the leaves and the larvae will attach their hind ends to a leaf that is uninjured and pupate. If you see a skeletonized leaf, start looking on the underneath sides of leaves for yellow orange egg clusters.

NATURAL REMEDY
Release the parasite wasp, *Pediobius foveolatus* to eliminate the infestation in about 1 week or handpick the beetles and their eggs.

MORE ACUTE REMEDY
Mix up a batch of pepper, garlic and onion juice in 1 quart of water and spray them. Pyrethrum spray will kill them and soap and lime spray will cause them to vacate your premises in a hurry.

MIXING POTATOES WITH BEANS
If you plant potato plants among the bean plants chances are you will never see a Mexican bean beetle or the standard bean beetle. They hate potato plants and will avoid areas where they are planted.

PICK A BEETLE
The best line of defense is to just pick the beetles off the plants and drop them into a bucket of soapy water or water topped with kerosene.

POWDERPOST BEETLE

GET OUT THE PAINTBRUSH
These beetles are commonly found in wood furniture and are brought into the house. They are also very common on posts around yards and cattle pens. Once they lay their eggs it is almost impossible to stop them. The best method is prevention, which involves placing a covering on the wood, so that when they land on the wood to test it for starch and sugar content, to make sure that there is enough to feed their young, they will reject the wood. Cover the wood with paraffin wax, varnish, shellac or just paint the surface to stop them.

ROSE CHAFER

This a tan, long legged beetle that haunts rose bushes and skeletonizes the leaves as well as leaving excrement on the leaves. It especially likes white roses and will feed on the petals. The larva is white with a brown head and likes to feed on the roots of grasses and weeds. It is mostly found in the northeastern states but has been found as far west as Colorado.

PICK-A-BUG
Since these bugs are easy to spot, the best method of eradicating them is to handpick them.

MAKE A BARRIER
You can make a barrier that will stop these bugs by using cheesecloth or mosquito netting. Place the netting on poles covering the roses for the period of time that you notice they are bothering the roses. They cannot fly well and will leave the roses alone for greener pastures.

SAW-TOOTHED GRAIN BEETLES

These bugs have a saw-like projection at the midsection of their bodies that protrude on either side. They are not fussy eaters and will eat almost anything but prefer grains and grain products. They have very active larvae that will be found crawling about looking for different foods to eat.

BAY LEAVES TO THE RESCUE
These beetles do not like bay leaves. Place them around your pantry and even into some of the flour or grain products if they cannot be sealed up in a plastic container. A stick of spearmint gum in the product also works great.

SQUASH BUG

Identification:
This is a brownish-black, shield-shaped bug with long legs and antennae. They will suck the juices out of your plants and will be found on the leaves. They lay brown-gold shiny eggs on the underneath side of the leaves that change to reddish-brown. The adult will spend the winter in an old pile of leaves. The new hatchlings will have a reddish head and legs and green bodies.

General Information:
They feed by inserting their needle-like mouthparts into the plant tissue and drawing out the juices. They will also release a toxin that will cause the plant to wilt. If these bugs are disturbed or crushed they will release a foul-smelling odor. They prefer to eat squash, pumpkins, melons and cucumbers. Vine crops; are easily killed by these bugs, especially during the early part of the growing season.

PRAY FOR A MANTIS
One of the best deterrents is to have some praying mantis around your property. If you don't have any and this bug is around it would be best to import some. They will eat the eggs as well as the nymphs.

PLANTS TO THE RESCUE
There are a number of plants that will ward off these pests if planted around your garden. They are the radish, nasturtium, onion, tansy and marigold plants. If you plant mustard greens near you garden they will go for that and leave all other plants alone. Planting peas in the rows will also deter them.

SOAP THEM UP
If you wan to kill then, just use an insecticidal soap spray. You can also use a spray prepared from imitation vanilla extract and water.

HANDPICKING IS THE ANSWER
This is one bug that handpicking really works well. Wear gloves since they will release their foul-smelling chemical when you touch them.

PLANT BUG RESITANT VARIETIES
There are a number of bug resistant varieties that will fare better than most. These are Table Queen, Royal Acorn, Early Golden Bush Scallop, Early Summer Crookneck, Early Prolific Straightneck and Improved Green Hubbard squash.

TREE CRICKETS

Identification:
Sometimes called the blackhorned tree cricket is a problem for raspberries and blackberries. It is a greenish-yellow bug with feelers projecting from the front of its black head.

General Information:
They will also attack a number of wild shrubs and love fruit trees when they can get to them. If you have a square field you will have less damage than if you have a long narrow field. The berry canes that are injured will show areas of split bark in an irregular line. If you look inside the splits you will see numerous small holes that will extend into the pith.

IT'S A PITHY
Since the damage extends into the pith it is best to remove all the injured canes and burn them. The more numerous the rows of holes are the more likely that the canes will just fall over. Burning is the best method of eliminating the eggs. The chemical rotenone is also used successfully on these bugs.

WEEVILS

Identification:
This long snout beetle loves grains. They have a strong pair of mandibles at the end of their snout that is capable of opening most seeds, which they then lay their eggs in. The eggs hatch into larvae; that will eat the inside of the seed and allows the shell to remain intact.

General Information:
Weevils are one of the hardest beetles to control. They may also attack fruit trees, cotton, rhubarb and a variety of vegetables. The bean weevil loves beans and peas; however, if none are available they will eat almost any other vegetables.

WORM THEM OUT
Best to eliminate them with Nc nematodes, which has been found to be one of the most efficient methods of controlling weevils.

GLUE THEM UP
Weevils normally crawl to your houseplants, especially vine weevils. However, the weevils can be stopped, by placing a thin bead of non-setting glue or Tanglefoot™ around the plants. This can get a bit messy but it does work well.

PEPPER THEM
Black pepper can be placed into foods that you ordinarily place it in to keep the bugs out. Even some beetles that will consume red pepper will not eat black pepper in most instances. Black pepper will actually kill the pests. The USDA found that 500 parts per million of black pepper will kill 97% of the weevils in wheat.

COWPEA CURCULIOS (BEAN WEEVIL)

These are small black or brown beetles that have a snout and have reddish legs and antennae. They lay their eggs in holes that are chewed along the bean pod seams. The tiny white grub then feeds on the young seed and tends to come out when the beans are in storage and leave a small round hole when exiting.

They prefer southern peas and love Lima beans. Praying mantis, love to dine on these bugs. Spray the pods with a soap and pepper spray and they won't lay their eggs. Nc nematodes also will eliminate the problem. Stored dry beans; can be protected by heating them to 135°F for 3-4 hours or suspending the seeds in a bag of tap water and heating it to 140°F before drying them very rapidly.

SCARE THEM OFF

Weevils tend to take up residence in dried beans and most grains. However, if you place a dried hot chili pepper in with the beans or grains you will never find another weevil or other insect in your beans and grains. Placing the beans in the foods will not affect the foods.

LEAF NOTCHER

The black vine weevil is a very shy bug that only feeds at night and will munch notches around the edges of the leaves of the yew tree, rhododendron bushes, azaleas and most other ornamental shrubs. It will lay its eggs in the soil, which hatch into white legless grubs, which will feed on the roots of your plants. They hide in mulch and leaf litter during the day. Place Tanglefoot™ around the trunk of bushes and trees to keep them off. Rake in Nc nematodes to be rid of them permanently.

NUTTY WEEVILS

These go by a number of nutty names such as the pecan weevil, chestnut weevil and the other nut weevil. All three are similar and have long snouts, which are actually as long as their bodies. The females use their snout to bite holes in developing nuts, which is where they lay their eggs. The eggs hatch about the same time as when the nuts are ready to fall to the ground. If you spread Nc nematodes under the tree in the late summer when the nuts fall it will eliminate the problem.

STRAWBERRY ROOT WEEVILS ARE SHY

These weevils feed on the upper parts of the plants and then lay their eggs in the soil. Their grubs feed on the plant roots and heavy infestations will easily kill the plant. Mulch containing Nc nematodes and a somewhat sandy soil around the plants will solve the problem. You can hand pick them, however, the adults only come out at night and are very shy.

SWEET POTATO WEEVIL

This beetle looks like an ant and has a snout and a black body. They mainly eat foliage and lay their eggs on the stem and tubers of plants. When the grubs hatch they will eat down the stem into any tuber or potato that is available. These are normally only found in the southern United States. It also like to eat stored sweet potatoes. If you get an infestation it would be best to burn the crop, however, Nc nematodes do work as a good preventive measure.

GETTING THEIR GOAT

Goatweed is a natural enemy of the weevils. You can powder the plant and place the powder in areas that you are having a problem in. You can also plant goatweed to protect plants from a number of pests.

FEED THEM THORN APPLES (Jimson Weed)

This is a very effective method of controlling seed weevils. Just dry the leaves and stems of the plant and use it as a dust to dust the crops that are affected. This plant can also be made into a spray by crushing a handful of the leaves in 4 cups of water and add 3 drops of liquid soap, strain and spray. **This plant is poisonous to humans and animals and should be handled accordingly.**

REFRIGERATION WORKS

A number of large companies that sell and store grain in the United States found that they do not have any problems with grain beetles if they store the grain products at 40°F. Most refrigerators maintain this temperature. Most companies now recommend that you store your grains in the refrigerator as soon as you bring them home from the store.

USE A COOKIE SHEET

If you are not sure if a problem exists in your flour or grain product, just spread out the product on a cookie sheet and place it in a 135°F oven for 30 minutes. Check the oven with a thermometer since if you have a pilot light the temperature may be around the degrees you need without turning on the oven.

PLAY DROPSY WITH THEM

The arbovitae weevil is a small black beetle covered with metallic green scales and emerges from the soil in early May. They like red and white cedar roots and the adults will eat foliage of adjacent plants as well. The best way to remove the beetles is to place a sheet under the plant or tree and shake for all your worth. They readily fall off and can be captured and disposed of with extreme prejudice.

PEA WEEVILS PREFER THE WEST COAST

The pea weevil is a coast-to-coast pest, however, they seem to prefer the states of Utah, Washington, Oregon and California the best. The adult beetle is a brownish color with scattered white and gray markings. It loves to feast on pea blossoms and lays their eggs on young pods. The worms them burrow through the pod and into the pea flesh for their meal. Most remedies for weevils will work on this pest.

If you are going to use peas for seed it would be best to heat them to 125^0F for about 5-6 hours to be sure there are no eggs on the peas. This will not damage the pea for seed purposes. The weevils will settle when in flight as soon as they get the scent from pea blossoms and the edges of the fields are more susceptible to damage than the rest of the field.

CHAPTER 9

FLIES

FLIES

There are over 100,000 species of flies. They are disease spreaders and should be eradicated whenever possible. An adult female housefly is capable of producing up to 2,400 eggs in her lifetime. Every egg that hatches turns into a maggot. In hot weather flies can multiply in 2-3 weeks, especially if they have a good supply of fresh warm excrement from a family pet. If you ingest fly eggs they can cause a stomachache. Flies have 4,000 faceted eyes and have ultra-sensitive hairs that can detect even the slightest change in air currents. Flies take off somewhat backwards and if you aim a flyswatter toward their back you will kill more flies.

When you see fly specs, the dark specs are excrement and the light specs are regurgitated food and saliva.

- A horsefly can actually bite through leather and can inflict a painful bite in humans.
- The stable fly has a proboscis like a hypodermic needle and draws blood, usually from a person's ankle, socks or no socks. Best to wear boots around stables.

NATURAL METHODS OF ELIMINATION

MAKING FLYPAPER WITH MAPLE SYRUP
The following ingredients will be needed:

1	Tablespoon of brown sugar
1	Tablespoon of granulated sugar
¼	Cup of an inexpensive maple syrup
1	Brown paper bag
1	Cookie sheet

Place all the ingredients in a small bowl and mix thoroughly. Cut 8-inch strips, about 2 inches wide from a brown paper bag and place them on the cookie sheet. Pour the mixture over the strips and allow the strips to soak overnight. Hang up the strips where needed.

GARBAGE CANS ARE A PROBLEM
Sprinkle dry borax into garbage cans after you wash them out, this will deter and kill them if they get it on them.

FLIES, WHERE THERE SHOULD BE NO FLIES
If you have a fly problem and your home is clean and there is no garbage around, it may be caused by a dead mouse or other small dead animal somewhere in the house, attic, basement or ? The problem will not go away unless you remove the cause or it will eventually decay eliminating the problem.

124

FRUIT FLIES AND BIRDS
If you own birds and feed them fruit, you may develop a fruit fly problem. There is a pyrethrum aerosol spray that is safe to use around birds called Misty Miser XX™. This will work as a short-term problem solver, but removing the food supply is the best answer. This spray is also one of the best methods of ridding your yard of flies.

FRUIT FLY LURE
Citronella grass is very effective in luring fruit flies into a glue-coated trap. If you have a problem with crops, just spray them with a diluted citronella oil spray.

GRAIN WILL KILL FRUIT FLIES
If you crush 1 cup of the grass-like grain called finger millet and place the powder in 1-quart of warm water then spray it works great for small areas or just a few trees.

MAKING FLYPAPER WITH HONEY
The following ingredients will be needed:

9	Parts rosin
3	Parts canola oil
1	Part honey

Place all the ingredients into a saucepan and melt together, stir well and apply to the paper while still warm. The paper should be prepared cutting strips of paper and folding them over and stapling them so that they will strong. Size the paper with shellac or varnish to prevent the mixture from spreading too far.

KEEPS THEIR BREATH FRESH TOO
Trying crushing some fresh mint and placing it into 1-2 sachets, then hang the sachets around the home or on the patio to repel flies.

HERBAL REMEDIES
- Use bay leaves, pennyroyal, eucalyptus or cloves in a muslin bag and hang them around the house. Pound them to release the essence before placing them into a bag.
- If you place some sweet basil in a small container in the kitchen or near a pets food dish it will repel flies. You can also plant sweet basil or rue around the doorways.
- Place a cotton ball with a few drops of eucalyptus oil on it in a shallow container in the kitchen.

FLYPAPER 101
To make your own flypaper, just mix together:

¼	Cup Karo® syrup
1	Tablespoon granulated sugar
1	Tablespoon of brown sugar

Cut strips of brown craft paper and soak it in the mixture, then allow it to dry overnight. Place a string in a small hole on top and hang wherever you have a problem.

MAKE A FLY OMELET
Beat 1 large egg yolk with 1 tablespoon of molasses and add 2 pinches of finely ground black pepper, then place the mixture in a shallow paper plate.

WHAT'S GOING ON DOWN THERE?
If you notice a number of very small flies and don't know where they are coming from it is probably from your kitchen drain. They are called drain flies and live in the drain on rotted foods. To trap them just place some duct tape over the drain at night, sticky side down. Pour vinegar down the drain and rinse out after a few minutes.

DUST OFF THE DOO, DOO
If you don't want to pick up after the pet, then dust the pile with garden grade diatomaceous earth (DE). DE can be fed to your pet and the flies will stay away from their feces. For cats feed ½ teaspoon every week, dogs should get ½ tablespoon each week and horses can get ¼ cup added to each meal. The flies won't even go near the horse manure.

SEND YOUR FLIES TO PEACEFUL VALLEY
This will be a permanent vacation for the flies. The trap is called the Peaceful Valley Fly Trap and is sold through most farm supply house. It will accommodate up to 25,000 flies. The trap used yeast and ammonium carbonate to attract the flies.

CARPET THE AREA
Cabbage root flies tend to lay their eggs close to young cabbage plants. To stop them from laying their eggs too close, just place a small circle of carpet with a slit so that it will wrap around the small plant and protect the base.

KEEP YOUR CAN CLEAN

Garbage cans and trash compactors can produce 1,000 or more fly eggs per week unless they are sealed tight. The problem can be solved with lavender oil. If you have a fly problem place a few drops of lavender oil on a piece of cotton and place it in the garbage can or an empty trash compactor bag before you start adding garbage.

You can also place a mint sprig in each can every week. Better yet just sprinkle the bottom of the can with insecticidal soap.

ESSENTIAL OILS TO THE RESCUE

There are a number of essential oils that will repel flies very effectively. The most effective are oil of peppermint and oil of cloves. If you place oil of lavender on a sponge and leave it in a room it will repel flies.

CLEAN UP AFTER YOUR PET

One of the preferred spots for flies to multiply on is your pet fecal material. It would be best to clean up after your pet daily to reduce the fly population around your home and garden area.

WHEN IS A FLY NOT A FLY?

When it is a whitefly, which is really a member of the insect family and not a "real" fly. They have four wings while flies only have two wings. They will suck the juices from plants and like to hang around greenhouses as their preferred residence. They lay their eggs on the underneath sides of leaves. They can be controlled in a greenhouse if you release the parasite *Encarsia formosa*. Also, ladybugs and lacewings enjoy munching on these bugs. A soap spray with a small amount of rubbing alcohol and coconut oil will dissolve the waxy coating on their larvae and kills them.

LEMON GRASS VERY PRETTY

If you have a problem, keeping flies away from your plants, just rub the leaves of the lemon grass plant on their leaves. By just rubbing the leaves on your plants it will provide the plant fly protection.

CAMPHOR TREE DOES THE JOB

If you plant a camphor tree near your kitchen it has the ability to repel flies. Chinaberry trees will also do the job.

FIGHT FLIES WITH FLIES

Wherever manure is you will find flies, especially around chicken ranches and stables. There a number of companies that sell fly parasites that can be released in these areas to control the fly population. The parasites deposit their eggs on the fly larvae or pupae in the manure and prevent them from becoming flies.

FLY MINTS

If you crush up some fresh mint and rub it on an animal, especially a horse it will keep the flies away for some time. The flies will not even land on them.

SOUTH OF THE BORDER

If you enter a dog kennel or stables and wonder what the plants are hanging from the doorways, it is probably Mexican marigolds. This plant has been used as a fly deterrent for hundreds of years and is still in use today.

LITTLE GAME HUNTER
There are a number of commercial flytraps sold on the market. If you do purchase one be sure that it is not placed in direct sunlight, since filtered sunlight works best. Ripened fruit works best in the trap, but if that is not available a combination of cornmeal mixed with molasses works almost as well.

ZAPPERS DON'T WORK WELL WITH FLIES
Flies are unable to see ultraviolet light during the day so placing a zapper outside in daylight will not work well and at night flies are inactive. All you end up doing is killing the beneficial insects.

GET A GIANT FLYSWATTER AND AIM FOR THEIR BACKSIDE
One of the best methods is still the good old flyswatter. For every fly that you kill, hundreds will not be born. A mesh flyswatter with a metal handle works the best. Be sure and wash the flyswatter in hot soapy water because of the bacteria and disease that they could harbor.

CHASE THEM WITH HAIRSPRAY
Better be sneaky and have a good aim, however, this works really well and is a bit challenging.

FAN THE FLIES
Flies do not like fast moving currents of air and will avoid them at all costs. If you have a fan over ever doorway that opens into the house, you will never have any flies in your home.

SPRINKLING MANURE
If you have areas with manure in piles it would be wise to sprinkle diatomaceous earth (DE) on the manure to reduce the fly population.

WON'T WORK LIKE MISTLETOE

If you hang a small sprig of ragwort over a doorway it will repel houseflies in the summer. Be sure that you are using the "real" thing. Ragwort has the botanical name of *Senecio jacobeae* and is part of the family *Compositae*. Look for feathered leaves and clusters of bight orange flowers that look like daisies. Since it has a somewhat pungent smell, best to hang it just outside the door.

CARROT RUST FLY

Identification:
This fly has a shiny greenish-black body, big red eyes and a yellowish head and legs. The larvae are yellowish-white maggots. The maggots will hatch from eggs that are laid around the carrots crown. After they hatch they burrow down into the roots. The tunnels they make are rusty in color from the maggot's excrement, which gives them their name. Their damage leads to soft-rot bacterial problems.

General Information:
This is a sneaky little fly that damages the plants underground and the damage is not noticeable until its too late. Loves to munch on carrots, parsnips, celery, parsley, fennel and dill. The carrots will have minute tunnels with a light-colored fecal matter. These bugs hang out in the northeastern states, coastal Washington and parts of Oregon and Idaho.

A SPOT OF TEA WITH YOUR SEEDS

Save your used tealeaves and place them into your carrot seeds when you plant. This will prevent any problems from carrot maggots.

PLANT REPELLANTS

There are a number of plants that when planted near the carrots and other similar vegetables will repel bugs. These include leek, onions, garlic, pennyroyal, rosemary, sage, black salsify and coriander.

DUST OFF THE PLANTS

If you prepare a dust composed of either wormwood or rock phosphate it will keep the flies from laying their eggs on the plants.

ONION FLY SOLUTION

The onion fly can be a real problem if you are growing onions. The fly lays its eggs in an onion and the resulting maggot does a good job of ruining the onion. If you scatter wood ash around the base of the plant it will help keep their number down since the flies will shy away from wood ash.

ROOT MAGGOT FLY

This fly looks like the common housefly but likes vegetables. There are a number of species all preferring their own veggie. The adult female lays her eggs on the roots of the vegetables and when the maggots hatch they proceed to live off the roots thus weakening the plant.

WOOD ASHES TO THE RESCUE

If you sprinkle a goodly amount of wood ashes around the roots it will keep these flies at bay and save your vegetables. Fireplace ashes will also do a very efficient job of keeping them away.

TAR PAPER WORKS

Place circles of tarpaper around the plants making a slit in each so that it will fit fairly snug around the plant.

DIG UP THE SOIL

One of the best methods of getting rid of root maggot flies is to dig up the soil in the fall and leave the pupae of the root maggots exposed to the cold of winter. This will also provide feed for hungry birds.

CHAPTER 10

MOSQUITOES

MOSQUITOES

KILL THOSE LITTLE BLOOD SUCKERS
Luckily, only 50% of the mosquitoes worldwide suck human blood. The female mosquito needs the protein from human blood to develop her eggs and lay them. When they don't get the blood meal they have to consume their own wing muscles. There are 2,500 different species of mosquitoes worldwide and they only weigh in at 1/25,000th of an ounce. They are so light that they are able to walk on water. The mosquito saliva, which they leave when they bite you, is what causes the itching.

In the United States alone there are over 150 species of mosquito and most can mature from an egg in one to two weeks. Mosquitoes need water to reproduce and they can usually find some standing water in pets dishes, drainage ditches, fishponds, old tires, damp mulch, rain gutter lines, sewers, planters, leaks around spickets, etc. Mosquitoes like to live near your home and are smart enough to know that there are plenty of free meals there; you and you're family.

During the day they will seek shelter from the sun and are more active when it cools down or in a shady spot. They will never go too far from water. Getting rid of any location that has even the slightest amount of standing water should help to eliminate the problem. They don't like windy condition and prefer still air areas. Using a fan in the home will keep them out as well.

The female mosquito eats a blood meal and then lays an egg on the surface of water. The water must be still so keep this in mind regarding mosquitoes on your property. If you have any standing water and there are mosquitoes in the neighborhood you will have eggs hatching in your backyard. They prefer very shallow water so it doesn't take much to make them happy. They will feed on bacteria in the water after they hatch then they will turn into pupae. It only takes several days for mosquitoes to turn into an adult and go looking for you.

It only takes 1 pint of water to nurture 500 mosquito larvae.

Your best protection against mosquitoes is to be sure that they do not have a point of entry into your home. Be sure and seal off any openings and especially holes in screens.

NATURAL METHODS OF ELIMINATION

MOSQUITO REPELLANT #I FOR ARMS AND LEGS
The following ingredients will be needed:

| 4 | Parts glycerin (from pharmacy) |
| 1 | Part eucalyptus oil |

Place the ingredients into a small bowl and mix thoroughly. Place in a well-sealed container. Rub a small amount on arms or legs to keep mosquitoes from biting.

WATER, WATER, EVERYWHERE
Be sure that there is no standing water anywhere on your property. Mosquitoes like pets, water dishes and birdbaths. If you sprinkler system is leaving a puddle that does not dry up in a short period of time, be sure and fix it.

NUMERO UNO MOSQUITO KILLER
If you don't have a cat this is the best mosquito killer that is available. Catnip placed in a sachet and placed around the home will deter any and all mosquitoes in short order. Catnip contains the essential oil nepetalactone, which is at least 10 times more powerful than any commercial mosquito killing solution. A tea made from catnip can also be placed into a spray bottle and sprayed anywhere you have a problem.

REPEL MOSQUITOES WITH YOUR BARBECUE
It doesn't matter if you use real charcoal or artificial charcoal, just place a few sprigs of rosemary or sage on top of the coals and you wont see a mosquito for some time.

GETS RID OF VAMPIRES AND MOSQUITOES
Mix 1 part of concentrated garlic juice with 5 parts of water and place in a spray bottle. Spray in any area that they frequent. This treatment will be effective for 5-6 hours and you will have great smelling mosquitoes.

MOSQUITO REPELLANT II
The following ingredients will be needed:

1	Ounce of oil of citronella (from health food store)
1	Drops of corn oil

Place the ingredients in a small bowl and mix well. Rub the mixture on your skin before going into mosquito-land.

SOLUTION FROM INDIA

A natural vegetable oil that is extracted from an Indian tree called the "Neem tree" is very effective in repelling mosquitoes. The seeds and the leaves contain the chemical sallanin, which has been used for hundreds of years in India to repel flying insects. It is natural and more effective than any commercial product on the market. One Internet site to get the product is www.nutraceutic.com.

A GRASS THAT REPELS MOSQUITOES

A very effective substance that repels mosquitoes is citronella. Citronella can be found in lemon grass and in the natural oil form, found in the grass, which is even more effective than the citronella that you purchase from the store. It is also called Thai grass and is available at most garden stores. Use the scallion-like stem of the plant, crush it and use it on your arms, legs and neck to repel mosquitoes. You can also make a spray by making a tea from the stem.

HERBS 101

To get rid of flying insects, just place some fresh basil in a muslin bag or two and hang them around the house or on the porch. Flying insects do not like the smell of basil and it will repel almost every flying insect.

MOSQUITO REPELLANT III

The following ingredients will be needed:

3	Cups of rubbing alcohol
1 ½	Cups of red cedar wood shavings
½	Cup of eucalyptus leaves
1	Spray bottle

Place all the ingredients in a large bowl and mix well. Cover the bowl and allow it to stand for 6 days before straining the solution through a piece of cheesecloth. Place the liquid in a small spray bottle and spray on skin as needed.

SCARE THEM AWAY WITH BEANS

If you want an easy solution to ridding your home and garden of mosquitoes, just purchase some castor bean seeds and grow a few plants. Castor bean plants grow like weeds and will repel mosquitoes. The chemical in the castor bean is ricinine and when extracted it is a deadly chemical.

GROW SOME BAMBOO PLANTS

Dragonflies are attracted by bamboo plants and are safe around people. They like to live among the long bamboo shoots in warm and sunny areas of your yard. One dragonfly will consume at least 100 mosquitoes in 30 minutes and will eat their larvae as well. They can spot a mosquito 25 yards away and go after it at 60 miles per hour. Dragonflies can be found in most areas of the United States.

MOSQUITOES VS ZAPPERS

Studies have shown that electric bug zappers have no effect on mosquitoes. They seem to have a special sense that keeps them away from electrical magnetic fields.

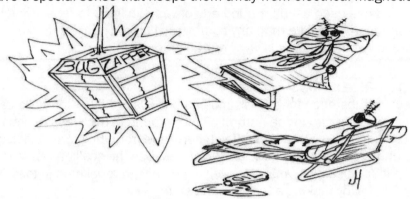

GET BATS IN YOUR BELFRY

If you don't have bats in your neighborhood you might consider purchasing a bat house. Most garden supply stores will sell a bat house for about $25.00. This will eliminate thousands of unwanted insects every night. Bats will not bother people, however, if you have a pool or birdbath they will swoop in for a drink occasionally.

BIRDS LOVE INSECTS

If you place a number of birdhouses on your property to attract birds it will decrease your insect population significantly. To be sure that the birds don't eat your plants you will need to have a few bird feeders around with birdseed and keep them filled.

NATURAL REPELLANT PLANTS

There are a number of plants that will repel mosquitoes very effectively. They are tomato, basil, germanium, citrosa, lemon thyme, citronella grass and eucalyptus. These plants tend to give off oils that repel mosquitoes. You can crush up most of these plants and make a natural mosquito repellant, but be sure and try a small area of your skin to be sure that you do not have an allergy to that particular plant.

A LITTLE BOUNCE™ WILL DO YA

Florida's national insect is the mosquito or at least should be. When you are in Florida and see people with a Bounce™ fabric softener sheet sticking out of their clothing, they are wearing them to repel mosquitoes. This seems to be a very effective method of keeping them away from you.

POSSIBLE REPELLANTS

Rumor is that rubbing apple cider vinegar, peppermint, bay cloves, vanilla bean, sassafras, cedar, eucalyptus or parsley on your skin will repel mosquitoes for a short period of time.

CLEARING THE ROOM
If you open a bottle of pennyroyal or citronella oil and leave it open it will eliminate all the flying insects in the room. Just be sure and leave them a way out.

THE MOSQUITO HUNTERS
Both toads and bats consume thousands of insects. Mosquitoes are one of their delicacies and they can consume thousands of mosquitoes every night. If you live in an area where toads live and want them in your yard, just build them a "toad house." They like to live in clay flowerpots so just place a flowerpot upside down and break a hole near the top (which is the bottom now) and they can easily jump in. They like cool, dark homes to get away from the heat of the day.

MOSQUITO REPELLANT IV
The following ingredients will be needed:

1	Cup peanut oil
½	Cup dried chamomile
½	Cup of dried nettle
½	Cup of dried pennyroyal
¼	Cup of sweet basil
½	Cup of sweet orange oil
1	Teaspoon of boric acid

Place all the ingredients in a double boiler and crush the herbs into the oil, then heat, stirring occasionally for about 45 minutes. Cover the mixture and remove from the heat and allow it to cool. Strain the mixture through a fine sieve, mashing the herbs to acquire the most fluid possible. Store in a well-sealed container in the refrigerator until needed. It will not take very much to do the job. Rub on exposed areas.

JUST ONE LITTLE CANDLE
Candles will attract mosquitoes and will kill them when they get too close. Just don't use citronella candles inside the home since the fumes are harmful to your health.

THE NEW MAGNET

There is a new device on the market called the Mosquito Magnet®. This device employs propane and in a Florida swamp test no one had a single bite.

THE YOLK IS ON THEM

If you break open a few egg yolks and allow them to spread over the surface of water or a pond it will suffocate the mosquito larvae and last for several days.

THE MOSQUITO FISH

If you have a pond or small lake on your property you may consider stocking the lake with *Gambusia affinis*. These fish thrive on mosquito larvae.

PAMPER THE MARLINS

Purple marlins love mosquitoes and will consume a great amount of the adult mosquitoes. They like apartment-style birdhouses and make the entrances 21/8 to 2½ inches and allow the depth from the hole to the bottom of about 6 inches. They are very fussy where they live. Make sure that you drill a small drainage hole in the bottom.

TINY MOSQUITO HUNTERS

Minnows can make excellent mosquito larvae and pupae hunters and finds them one of their favorite foods. They will also catch a female while they are laying their eggs on the surface of the water.

CHANGE THE SURFACE TENSION

Mosquitoes like water and if you spray the surface of the water with Safe Solutions, Inc Enzyme Cleaner with Peppermint (from garden supply store) it will make it almost impossible for the mosquito larvae and pupae to survive. The adult mosquitoes cannot maintain surface contact if the spray is used. Another chemical, which will change the surface tension of the water, is "isostearyl alcohol ethoxylate." It is a non-irritating alcohol that comes from plants and has no odor. It is commonly used in the cosmetic industry.

FLOAT THE KILLER

If you float rings of Bti, which is a special strain of Bt it will kill only the mosquito larvae in your pond or small lake. The crotches of trees that extend into the water are especially a problem area in which Bti will do the job. Soap spray is very effective as well and changes the surface tension of the water.

BURNING GRASS?

If you place some lemon grass in a safe metal container and burn it, it will repel mosquitoes. If mosquitoes are frequenting a plant and you don't want them, just rub some lemon grass on the leaves.

OIL THE WATER

If you spray any aerosol oil on any standing water you must have on your property it will kill the mosquito larvae and pupae by suffocating them.

BARBECUE THEM

Next time you barbecue and want to keep the mosquitoes away, just throw some sage or rosemary on the hot coals. Both of these herbs work great on the barbecue and will keep all flying insects away.

ITALIANS RARELY GET BITTEN

People who consume garlic on a regular basis; rarely get bitten by mosquitoes. Mosquitoes hate garlic flavoring in your blood. One of the best biological control of mosquitoes utilizes garlic oil emulsion. The active ingredient *allyl sulfide* is a known mosquito killer.

CHAPTER 11

MISCELLANEOUS FLYING INSECTS

MISCELLANEOUS FLYING INSECTS

GNATS

BAIT & TRAP
Gnats are easy to trap and eliminate from your home using a vinegar and water trap. Just fill a small jar about ¾ full of water and add 1 tablespoon of apple cider vinegar. Place the jar on your kitchen counter near a ripening fruit or even better an overripe fruit. The gnats will investigate the jar and will be killed. To control the gnat larvae in the soil use a natural organic product called Neem™. Neem™ can be purchased in any garden shop.

BLACKFLIES ARE REALLY GNATS
Blackflies are gnats that can be a really big pest to gardeners. They are bloodsuckers and prefer the areas around your head and neck. They prefer to lay their eggs in moving well-oxygenated water and then hatch into round black maggots. One small stream can produce millions of these pests. The best control method is to spray Bti, which is a special strain of Bt in areas that the gnats frequent in late summer or early fall.

MOTHS

Never use mothballs in your closets: or even have them around the house, they are very poisonous and many pets have died from eating them and they have made hundreds of children very sick. The adult moths are not the guilty ones when it comes to eating your clothes and leaving holes, however, it is their larvae; that actually does the damage. The female moth lays her eggs on fabric and if the fabric is moved will easily dislodge them. The larvae, uses any stains that contain food, urine or sweat to get their vitamins.

If you leave sweaty clothing in a closet the moths will find it and set up housekeeping and lay eggs.

HIT THEM WITH A CHILI POD
To prepare a potent spray for moths, just follow the recipe. Grind up 2-3 handfuls of ripe hot peppers then allow the to soak in 1½ quart of water for 24 hours. Mix well, strain and add 3 quarts of water and 3-4 drops of Ivory liquid soap. Strain again and place in sprayer. This is meant for the outside, do not use in the home. Before you spray all the plants check and be sure that the mixture is not too strong and will damage the plants.

THE VINEGAR TRAP
If you are curious as to what kind and how many moths you have, just place a shallow dish or bowl with white vinegar in it on the shelf to trap them.

THE FEMALE TEMPTATION ALWAYS WORKS

In the late spring, try hanging pheromone traps in the apple trees. They contain sticky paper and a capsule of the female hormone to attract the male. If you trap the males then they cannot fertilize the females and no eggs.

WAX THOSE MOTHS
To make moth repellant paper, just mix together 4 parts of naphthalene and 8 parts of paraffin wax. Melt both together and paint it on a piece of thin white cardboard while the solution is still warm.

HERBS TO REPEL MOTHS
The following herbs can be placed in your closet to repel moths. Try using pennyroyal, wormwood, sage, santolina, lavender and mint.

CABBAGE MOTHS

TAR PAPER TRAPPER
Roofing felt or tarpaper can be very effective against cabbage moths. These very small pale purple moths kill young sprouts. Make a slit in the paper and place it fully around the plant. This will stop the cabbage moths from laying eggs around the base of the cauliflower; cabbage, broccoli or Brussels sprout plants. The plant will open the slit more and more as it grows.

CLOTHES MOTHS

CEDAR CHEST NO HELP
Since cedar loses its oils and effectiveness after 2-3 years don't expect much protection from cedar for any extended length of time.

KILLING THE EGGS
If you are worried that you may have moth eggs in your woolens, just place the garment in a plastic bag and place it into the freezer for 24 hours. This will kill the eggs permanently.

WHOOOOSH

If you vacuum your clothes it will eliminate the problem, however, you should do the carpet as well while you are at it.

SKIP THE MOTHBALLS

You will never have a moth problem if you place one hedgeapple in every closet and change them about every 2 months. They work better than mothballs without the offensive odor.

GIVE THEM THE COLD SHOULDER

If you have a problem with moths it would be best to place the suspect garment into a plastic bag and freeze it at -4^0F for 7 days to kill off all eggs and larvae.

TURN UP THE HEAT

Heat can disinfect your clothing and kill all stages of moths. If the clothes are exposed to 122^0F for about 12 minutes or 140^0F for 1 minute that should do the trick and the clothes will be free of moth problems. Woolens, however, may not take the heat well and would be better in the cold.

MOTH REPELLER

The following ingredients will be needed:

All herbs may be purchased at a health food store

4	Teaspoons of orris root powder
1	Cup of wormwood
½	Cup of lavender
1 ½	Cup of yarrow
1	Cup of mint
10	Drops of oil of cloves
1	Cup cedar chips
10	Bay leaves
1	Tablespoon whole cloves
3	Clothespins or bag clip
1	Stainless steel fork

Place the orris root powder in a small bowl and add the oil of cloves, then mix well (crush any lumps) with the stainless steel fork. Place all the other herbs in a brown paper bag and shake to mix. Add the oil and orris root to the bag and shake well to mix. Seal the bag with the clothespins or a bag clip and place the bag in a dry, cool location for 2 weeks. After the herb mixture has mellowed, place a portion in a number of old socks and hang them up in the closets. You will never see another moth they will be fighting to get in next door.

A LITTLE HERE, A LITTLE THERE

Diatomaceous earth (DE) powder sprinkled in the corners of shelves. To make the DE more effective mix half pyrethrum and half DE.

HANG UP A SACHET OR TWO
Make a sachet to hang in the closets using dried mint, peppercorns, rosemary, lavender, bay leaves, whole cloves and cedar chips.

KILLING CLOTHES MOTHS
These moths are rarely seen since they only come out at night to feast on your clothing. They prefer protein-based fibers such as woolens, carpets and furs, which are a delicacy, pet hair and even your hairbrush hair.

SEND THE MOTHS TO THE CLEANERS
Dry cleaning will kill the moths as well as their larvae but will not stop other moths from attacking the clothes after you wear them and the chemicals wear off. After you dry clean them, place them into a plastic bag and place them into cold storage for safe keeping if you are not going to wear them for a while.

PUT A SUNLAMP IN THE CLOSET
Moths hate the sunlight! If you bring your clothes outside when it's sunny for 30 minutes you will eliminate the problem. Best to give them a little beating to be sure they all fall off, including the larvae and eggs.

NATURAL ELIMINATION, TOGA PROTECTION
Place cedar chips in a porous cloth bag; then hang it in the closet. Moths do not like the aroma of cedar. You can also place cedar oil on a piece of absorbent cloth and hang that in the closet. Cedar oil tends to work better since cedar chips will lose their effectiveness after several months and the oil dries out. The Romans used oil of cedarwood placed on backs of parchment to get rid of the moths that were eating their togas.

HERBS VS MOTHS
Make a sachet using a combination of rosemary, lavender and rose petals and hang in the closet. Dried lemon peels also do very well to deter moths just placed in the closet.

CODLING MOTHS

Codling moths can be found wherever apple and pear trees are grown. They love apples and when you see what looks like a worm in your apple it is probably a coddling moth worm. They lay their eggs on the branches of the trees and when they hatch the caterpillars tunnel into the fruit and consume the core while leaving the rest of the fruit for us.

They spend their winter in cocoons just under the bark of the tree and usually in the lower three feet.

Spring is the best time to get rid of them and they can be scraped off the bark without too much trouble. In winter it is best to spray the tree with quality horticultural oil.

TRAPS WORK GREAT

Pheromone traps are available through garden or agricultural supply stores and work great. However, don't expect immediate results since it will take about 2 years to get rid of the pests.

DON'T CODDLE THEM

About mid-summer, scrape off an area on your apple trees and wrap the area with a piece of burlap (tie it down good). When the caterpillars climb up the tree to pupate they will hide in the burlap. The burlap can then be removed and discarded.

TRICHING CODDLING MOTHS

If the trichogramma wasp is released at the beginning of spring it will eliminate or at least greatly reduce the infestation. Also, spraying with an Nc nematode solution in late winter will make a big difference.

WRAP THE TREES

In early summer you can wrap the tree trunks with a sticky paper or use Tanglefoot™ and trap the caterpillars as they go down the tree. Best to keep them wrapped all summer if you have this problem.

DIAMOND BACK MOTHS

WILD SUNFLOWER VS DIAMOND BACKS

To eliminate diamond back moths, just use wild sunflowers. Pound the leaves and extract the juice and use as a spray diluting the juice of 1½ pounds of leaves with 4 cups of water, strain and spray.

GYPSY MOTH

These were brought to the United States by a Frenchman hoping to breed them with silkworms. The northeastern Unites States is the hardest hit by gypsy moths attacking oak, birch, willow, linden, basswood and apple trees. They tend to defoliate trees and have become a major pest.

The adult moth hardly eats anything and the female cannot fly. The problem is, however, the larvae is a voracious eater and is very mobile. The larvae, eats at night, most of the time and is difficult to spot.

The female moth lays her eggs in large clusters that can reach up to 1,000 eggs, under stones or on tree trunks. You can even find the eggs on patio furniture or on your car. The caterpillars can travel as far as ½ mile on a strong current of wind. For some reason when the moth population, builds up too high, they are killed off by a virus.

CALL FOR REINFORCEMENTS
One of the best methods is to call for a professional if the infestation is a major one. If not spraying with Bt or Neem™ will solve the problem without the use of pesticides or harmful chemicals.

USE THE SEX ATTRACTANT
Pheromone traps have been very effective in catching these pests. They should be coated with Dispalure® or Gyplure® (Gyptol) to lure in the male moths.

NATURAL ENEMY
A ground beetle called *Calosoma frigidum* eats the caterpillar and hunts it down. The beetle has a black and greenish shine and is a night hunter. Another beetle that goes after the gypsy moth larvae is the *Calosoma sycophanta* and is another excellent caterpillar hunter.

JAPAN HAS THE ANSWER
Biological control of this moth has been very successful. The Japanese insect *Oercyrtus kuvamai* is now produced by the USDA labs and has been released in several states including New Jersey, New York and Pennsylvania. The female of this parasite lays her eggs, in the eggs of the moth and destroys the majority of them.

DRIVE THEM CUCKCOO

If you have a black-billed or yellow-billed cuckoo living in your neighborhood, it would be wise to entice them to your property since they are the number one bird predator for gypsy moths. There are many other birds that like the moth for dinner but the cuckoo has a real thing for them.

FOREST SERVICE USES NPV

The U.S. Forest Service uses a Nuclear Polyhedrosis Virus (NPV) and marketed as Gypchek®. This spray is non-toxic to all other insects and animals but kills the gypsy moth. The forest service recommends two spraying to eliminate the problem.

INDIAN MEAL MOTHS

POSSIBLY WEARS SUNGLASSES

This is a very small moth that is not attracted to light. The moths can lay up to 350 eggs, which develop into small worms that love to consume all types of grains, crackers, candy, dried fruit, red hot peppers and they love dog and cat food for dessert. They leave silk threads as they eat, which causes foods to clump together. Best to freeze foods if you have the problem, which will kill them.

MEAL MOTHS

HOW TO PREVENT THEM

Meal moths are a problem when food is stored in moist areas or the humidity is high. They normally reside in grains or grain products such as cereals.

- Exposed grains attract them.
- They love cookie crumbs and especially dry dog food.
- Toasters are their favorite place to hangout especially when they are not used for a while.
- They will come for a visit in loose grains that are purchased in markets or health food stores.
- They will chew their way into cardboard boxes without any trouble. Best to inspect boxes every once in a while for holes.
- If you have rodents and they steal pet food the moths will find it.
- Vacuum all cracks and crevices in food areas regularly.

STALK BORER MOTHS

GUMMING THEM UP

If you have a problem with stalk borer moths all you have to do to control them is to grind some young leaves from the gum tree into a fine powder and use it for dusting. You can also crush some young leaves and allow them to soak in water and add a few drops of a liquid soap. Soak the leaves until the water is green then use the water as a spray. Best to use the spray when the moths are active. Test an area of your plants since this mixture may burn the plants.

WASPS/YELLOW JACKETS/BEES

Identification:

The adult wasps are about 1-inches long and a bright yellow and black or sometimes have white and black patterned bands on the abdomen depending on the species. Their wings are clear and folded neatly back when not flying. The queens are twice the size of the workers.

General Information:

Wasps are beneficial insects that will not bother humans unless agitated. They consume insects that are pests and should only be eliminated from your immediate environment when they are pesky. Wasps are active in pollinating a number of crops including melons and spinach. Stay as far from their nesting places as possible since they will attack you if you get too close. If you see more than one wasp in your home they may be making a nest and you need to investigate thoroughly.

Only 50 species of wasp out of about 2,500 species will sting you

Yellow jackets are wasps that are very aggressive and feed on sweets and meats. A nest, usually only lasts for 1 year then the queen flies away to start another nest and the workers die off. A nest that is left over will not be used again.

REMOVING A STINGER

If you get stung by a bee, yellow jacket or wasp be sure that you do not pull the stinger out. When you try and remove it you may cause more venom to enter the body by squeezing it. The best method of removal is to use a credit card and scrape it off at an angle until it is dislodged. This will stop the poison from entering the skin.

HAIRSPRAY TO THE RESCUE

Hairspray will give you some temporary relief if you have bees or wasps hovering around your lawn eating area. Just spray them with hairspray and it will coat their wings so that they can't fly. However, eventually it will wear off and you do not want to be around when it does.

LEAVE THE VIBRATOR IN THE HOUSE
Wasps and yellow jackets are very sensitive to vibrations such as running, yelling or any other fast movement anywhere in the vicinity of their nest. They will investigate and take action if they feel threatened.

ZIG-ZAG PATTERN
If bees are chasing you it is best to run in a zig-zag pattern to confuse them. This may save you from getting stung too many times.

WASPY FACTS
- Wasps will be attracted to protein foods and they love being a guest at barbecues.
- A dish of pet food outside will attract them.
- Wasps imprint foods and even when they are removed they will return to that same area.
- In late summer and early fall wasps like sweets and are more aggressive.
- If you step on a wasp and kill it they release a pheromone, which attracts other wasps.
- Rotting fruit will attract wasps.
- Bright clothing attracts wasps.
- Perfumes should not be worn if wasps are present in the area.
- Wasps are attracted by yellow light.
- Remove nests at night only. Place a cloth over the entire nest and seal it.
- Burning a nest will make them very mad at you.

DON'T USE A BRIGHT LIGHT
If you decide to eliminate the wasp or yellow jackets nest at night when they are dormant, be sure that you do not use a flashlight or cast a shadow on the nest. Best to place some red cellophane paper over the lens since red light does not bother them.

PUT THEM IN A FISHBOWL
If you locate a nest on the ground, try covering it with a large glass bowl and allow it to remain for 2 weeks to kill off the nest.

ICE THEM
Placing dry ice around a ground nest will eliminate the nest by putting carbon dioxide gas into the nest. The CO_2 is heavier than air and will enter a nest that is partially underground.

INSULATE THEIR NEST
If you inject aerosol foam insulation into their nest at night (using a red light) this will eliminate the nest. This method is frequently used in tree cavities or logs.

BAIT THEM
Sweet attractive bait can be prepared by using a 5% food-grade DE or sodium borate (borax) and honey or jelly. Form small balls and leave it in areas that they frequent. Make sure it is not near any pets or children since it is not safe for them. They also love soda cans that are left around by the kids.

USE A FIRE EXTINGUISHER
CO_2 fire extinguishers work great for getting rid of stinging insect nests. Use it at night for the best results.

CALL FOR PEPE LE PEW
Yellow jackets frequently make their nest in the ground. There are two animals that love to dig up these nests; they are skunks and raccoons. They will prey on the yellow jackets when they can find them.

BOTTLED YELLOW JACKETS
If you place some sweet soda pop in a tall plastic soda bottle and leave it out the yellow jackets will go in get confused and will not be able to get out. A piece of fresh liver or ham placed away from your area helps as well.

WHITEFLIES

Identification:
These are moth-like flies that are milky white and covered with a waxy powder. Their eggs are laid on the underneath side of the leaves. The eggs are yellow and will turn to gray as they mature. If you shake a plant that you think has been infested with whiteflies, these tiny moth-like bugs will fly up from underneath the leaves. They look like "flying dandruff" and multiply very quickly.

General Information:
Whiteflies excrete sticky honeydew that will also damage a healthy plant. These are a real pest in greenhouses or on indoor plants since they like warm, sheltered areas. They are more prevalent in the southern United States. They are not fussy eaters and will damage almost any plant, especially if a plant is deficient in magnesium and phosphorus.

DOCTORS ANSWER TO WHITEFLIES
Try using 10 tablespoons of Dr. Bronner's Peppermint Soap™ to 1 gallon of water and add 1 tablespoon of pyrethrum and 1 tablespoon of sunflower oil to the mixture. This spray is usually only used for a serious infestation. For a minor infestation use Jungle Rain™. Remember if you don't control the ant population you can't control the whiteflies since their favorite food supply comes from aphids, which are herded by ants and produce honeydew.

WHITEFLIES LOVE YELLOW
Whiteflies will damage your tomato plants unless you protect the plant. All you have to do is to place a small can (vegetable can) that has been painted yellow over the top of the stake that supports the tomato plant then place a small baggie over the can and rub Vaseline® on the baggie. This will eliminate the whitefly problem.

BIO-CONTROL TO THE RESCUE
The parasite *Encarsia formosa* will attack the larval stage of the bug and eliminate the problem. Ladybugs and lacewings find them a tempting dish to dine on.

WHOOOOOSH
If you have a portable hand vacuum it will come in handy. Just vacuum the plant and you will eliminate the whiteflies. Be sure that the vacuum is not too powerful that it will damage the plant when you try this.

CHAPTER 12

PETS

PETS

MISCELLANEOUS TIPS

DE-BURR-DEN YOUR PET
If your pet gets a burr in it's coat, just apply a small amount of vegetable oil to the burr and allow it to remain for 5 minutes before combing it out. Sometimes if you crush the burr first with a pair of pliers it may hasten the removal.

CURING THE PAW-CHEWER
To cure a dog of paw, chewing, just paint the paw with oil of cloves. This will stop them from chewing instantly and wait until you see the look on their face.

DOES YOUR DOG LIKE TO PLAY TERMITE?
Puppies like to chew on wood, which can make the owner very unhappy if the wood is a good piece of furniture leg. Just paint the leg with oil of cloves to eliminate the problem.

FLEAS

MY DOG HAS CAT FLEAS
Fleas are usually brought into your home by your pet or visitor's pet. If you find one flea there is probably 100 more for every one you find somewhere in your pets environment. Fleas can jump 150-200 times their body length and one pair of fleas can produce 250,000 more fleas or up to 1 trillion in a year. They are like little vampires and like warm-blooded hosts.

The most common flea is the "cat flea," which can be found on your dog. It would be best to treat areas that fleas may frequent before you have a problem, because afterwards it is really hard to get rid of them. The flea cycle is as follows: the flea jumps on your pet and has a warm blood meal. If your pet is not available, you are next. Once they have fed, they will mate and lay eggs (and are not fussy where they lay them).

It will take 2-3 weeks to hatch the hundreds of eggs, which release small caterpillar-like (larvae) creatures, which feed on almost any organic matter they find. After it has fed, it spins a cocoon (pupae stage). When the flea is in the pupae stage it cannot be killed in the cocoon. No chemical spray will penetrate the cocoon. When it hatches, you have more fleas. Treating your yard is one of the best methods of controlling a flea population. Professional help is usually needed if you have a bad infestation.

One of the most common reasons pets get fleas is that they have dry, flaky skin, which makes it easier for the fleas to get a foothold and is easier for them to obtain their meal of blood. If the animal gets adequate exercise they will not have as many fleas.

SWEET SMELLING FLEA SHAMPOO FOR PETS
The following ingredients will be needed:

1	Cup Castile™ soap (liquid)
1/8	Ounce of essential oil of pine
1/8	Ounce of essential rose oil

Place all the ingredients into a jar with a lid and shake to mix well. Add the mixture to your pet's bath water and the fleas will be very unhappy.

ANIMAL DRY BATH FOR WINTER
The following ingredients will be needed:

1	Tablespoons of trisodiumphosphate (TSP)
2	Tablespoons of borax
4	Tablespoons of sodium carbonate
12	Tablespoons of talc
1½	Cups of starch

Place all the ingredients into a container and mix well. Rub the mixture on the animal against the direction of the hair; then brush well or vacuum to remove the dry shampoo. If you would like to leave your pet sweet smelling, just add a few drops of your pets' favorite essential oil to the mixture.

OINTMENT FOR ANIMAL FLEA SORES
The following ingredients will be needed:

8	Ounces of lard
4	Ounces of beeswax
4	Ounces of rosin
½	Ounce of carbolic acid

Place the beeswax, lard and rosin in a double boiler and heat while stirring until melted, then add the carbolic acid and mix thoroughly. Remove from heat and allow the ointment to cool, then store in a well-sealed container until needed.

DO-IT-YOURSELF FLEA COLLAR

To rid your pet of fleas make your own all-natural flea collar, just cut a strip of cloth about an inch larger than the size of your pet's neck. Fold the cloth over with an opening in the center then sew one end shut as well as placing a seam down the strip. Using a funnel fill the opening with a combination of 50/50 rosemary and oregano then sew or tape a piece of Velcro to close up the open end and attach it to the pet using a Velcro closure. Do not put pyrethrums in a cat collar but it can be used in a dog collar.

BASIC PET SHAMPOO

The following ingredients will be needed:

½	Cup of Castile™ soap (grated)
2½	Tablespoons of glycerin (from drug store)
3	Drops of pine oil or any scent your pet prefers
2	Tablespoons of denatured alcohol
1½	Cups of warm tap water

Place the soap and water in a double boiler and warm to melt the soap into the water, then add the glycerin and mix well. Remove the pan from the heat and allow the mixture to cool. As it cools, add the alcohol and the pine drops, then mix well.

FLEA POWDER

Powder ½ cup of the following herbs and dust the animal. Use wormwood, fennel, rue and peppermint.

SCRUB-A-DUB-DUB

Best to give your pet a bath regularly using just a mild soap or soap for pets from your pet store. When you brush your pet and find a flea soak the brush or comb in soapy water to kill the fleas. Also, if you add 1 teaspoon of white vinegar to 1 quart of water for every 40 pounds of body weight it will also help.

MAKE SOME FLEA-ADE

Citrus oil is an excellent flea deterrent. Just slice up a lemon, score the skin to release more of the oil and then pour 1 cup of boiling water over the lemon and allow the lemon to sit overnight. Use a clean sponge and sponge the lemon water on your pet to instantly kill the fleas. Best to give the pet a bath afterwards or they will smell like lemonade all day. If you buy a citrus product be sure it has D-limonene in it, since this will also kill ticks.

FLEA-ELIMINATOR FLOOR CLEANER

The following ingredients will be needed:

1	Tablespoon of liquid dish soap
4	Lemons (sliced thin)
5	Drops of pennyroyal (from health food store)
1	Gallon very warm water

Place the sliced lemons in a medium saucepan, cover with cold tap water and allow them to simmer on low heat for 1 hour. Remove the juice from the lemons and strain well. Place the juice into a bucket and add the soap, pennyroyal and water. Mix the solution very well before applying with a damp sponge mop. Allow the floor to dry before rinsing with a clean damp sponge mop.

DO-IT-YOURSELF FLEA COLLAR

To make a flea collar, just soak a store-bought leather collar in the lemon juice (citrus oil) solution. You can also use a piece of cloth with a Velcro fastener. Most commercial flea collars use a pesticide, which are damaging to the environment.

VITAMIN B TO THE RESCUE

Your vet can recommend a vitamin B supplement for your pet. Fleas will not remain on a pet if they are on a vitamin B supplement.

FLEA-A-WAY FOODS

If you add a small amount of brewer's yeast, apple cider vinegar or crushed garlic to your pet's food, it will keep the fleas away. The garlic is questionable since he will smell garlicky for some time. Brewer's yeast can also be powdered on your pet and allowed to remain for 5-10 minutes before vacuuming the pet off.

ODE DE DOGGIE

To keep fleas out of your pets bedding, just sprinkle a few drops of lavender oil in their bed. Lavender oil can be purchased in most health food stores.

PET'S BEDDING FLEA ELIMINATOR

The following ingredients will be needed:

½	Cup of pennyroyal
2	Tablespoons of dried thyme
2	Tablespoons of dried wormweed
2	Tablespoons of dried rosemary

Place the herbs in a food processor and powder. Place the herbs inside your pets pillow by opening up a seam, inserting the powder and sewing it back up making sure that the powder is as evenly distributed as possible.

FLEAS HATE SAGE

Fleas do not like the odor of sage. Crush up sage into a fine powder and rub it on your pets skin, then allow it to remain for 15-20 minutes before brushing it off or vacuuming the pet if it is a big pet. Vacuuming mini Chihuahuas is not recommended or they may be staring out from the clear plastic dirt tank.

GREEN BAN FROM DOWN UNDER

This shampoo is usually available from most pet stores or vets office. It is fresh smelling and contains pure essential oils that will eliminate the flea problem and leave your pet smelling spring fresh.

MAKING DOGGIE BISCUITS

The following ingredients will be needed:

¾	Cup of rye flour
1¾	Cups of whole wheat flour
¾	Cup of bulgur
½	Cup of cornmeal
½	Cup of Brewer's yeast (fresh from health food store)
1	Teaspoon of dry yeast
½	Cup of reduced fat dry milk
¼	Cup of warm tap water
1	Cup of de-fatted chicken or turkey broth
¼	Cup of dried parsley
1	Large egg (beat with 1 tablespoon of whole milk)

Place the warm water and dry yeast in a bowl and stir until all yeast is dissolved; then add the chicken or turkey broth. Place the flours, Brewer's yeast, bulgur, dry milk, cornmeal and parsley in another bowl and mix well. Stir the liquid mixture into the dry mixture and mix well into stiff dough. If the dough is too difficult to work, add a small amount of warm water to loosen it up. Roll the dough out on a floured surface to about ¼ to ½ inch thickness, then cut with a cookie cutter into biscuits. Place the biscuits on a cookie sheet and lightly glaze with a beaten egg and bake at 300°F. for 40 minutes. Allow the biscuits to remain in the oven overnight to thoroughly dry out.

A SPOT OF TEA

A cup or two of cool peppermint tea added to your pets' bath water will also eliminate the fleas very effectively.

CALL FOR REINFORCEMENTS

Nc nematodes to the rescue! These beneficial worms will eliminate almost all of the flea larvae and pupae within 24 hours after the product is released. It is safe on vegetable gardens as well as lawns. Best to spray the entire lawn area.

HERBS FOR YOUR PET

There are 3 herbs that you can feed to your pet to help keep fleas off; they are fennel, rue and rosemary.

DOG DEODORANT

The following ingredients will be needed:

2	Large size box of baking soda (fresh)
2	Pounds of cornstarch
2	Cups of dried pennyroyal
2	Cups of dried lavender
1¼	Cups of dried rosemary
15	Drops of essential lemon oil
15	Drops of citronella oil
20	Drops of essential rosemary oil
25	Drops of essential lemon oil
25	Drops of essential pennyroyal oil

Place the dried herbs in a blender and powder. Place all the ingredients into a small bucket, mix and allow it to stand in a cool, dark location for 2-3 days. Mix well and sprinkle where needed.

GETTING MISTY OVER FLEAS

Daily spraying of a fine mist prepared from Dr. Bronner's Peppermint Soap™ should do the trick, however, it needs to be done daily for the first week, then once a week for control for the next 4 weeks.

POWDER YOUR PET OR A NEIGHBOR WITH A PROBLEM

An excellent method getting rid of fleas on pets is to powder the pet with pure pyrethrum powder. It is safe for pets and people and works great. The animal should be powdered once or twice per week for the best results. If you dust the bedding and carpet areas around the bed then vacuum it will help control the flea population. The pyrethrum powder should remain in place for about 1 hour before vacuuming any area that you powder.

PENNYROYAL BATH

Make a pot of pennyroyal tea and after it cools add it to the pets bathwater to eliminate the fleas. Dried pennyroyal also works in the pets bedding to get rid of fleas.

DIGGING DOG SPRAY

The following ingredients will be needed:

1	Clove of garlic (crushed)
1	Small yellow onion (chopped fine)
1	Teaspoon of Tabasco Sauce™
½	Teaspoon oil of peppermint
½	Teaspoon of cayenne pepper
1	Quart of warm tap water

Place all the ingredients into a large jar with a good lid and shake well. Allow it to sit for about 8 hours before placing the solution into a spray bottle. Spray the dogs' favorite spot to dig in. The dog will dig no more, or sneeze a lot.

THE FLEA HOTEL

Vacuuming is one of the most important things you can do to control the flea population on and around your pet. However, if you do not dispose of the vacuum bag or clean out the dust container after every vacuuming, it will turn into a flea hotel.

COMB 'EM OUT, BUT DO IT OUTSIDE

A metal flea comb should be used if you have a serious flea problem. The comb will not only remove fleas but will get their eggs as well. If you do have a problem you should comb your pet twice a day for the best results.

WASH THEM FLEAS

Boil 1 quart of water, then add 1 cup of dried rosemary (fresh OK). Cover the pot and allow the mixture to steep until it is cool. Use to wash the pet, working it in and make sure you rinse the pet well.

FLYING INSECT POTPOURRI
The following ingredients will be needed:

½	Cup of pennyroyal
1	Cup of southernwood
1½	Cups of lavender flowers
1½	Cups rosemary
½	Cup of spearmint
3	Tablespoons of orris root
½	Cup of santolina
¼	Cup of tansy
8	Yellow tulips (dried well)
¼	Cup of mugwort
¼	Cup of cedarwood chips (fresh as possible)

Place all the ingredients into a container and blend well, then place into a few potpourri baskets around the house. The aroma is pleasant except to flying insects.

HERE LITTLE FLEA
Check with your hardware store or garden supply house for a flea trap that uses a light bulb to attract them and a sticky base to capture them. These are very effective and inexpensive.

DON'T CROSS THE LINE
To keep your pets food safe from ants, just draw a line around the food dish with a piece of chalk. Ants will not cross the chalk line.

BUILD A FOOD DISH MOAT
If you place your pet's food dish in a shallow dish of soapy water so that it surrounds the food dish it will keep the ants out of the pets food.

FLEA, CONTROL
The following ingredients will be needed:

1	Pound of diatomaceous earth (from nursery)
8	Ounces of table salt
2	Ounces of peppermint powder

Place the ingredients into a container that you will be able to sprinkle it out of. The container should have a sealed cap for shaking and mixing it and another cap with holes for sprinkling it out. Shake the powder (try not to breathe in the mixture) on carpets where there may be a flea problem, then allow the powder to stand for 1 hour before thoroughly vacuuming it up. Keep kids and pets off the carpet until it has been well vacuumed.

A PILLOW FOR YOUR PET DOG
Most dogs like to rest their head on a pillow. To make a safe pillow that will not attract fleas, just place 2 ounces of pennyroyal, 1 ounce of thyme and 1 ounce of wormwood mixed together inside the pillow.

A PILLOW FOR YOUR PET CAT
Cats will love this pillow contents and it will keep fleas away. Mix together 2 ounces of pennyroyal, 1 ounce of catnip and 1ounce of chamomile then place it inside of your cat's pillow.

DOGGIE TREATS
The following ingredients will be needed:

1	Cup of chicken
1	Cup of whole, wheat flour
2	Cups of standard oats
2	Large eggs
1¼	Tablespoon of garlic powder
1	Tablespoon of parsley
2	Tablespoons of soy sauce
¼	Cup of powdered whole milk

Place the chicken in a medium saucepan and cook in chicken fat for 15 minutes then simmer for 35 minutes adding a small amount of water. Remove from heat and allow the chicken to cool for about 20-30 minutes. Slice into small pieces and place all ingredients into a food processor and blend, but do not liquefy. Place tablespoon size or larger globs on a cookie sheet and bake at 250⁰F for 40-50 minutes, then allow to set-up in the sun (out of dogs reach) to fully dehydrate for a few hours. Allow the biscuits to cool for another 12 hours before allowing your pet to devour them.

POWDER FOR FLEAS
The powder formula works on both cats and dogs and should be used whenever needed. Mix together 2 ounces of pennyroyal, 1 ounce of wormwood, 1 ounce of rosemary and a dash or two of cayenne pepper. Try not to get the mixture in your pet's eyes.

DUST THEM OFF
If you think your pet has fleas or ticks, just dust them with diatomaceous earth (DE), then allow it to remain for a few minutes before vacuuming the pet off.

SPRINKLING WITH DE
Just prepare a mixture of DE and water and place the mixture in a watering can and spray the areas outside that your pet frequents the most. If you want a safer method, just use safe flea soap in water.

POP GOES THE FLEA

Before this flea information was available grandpa used to catch the fleas and squeeze them until she heard a "pop." This is the oldest form of flea removal ever recorded. However, this was not very practical since a flea can lay 1 egg per hour. This is by far the worst method ever used, since the flea may contain a disease and by crushing it, would release the disease.

SWIMMING POOL FOR FLEAS

If you would like to catch the fleas, use a shallow pan half-filled with soapy water (use Ivory Liquid Soap™). Place a light over the pan to attract the fleas. The fleas like the heat from the lamp and jump for the heat, fall into the water and lack swimming skills, so they drown. The soap eliminates the surface tension of the water and the fleas can't bounce out.

MAKING EARWAX REMOVER FOR PETS

The following ingredients will be needed:

¼	Cup of isopropyl alcohol
10	Drops of glycerin

Place the ingredients into a small bottle and shake to mix well, then place a small amount (at room temperature) on a cotton swab and clean the pet's ears, very gently. The pet will probably shake their head, which will help clean out the wax. Be careful to remove the swab if the pet shakes their head to avoid damage to the eardrum.

THE ORANGE RUBDOWN

Just score the peel of an orange and rub the peel on the animals skin. This will repel fleas on most animals. You can also use the peels from 3-4 oranges or lemons and place them into a blender then rubdown the pet with the solution using a sponge. You might want to give them a bath 30 minutes after and keep them outside until the bath time.

THE FLANNEL TRAP

Place a piece of flannel in your dogs bed and let him lay there for a few minutes then get him up and check the flannel for fleas. This is a good test to see how bad the infestation really is. Wash the flannel immediately in hot water.

SOCK IT TO THEM

If you walk around the house with a pair of athletic socks they will pick up fleas. Just check the socks for fleas and throw them into the washer immediately.

ANTI-TICK GROUND COVER

There are a number of ground covers that seem to repel ticks or at least discourage them from staying around very long. They are molasses grass, sage, pyrethrum and lavender. Studies have shown that there are fewer ticks in areas where these ground covers grow.

PARASITES

PREVENTION IS BEST

If you add some powdered pumpkin seeds and a small amount of garlic to your pet's diet they will probably never get worms and if they do, the worms will probably pack up and leave.

TICKS

Ticks are related to spiders and can harbor a number of different diseases. There are hard ticks and soft ticks. The hard tick can produce up to 10,000 eggs after one feeding. Soft ticks can feed several times and lay 30-50 eggs after each feeding. If you feel that you have been bite by a tick, it would be best to see your doctor as soon as possible. Ticks take their time when feeding since they do not fall off easily they are in no rush and can enjoy their meal. They are actually more dangerous than fleas and mosquitoes.

There are over 800 species of ticks in the United States and they will feed on animals, birds and humans. They wait on a tall piece of grass until a suitable host passes by and then jumps or flies on them. A tick will not bite a human immediately and will search for the best spot. It has a curved set of teeth that hang on then secretes a cement-like substance, which helps it stick on to its host. Ticks can feed for several days on a host if not found.

TICKS THAT CAUSE DISEASE

- *American dog tick:* These ticks are common on the east coast but can be found in most parts of the country. They are brown and have silvery-gray marks on their backs. It normally prefers dogs but if none are available it will go to a human host. This tick can transmit tularemia and Rocky Mountain spotted fever and can cause a special tick paralysis in susceptible dogs and people.

- *Deer tick:* This tick loves deer and is usually found in the East. It prefers white-tailed deer as its source of food and transmits Lyme disease. In the Midwest the same tick is called the bear tick. It is a very small tick and the nymph is about the size of a black pinhead. Because of the ticks size you will hardly know if you have been bitten.
- *Lone star tick:* This tick has a white mark on its back and is reddish-brown in color. It is usually found in the southwestern United States and will feed on humans and deer as its preferred meal. It can transmit tularemia (rabbit fever) as well as Rocky Mountain spotted fever.
- *Rocky Mountain wood tick:* Similar in appearance to the American dog tick and is usually found west of the Rocky Mountains. It transmits Rocky Mountain spotted fever, tularemia (rabbit fever), Colorado tick fever and tick paralysis.
- *Western black leg tick:* This tick is found in the Western states and may be called the "cowboy tick". It can transmit Lyme disease and is about the same size as the deer tick. It is reddish-brown and has black legs.

BASIL WILL WORK

Crush the entire basil plant and place the basil into 2 quarts of water. Allow it to remain for 2 hours before straining and using in a sprayer. Has been used to control ticks for hundreds of years.

BASIL WILL WORK

Crush the entire basil plant and place the basil into 2 quarts of water. Allow it to remain for 2 hours before straining and using in a sprayer. Has been used to control ticks for hundreds of years.

USE A LINT ROLLER

Lint rollers that you can usually purchase at your dry cleaners are a roller with sticky tape on them used to pick up lint. These can be used very efficiently to roll over a dog or cat and pick up fleas and ticks.

A CHILLY SOLUTION

Ticks are attracted by carbon dioxide, which is expelled by all animals. Ticks can be trapped using the dry ice method. You can make a dry ice trap by following the directions:

1. You will need a covered bucket approximately 6X6X12. Any type of container will do as long as it is about the right dimensions.
2. Drill or cut four ¾ inch holes near the bottom of the container spaced evenly. This will allow the dry ice vapor to be released and attract the ticks.
3. Drop about 2 pounds of dry ice into the container, which will last about 3 hours before it will dissipate. It will capture all ticks in about a 75-100 square foot area during the 3-hour period.
4. Place the container on top of a piece of plywood and place masking tape sticky-side up on top of the plywood. Attach the tape with staples and remove the masking tape and replace it as the ticks are trapped

TICK REPELLANT

Crush up the following herbs and place the mixture into a small muslin bag, then leave the bag near the pets bedding. Use about ½ ounce of each.

Dried peppermint, eucalyptus, bay leaf, sage, rosemary, cloves and marjoram.

FLEA AND TICK COLLARS

Use a pyrethrum-based flea collar for best results. *DO NOT USE A PYRETHRUM COLLAR ON A CAT.* Cats are allergic to pyrethrum and may break out in a rash.

TICKS HATE GARLIC

Finely chop 5 cloves of garlic and allow them to soak in 4 teaspoons of water for 24 hours. Strain the mixture and use 1 part per 20 parts of water then place in sprayer. This will kill a number of insects as well as the ticks and fleas. Make sure that you only use garlic in glass containers since garlic may react with metal.

GIVE THEM A GREASE JOB

To get a tick off your pet, just rub a small amount of oil on the tick. This tends to suffocate the tick and they withdraw almost immediately. This will stop the tick from injecting its poisons and is the recommended method of removing them safely.

KEEP CATS OUT OF HOUSE PLANTS

Some cats love to dig in houseplants and can do a lot of damage. To stop this behavior, just moisten a cotton ball with lemon oil furniture polish and place the cotton ball at the base of the plant.

FLANNEL COAT YOUR YARD

If you think that you have a bad tick or flea problem in your yard, just take a piece of flannel with a string on it and pull it around the yard. Fleas and ticks are attracted to flannel and will jump on for the ride. Turn the cloth over to check to see how many you have trapped. If there is a lot you will need to spray and disinfect the areas.

WARNING: PET SHAMPOOS THAT CONTAIN PIPERONYL BUTOXIDE MAY BE HARMFUL TO BOTH YOU AND YOUR PET

CHAPTER 13

BENEFICIAL INSECTS & CRITTERS

BENEFICIAL INSECTS & CRITTERS

Your garden and yard contains million of insects and small creatures, some good and some bad. There are on the average 1,000+ insects in every square yard of your yard. Only about 1% of all insects can be considered a pest and will do damage in your yard. The beneficial insects can do a great job of reducing the number of bad insects providing you do not kill them off while hunting down the bad bugs.

If you do order beneficial insects or critters to assist in keeping the bad bug population down, be sure not to use and harsh chemicals or pesticides for at least 2 months before they have been released.

ANTLIONS

These look a lot like damselflies and have been called **"doodle bugs."** They can dig small pits in dry earth or sand and then just wait for their victims to fall in. They then throw sand in the air to confuse the prey, jump on them, paralyze them and suck out their fluids. They will them throw what's left of the bug out of the pit and wait for the next victim to come along.

ASSASSIN BUG

These bugs resemble spiders and stab their victims, injecting a dissolving fluid before sucking the liquids out of them. They love to feed on leafhoppers, bed bugs, caterpillars and an assortment of other bad bugs. There are hundreds of species in the United States and Canada. These bugs have very broad bodies, sturdy front legs, a long beak and large eyes. These are good bugs to have around the garden, however, if you bother them they will bite you.

BIGEYED BUGS

These bugs love to live in weedy areas and eat aphids, leafhoppers, Mexican bean beetles and insect eggs. They need meat to reproduce and will only occasionally consume plant juices. They have large "bug eyes" are oval in shape and usually gray to tan in color.

BATS

Bats love night-flying insects and consume them voraciously. They locate their prey through *"echolocation."* The bat sends out sounds waves similar to sonar and then interprets them to locate the bug.

A colony of 200,000 bats will consume about 3 tons of insects every night. They are also involved in pollinating plants and helping to disperse seeds. Birds eat the insects that are awake during the day and bats go to work at night where the birds left off. Since mosquitoes are active at night and one bat can eat about 4,000 mosquitoes, try to be nice to them, especially when they live in your neighborhood.

Bats never attack people and only get near people when they need water. If you are in your pool at night they may come in for a drink but will then leave as soon as they have had their fill.

LIGHTING UP THE BATS
If you have a bat problem in your attic, just place few light up there and they will vacate the attic in short order and never some back.

FAN THE BATS
An attic fan will disturb the bats to such a degree that they will move to someone else's attic. Even a draft of cool air will cause them not to roost since they need a calm air, quiet, dark location.

BATS IN THE HOUSE
If a bat gets into the house, try not to panic since they are very gentle creatures and only want to get back out. Just close the bat off in one room and open a window in that room. When the bat feels the current of air it will immediately leave the premises.

GET A BAT HOUSE
There is an organization for bats and you can contact them regarding building or purchasing a bat house. They are called Bat Conservation International (BCI) and the house is designed especially for bats. The bat houses need to be located near a body of water or swimming pool and on a tree trunk about 20+ feet high.

BEETLES

There are about 3,000 species of beetles worldwide. Many are good and some are bad and sometimes it is difficult to tell the good guys from the bad guys. Professional gardeners will tell you that if the beetle is slow moving kill it and if it is moving fast it is probably in pursuit of another bug. All beetles have a straight line running down its back where its wings join.

BLISTER BEETLE
The only good thing about this beetle is that its larvae, consumes grasshopper eggs. If you touch this beetle it will give you a painful blister. Spanish fly is produced from this beetle.

CHECKERED BEETLE
Bright-colored beetle: that is covered with a thick coat of short hairs. The larvae are usually yellow or red and have a horn. Most have a checkerboard pattern and prey on wood borers, however, their larvae will kill many pest larvae and the eggs.

FIREFLY
These beetles are also referred to as "lightning bugs" and have a luminous area near the end of their abdomen. They use this light to signal for a mate so they will not be too happy when you catch them and interrupt their mating ritual. The larvae eat cutworms and many small insects. They love to eat snails and inject them with their digestive juices and then drink the liquefied tissue.

GROUND BEETLES
These night-hunting beetles can boast over 20,000 species worldwide and are rarely seen, making it hard to identify them. They are black and somewhat iridescent with bodies that are shaped like a shield. They may go by the name "caterpillar hunter." Their favorite foods include ants, cutworms, termites, spider mites, gypsy moths, mosquitoes, snails and slugs. They may even be seen climbing a tree to get to their prey. Some of these beetles will expel a foul-smelling gas if you go to pick them up.

ROVE BEETLES

This beetle looks more like an earwig (without the pincers) than a true beetle. It tends to prefer scrounging around in decaying material looking for prey and is especially fond of cabbage beetles, mites, bark beetles and cabbage maggots.

SOLDIER BEETLES

These beetles have a long rectangular body that is brownish in color. It looks like a firefly but without the taillight. The larvae enjoy feasting on many of the bad insects; however, the adults love an easy life of retirement and just hang around on a flower with their legs up taking it easy. The adult beetles will feed mainly on aphids and grow to about ½ inch in length.

TIGER BEETLES

These are the professional hunter beetles that are a pretty iridescent blue, green and bronze. They are speedy, large beetles that can grow to ¾ of an inch long. It prefers aphids and caterpillars but will not turn down other pests if they are readily available. This species is only found in the western United States. They usually lie in wait at the bottom of tunnels and wait for an insect to fall in for dinner.

CENTIPEDES

These creepy crawlers can actually have as many as 346 legs and sometimes as few as 30, which will depend on the species. They have a pair of claws that are venomous and can paralyze their victims. These are good to have around the garden since they eat snails, slugs, grasshoppers and many other pests. When you find them in the basement or house they are looking for cockroaches, flies and moths.

The very small centipede-looking bug, that you may see in your garden resembles a white centipede but are really "symphylan." These can do a great deal of damage to plants and are mainly found in greenhouses in the southwestern states.

COUNT THEIR LEGS

Centipedes are good for the garden and consume many of the garden pest, however, millipedes are not very good to have around.

DAMSEL BUG

These bugs are only about ¼ quarter inch long and have a body that narrows toward the head and have large front legs for grabbing small prey. They eat aphids, leafhoppers, treehoppers, psyllids, mites and small green caterpillars.

DAMSELFLIES

These look like a smaller dragonfly and prefer insects that have soft bodies. They can stand motionless in the air like a mini helicopter and just pluck aphids and scale off plant leaves. They normally only look for prey during the day and like to look for their meal near a body of water. If they find an area that has mosquito larvae they will literally gorge themselves.

DECOLLATE SNAILS

SNAIL HUNTERS
There is a snail that will hunt other snails and kill them. The decollate snail is somewhat smaller than the average snail and has a shell that resembles a seashell. It is a natural enemy of the brown garden snail and has the same habits as the brown snail. When it runs out of snails it will eat decayed leaves and help clean up the garden. It does need a source of moisture to survive. Poisons will kill this snail so try and avoid them, if you have a number of these snail hunters in your garden.

DRAGONFLIES

Dragonflies may be called by a number of different names such as horse stingers, darning needles or mosquito hawks. They are very fast and few prey, can avoid them when they are chasing them down. They grab their prey by using their hairy legs and look like they are carrying a shopping basket.

They cannot wait to dine and eat their victims while they are flying by sucking the fluids from them. They have been known to eat their own weight in 30 minutes or less. Their leg baskets are capable of carrying up to 100 mosquitoes, which is one of their favorite meals.

The dragonfly begins its life under water and then enters the air world for the majority of its life. It has an insatiable need for flying insects almost as if it a challenge for it to catch them. If you have them in your yard just hope that they remain.

EARTHWORMS

These are really one of the best good guys. They eat through the earth digesting organic matter and some minerals and turn them into better, more usable soil. The worms can also attract birds, which consume insects. If you don't have earthworms it would be best to order some. If you use chemical fertilizers or pesticides that are used to kill snails or slugs, they will also kill the earthworms.

EARWIG

Identification:
They are about ¾ inch long, brownish-black with a pincer on their rear end. They have very small wings that are almost useless and will lay white round eggs in the soil.

General Information:
They are fairly beneficial since they enjoy feasting on aphids and many other pest bugs. They clean up a lot of decayed materials and are active at night. When they are cleaning up the leaves and such, they find pests and kill them. If you don't want them around they can be eliminated using one of the following methods.

Rumor is that earwigs will crawl into your ear while you are sleeping. This is not true and they will not harm you even though they look menacing.

SAFETY FIRST
If they get into the house, one of the best repellants is to use diatomaceous earth placed around baseboards and windowsills. This will last a long time and still be an effective natural killer.

DAILY NEWS TO THE RESCUE
If you want to trap earwigs, just lightly spray a newspaper with water and then roll it up loosely and place it near an area that you have earwig activity. Allow it to remain overnight, then remove it and place it into a well-sealed container for disposal. Since they are beneficial this is only used inside a house.

OILING AN EARWIG
To make an earwig trap, just use a straight-sided container and fill it half full with canola oil. Leave wherever the problem exists and clean out whenever it has sufficient earwigs in it. The oil can be re-used. Use only if you are overrun with them.

GIVE THEM A HOME
If you place a small amount of dry moss in a few matchboxes and hang them from sticks around the plants they will climb up in them to spend the night and you can dispose of them every morning.

BANTAM HENS LOVE EARWIGS
Bantam hens will hunt for earwigs all day and will consume large quantities of them as well as other pests. They may peck at a few pieces of veggies or fruit but they do more good than harm.

FERRETS

Ferrets are a natural hunter and can be a real asset around the garden. They were brought to the United States from Europe where they were a "working animal." They would prowl shipyards, warehouses and farms eliminating rats and mice. They are related to minks, weasels and otters. They can even be trained to walk on a leash or ride on your shoulder. If you want one for a hunter get a females called "jills" since they are not as lazy as the males. They need to be fed mice and some commercial pet food. Best to get them when they are babies and train them.

They are not good diggers but if placed into a tunnel they will clear any animal out in short order. Gophers, moles and rabbits do not like ferrets.

FLIES

The following flies are not available through mail order insect houses. However, you may want to be aware of them so that you will leave them alone and allow them to do their job.

HOVER FLIES
Small hover or syrphid flies have a few small stripes on their back and are very beneficial since they consume aphids and a variety of other insect pests. They are attracted to yarrow, goldenrod, asters and black-eyed Susan's and will sip their nectar. Chances are if you plant these you will find that the flies will arrive if they are in the neighborhood. They will not sting you, however, they do resemble a wasp.

ROBBER FLY
These flies resemble bumblebees and can act very ferocious when attacking wasps and bees. They can be seen even chasing their prey when they are after small grasshoppers. Their larvae will feed on other larvae in the soil.

SYPHID FLIES (HOVER FLIES)
These are very colorful flies that are yellow-striped and somewhat resemble bees or certain wasps. This weird appearance keeps them safe from birds; who tend to confuse them with bees. They are relatively harmless to humans and animals and can hang motionless in flight similar to a hummingbird. They prefer to feed on aphids, scale, thrips and leafhoppers. You may spot one on rose bushes that look like a tiny green worm.

TACHNID FLIES
This bug looks like a large black housefly that needs a haircut. They can also be found in yellow, red or brown and are usually seen around leaves and flowers. They attach their eggs to caterpillars or on the plants that they consume. They do an excellent job of controlling the caterpillar population and especially European corn borers and gypsy moths. They prefer nectar or honeydew secreted by aphids and other insects. There are over 1200 species in North America. The adult bugs like buckwheat and if you plant some you will have these flies in your garden.

FLY PARASITES

These are mainly livestock parasites that kill flies that frequent cattle and other livestock. People hardly ever even notice these flies. The fly parasites lay their eggs inside of fly pupae and kill them before they can ever emerge. They look for their prey around manure piles in stables, kennels, barns and feedlots. Commercial composting operations are one of their favorite hangouts.

GREEN LACEWINGS

HERE, PRETTY BUG

The lacewing has long wings that look like a piece of old fashioned lace and very long antennae. They dine on aphids and their larvae as their favorite meal as well as other insect pests. They will be attracted to yarrow, black-eyed Susan's, goldenrod and the aster family.

The larva of the green lacewing also loves to feast on aphids and have been called "aphid lions". The larva of the brown lacewing dines on aphids and also many soft-bodied insects such as the red spider mite, thrips, mealybugs, scale and will eat the eggs of many pest worms. The lacewing larvae, is very cannibalistic and if they are near each other eggs they will eat their own eggs.

They can be ordered and will arrive with the eggs packed in feeding material such as rice hulls. This is done in case some hatch while in transit and hopefully will eat the rice hulls instead of the other eggs. They are so minute that 1,000 of them would fit in a small thimble. If you do see any movement you will need to disperse them immediately. Just sprinkle the eggs on the plant foliage, preferably on a warm day. If you want to keep them around they require some honey or sweet nectar.

BRRRRRRRRRRRRR

If you do buy lacewings don't refrigerate them, just keep them at room temperature. Watch the bottom of the container in case some of the kids hatch and start looking for food.

LADYBUGS

Identification:
These are round beetles that are about ¼+ inch long and are bright orange to red with a number of black spots and white markings on the thorax. They will consume about 400 aphids a day and an adult can eat thousands of aphids and scales during the season. The ladybug can produce 4-5 generations of offspring in one summer under ideal moisture conditions.

General Information:
There are almost 400 species of ladybug worldwide. The *convergent lady beetle* is one of the best predators and their favorite meal is aphids but won't turn down a good tasty meal of scales. They will also eat leafhoppers, thrips, and a variety of eggs and moths. In the late 1880's one of the ladybugs relative the *Vedalia beetle* was imported from Australia and became famous for saving the California citrus crop from the cottony cushion scale.

LADYBUG, LADYBUG WERE HAVE YOU GONE
Ladybugs are a common insect that enjoys munching on aphids, mites, scales and whiteflies. They love daisies, tansy or yarrow and will frequent gardens that have these plants.

If you do purchase ladybugs there are a few important facts you should be aware of

- Make sure that the yard is well watered before releasing the ladybugs or they may fly away looking for a more, moist location. They must have water droplets to live.
- Handle them very gently or they will get scared and fly away.
- Be sure and place them at the base of the plants but don't place too many in one location.
- They can be stored in the refrigerator (not the freezer) for up to two weeks and released gradually.
- Make sure you have food ready for them when you release them. Spray the plants with a 10% sugar or honey solution. You can also use a commercial food such as Control™, Honeydew™ or Wheast™.
- If a plant has an aphid or scale infestation, place the ladybugs on the plant and cover the plant immediately.
- Ladybugs: are easily killed by pesticides.

MEALYBUG DESTROYERS

These bugs are related to the ladybird beetle and destroy mealybugs. In fact in its larval stage it even resembles a mealybug. They will eat other garden pests, however, they need to be kept away from ants. Do not use any pesticides for at least a month before releasing these good guys.

MITES (BENEFICIAL)

The majority of mites are real pests, however, there are beneficial mites that will eliminate the bad mites. They are available commercially and shipped as adults and should be scattered by hand in the garden areas as needed.

The adults that you are releasing will then lay their eggs next to the pest mite on the underneath sides of the leaves. The beneficial mites will sometimes feed on nectar but will not harm the plants. The mites will not feed on aphids, whiteflies or scale and only feed on the bad mites.

Pesticides and fungicides will kill the beneficial mites so care needs to be taken if you are going to use them. It is best to catch the problem early if you expect good results. The minimum order by one mite sales company is 300 predatory mites, which will guard 15-20 plants that are lightly infested.

PREDATORY MITES COMMERCIALLY AVAILABLE

PREDATORY MITE	DESCRIPTION
Metaseiulus occidentalis	The most commonly released mite and is effective at high temperatures over 90°F.
Phytoseiulus persimilis	Likes mild humid conditions, especially in greenhouses up to 80°F. Higher temperature strains are available if needed.
Amblyseius californicus	Used in greenhouses and outside. Used at temperatures up to 85°F.
Amblyseius (Euseius) species	Will feed on all types of mites but is mostly effective against the citrus red mite on citrus trees in Southern California. Will not go into areas that are heavily infested with spider mites.

Nc NEMATODES

WORMING THEIR WAY IN

These beneficial nematodes are microscopic roundworms that are recognized as one of the safest methods of eradicating a number of pests. The bugs that respond well to "death by nematode" are wireworms, cutworms, Colorado potato beetle, Japanese beetle, grubs and June beetles. The beneficial nematodes will kill more than 200 species of pest insects. However, they will not harm earthworms, which make them a preferred method of control. They are capable of living in the soil for 2-3 months.

Nc nematode eggs can be purchased in most garden shops and usually come in a small sponge with about 1 million eggs. They hatch quickly and grow to adults in a very short period of time. Nc nematodes are harmless to pets and humans.

Nematodes enter their victim through any bodily orifice and most will introduce deadly bacteria into the victim or just eat their tissue. Never spray nematodes in direct sunlight or you may kill them.

PARASITIC WASPS

These wasps are one of our best insect hunters and eliminators. They will eat the pest's eggs and larvae and lay their eggs in the pests. The pest then acts as an incubator for the wasp eggs. They are available through many mail order companies.

BRACONIDS
These wasps look like small white rice-like drops that attach to the backs of caterpillars. These are actually the cocoons of the future wasp generation. The larvae, spends a small amount of time inside the body of the caterpillar before leaving and making their cocoon. It actually consumes some of the caterpillar's tissue without killing it. They then hatch and go looking for aphids and drill holes in the aphids back. The adults usually feed on nectar or honeydew.

CHALCIDS
These are very tiny wasp parasites that are found all over North America that attack and kill caterpillars, scale, aphids, whiteflies, mealybugs, leafhoppers and the larvae of many beetles. When you order them through mail order they will be shipped as adult wasps and will then lay their eggs on the pest as soon as they are released. The adults require flowers for nectar.

Recently, a new chalcid wasp is being sold called the "golden chalcid" *Aphytis melinus*. This parasitic wasp will be used to control California red citrus scale, San Jose scale and ivy scale. In cold climates they should be released in the spring.

ENCARSIA FORMOSA PARASITE
This wasp parasite prefers whiteflies and will lay its eggs on the scales of immature whiteflies. Then as the wasp gets bigger it will feed on the whitefly and kill it. If you see a whitefly with a black spec on its scales it is a wasp egg. These parasites are often used in greenhouses and will be at their best at temperatures over 70°F. When they run out of whiteflies to eat they will reduce their population.

If you place a rose geranium plant in the greenhouse the plant gives off a chemical substance that reduces the metabolic rate of the wasp and places it into a state of suspended animation. Remove the plant when you need the wasps again to clear out the whiteflies.

ICHNEUMON WASPS
These are unusual-looking wasps that have very long tubes that look like stingers but are really tubes to deposit their eggs with. They can use these tubes to bore through bark and lay their eggs on hiding caterpillars. They can locate their victims by sensing their vibrations.

They are dark-colored wasps that have clear wings and very long antennae. The adults will eat the host larvae and also consume honeydew and pollen. They are found in all areas of North America.

MUD DAUBERS
These wasps will attack their prey and paralyze them to death with their stinger. They prey on spiders, caterpillars and most other insects in the neighborhood. The adults will return to the colony with a portion of the prey and share it. They will sting humans if bothered while they are at work. You will notice a loud buzzing sound before they sting you.

TRICHOGRAMMA WASP
These wasps will not sting either humans or animals. This species can kill hundreds of pests and prefer armyworms, cutworms, gypsy moths, hornworms, corn earworms, leafworms and even bollworms. One wasp is can parasitize as many as 100 pests in its lifetime. When the wasp eggs hatch they live off the host and eventually kill them from within. They can easily be purchased through the mail and need to be kept in a warm, humid location. They must be released at the time when the moths are laying their eggs or when you first notice them in your garden.

PRAYING MANTIS

Identification:
One of the best insects to have around your garden is the praying mantis. They are large, about 5 inches long and usually green but may be found in brown. They have enlarged front legs, which work great for grasping prey.

PRAY FOR THESE INSECTS

The praying mantis eats its meals of insects while they are still alive then proceeds to groom afterwards. It is capable of consuming large numbers of insects including aphids, bees, wasps, beetles, caterpillars, grasshoppers and even a small frog, salamander or other small lizard. However, it is not too fussy and sometimes and may eat a beneficial insect for dessert. Another problem is that the praying mantis may also eat its own kind.

You can purchase praying mantis egg cases by mail order. They need to be attached to a low-growing twig in the fall. They will hatch in the early spring and disappear into the foliage immediately. They are very delicate when they first hatch resulting in a large number being eaten by ants and lizards. If you place the eggs in a brown paper bag and allow them to sit on a windowsill they will hatch. Be sure the area is not too hot or you will have **"fried mantis."** It takes about 8 weeks for them to hatch then release them as soon as their skin dries and hardens.

Praying Mantis' are found throughout the United States and Canada. They can easily be tempted into your garden if you plant raspberry canes.

TACHINID FLY

This fly looks like an ordinary black housefly, however, they may be seen in yellow, red or brown colors. They feed on nectar and honeydew secreted by other insects. These are a potent pest control parasite. Their larvae are deposited on the host and feeds on European corn borers, cutworms, armyworms, Mexican bean beetles and Japanese beetles. They love buckwheat and will be drawn to the grain.

TOADS

Approximately 90% of the toads diet is insects and the majority of them are pests that will damage your garden. There are 18 species of toads in the United States and all species are beneficial to man. Ponds will attract them and should be kept up in good order to keep them around. Toads do give off a noxious substance when handled and you should wash after touching one. Toads never drink through their mouth but absorb moisture through their skin. The female toad can deposit as many as 25,000 eggs, which turn into tadpoles.

DON'T KISS A TOAD, A PRINCE IS NOT A GOOD WORKER

Finding a toad in your garden is really good luck but you do not have to kiss it. A single toad will feast on over 100 slugs and snails, cutworms, grubs, caterpillars and an assortment of beetles and their larvae. If you are lucky enough to have a really big, healthy toad in top physical condition (one that works out) it can consume over 10,000 invaders in one season.

TURTLES

Wood turtles and box turtles are the most common turtle that people find visiting their gardens in search of snails and slugs. They may also be interested in low-lying berry patches. They do more good than damage and should be tolerated. If you have a garden pool or pond they will become regular visitors.

WHEELBUG

This is a real ugly bug that makes his home in your shrubbery. He is one of the good guys but not one you want to mess with. He has a wheel shape on his back to identify him, however, I don't think that you want to be that close. They eat other insects that do not have a hard shell and just sit and wait for a bug to go by. They do have a temper and will give you a stinging bite if bothered.

CHAPTER 14

MISCELLANEOUS INSECT PESTS

MISCELLANEOUS INSECT PESTS

BED BUGS

These little bloodsuckers have their way with us when we are sleeping. Each bug's meal lasts from 10-15 minutes and cause no sensation of pain. Their proboscis is so thin you do not feel it entering. Bed bugs have a pattern of three bites and you will notice three small red areas in a row, which is the telltale sign that you have been attacked. If you notice reddish-brown excrement that they leave around in your bed that looks like specks of dirt, it is really dried pieces of undigested blood. They do not fly and do not like daylight. They love to hang out in groups so if you find one there is definitely going to be more around. However, when they go on a feeding expedition they go it alone.

GIVE THEM A GOOD SWEAT

Bed bugs do not like excessive heat. If you want to kill them, just raise the temperature over 99ºF for 1-2 hours. Steam cleaning a mattress will also work great. Most steam cleaning carpet companies that do upholstery will be glad to steam the mattress. It should be done as a preventive every 6 months.

THEY DON'T LIKE COLD CLIMATES

Prolonged exposure to cold temperatures of 32ºF to 45ºF will kill the bed bugs in hours and even their eggs in about 30-45 days. If you live in a cold climate and close off an infected room it will eliminate the problem.

SEARCH & DESTROY

If you think that you have a problem but are not sure, just use a red light at night and search the area. You can find out where they are and eliminate their home base.

TREAT THE MATTRESS

One solution is to treat the seams, folds and especially the button areas if your mattress has some. The best solution to use is a mixture of ½ cup of borax in 1 gallon of water. Allow to fully dry before using mattress.

HERE DUCKY, DUCKY

Duct tape should be placed around the walls near the bed as well as around the legs with the sticky side out. Place masking tape around the edges of the tape to hold it in place. Try and place the tape wherever you think the bed bug activity is.

BLACKBERRY PSYLLID

This is a jumping pest that will injure cultivated plants, but is usually found on wild blackberries. The adult is yellow-brown and has three yellow bands on each wing. They will lay their eggs on the stems of the leaves and young shoots. The nymphs and adults will puncture the leaves and stems resulting in stunted or distorted growth patterns. Ladybugs like to feast on these bugs.

DUST THEM

A good dusting with diatomaceous earth (DE) will eliminate these pests if they do leave the blackberry patch and head for your garden.

CABBAGE ROOT MAGGOT

These are legless white maggots that have a black hook on their heads and prefer to feed on cabbage, radish, turnip, broccoli and cauliflower roots. They will kill a plant if not stopped and are capable of producing two generations every year. Their eggs are laid in the soil and the adult flies hatch in early spring.

WORMS WIN AGAIN

One of the best methods of eradication is to use Nc nematodes when planting in seed furrows or around areas that you are transplanting. You can also use a soap and lime spray to stop them from laying eggs.

CELERY LEAFTIER

Found throughout North America this bug will do a lot of damage to vegetables and ornamentals. They are pale green in color and have a white stripe running down their back. Eventually as they mature they will turn yellow. The worms will eat holes in the leaves and stalks and will fold the leaves together and tie them with their web material. Their eggs look like fish scales and are laid ion the underneath side of leaves.

BUG ELIMINATION

There are a number of methods of eliminating these bugs that work well. These include handpicking, using Bt and if the infestation is really bad you will have to use pyrethrum.

Pyrethrum is a natural botanical poison that will make the larvae so sick that they will leave their webs, pack up and head for greener, safer pastures.

CHIGGERS

Chiggers; are a relative of spiders that attach themselves to our bodies and proceed to feed. They can cause itching, illnesses and can even kill you if the infestation is not controlled. Chiggers can also inject an enzyme that will cause healthy cells to disintegrate. Baby chiggers will attack any warm body that gives off carbon dioxide. Their favorite method of getting on people is to jump on your feet and work their way up till they are right at home.

OUCH, OUCH

To get rid of the discomfort of chigger bites, try using a paste made from crushed aspirin and warm tap water.

SULFUR TO THE RESCUE

Chiggers can be eliminated with the use of powdered soil sulfur. Just place the sulfur in a broadcast spreader and spread the sulfur on your lawn early in the morning when the lawn has dew on it. Be sure and wear rubber gloves and a mask when working with powdered sulfur. Use an oscillating sprinkler and water the lawn good for about 15-20 minutes after the treatment. It takes about 5 pounds of sulfur to treat 100 square feet of lawn.

SPRAY THE YARD

Prepare a mixture of 4 tablespoons of dishwasher soap and 4 teaspoons of canola oil in 1 gallon of cool tap water. Spray the entire yard to kill off the chiggers.

CHINCH BUG

Identification:
These small black bugs with white, red or brown wings bugs tend to damage grasses by sucking the fluids from the blades of grass and replacing the fluid with toxic saliva, which interrupts the water conduction system of the grass and kills the blade.

General Information:
They are usually found in lawns that lack proper watering or have had too many chemicals used on them. If not removed, they are capable of wintering over in the grass. If your lawn is developing a bad odor you probably have a chinch bug problem. When the bugs are crushed, by stepping on them they give off a foul odor. These bugs like hot, sunny lawns like a schoolyard or football field.

THIS IS A CINCH FOR FINDING A CHINCH
If you want to find out if you have chinch bugs in your lawn, just use a tin can and cut out both ends then push the can into the lawn. Pour soapy water into the can and allow about 10 minutes to pass. Check the area and if you have chinch bugs they will come to the surface since they hate a soapy bath. This method is also used for grubs.

WORMING YOUR WAY OUT
One of the best methods of eliminating chinch bugs is to introduce Nc nematodes into your lawn areas. They will eliminate the problem in short order.

GIVE THEM THE OLD PEPPER SPRAY
A spray that combines onion, garlic and hot pepper will eliminate these pests in very short order. If you are doing a large lawn area a soap spray will work best.

2	Hot peppers or ¼ cup Tabasco Sauce™
1	Medium onion
4	Cups of warm tap water
7	Cloves of garlic
1	Teaspoon of Ivory Liquid Soap™

Place the garlic, peppers or Tabasco Sauce™, onion and 2 cups of water into a food processor and blend well. Allow it to stand for 24 hours, strain and add the balance of the water and the soap. Spray both sides of the leaves.

THERE'S A CHINCH FUNGUS AMONG US
A new strain of fungus in now available commercially called *Beauveria bassiana* that will kill the chinch bugs.

CRICKETS

Crickets; are a member of the cockroach family, the noisiest member. They will look for a warm location when the weather starts to get cold and can be a real pest. However, in many societies around the world they are considered lucky and are never killed or disturbed.

BAITS DO WORK
Place some molasses balls containing 5% food-grade DE or use borax or Comet®. This will kill them without a problem. **Make sure all baits are out of reach of pets and children at all times.**

A LITTLE SQUIRT WILL DO YA
You can prepare a spray that will kill the crickets in about 30 seconds if sprayed on them. Just mix 1 ounce of dishwasher soap in 1 quart of water. If you prefer to use vinegar use 4 ounces in 1 quart of water and it will kill them in about 60 seconds.

MOLE CRICKETS ARE SNEAKY
Mole crickets fly into the garden at night usually on very cloudy days and are drawn to light. These are large crickets and are about 1¼-inches long with sturdy shovel-like forelegs for digging into the soil. The northern mole cricket is a brownish-gray and the southern ones are usually more pinkish. They are most active in moist, warm weather and their tunnel tends to cut off the roots of seedlings. All deterrents that work for grasshoppers should be used.

EARWIGS

Earwigs; are a relative of the cockroach with over 1,000 species known worldwide. They love to feed on plants and can be a real pest in greenhouses. They do feed on aphids and are sometimes considered a beneficial insect.

A TUBULAR EXPERIENCE
Save your paper towel and toilet paper cardboard tubes to use as traps for earwigs. Stuff them with straw and the little pests will hide there and make it easy for you to locate and dispose of them. If you spray areas where they frequent with a soapy solution you can get ride of them that way as well.

SHOOT THE LITTLE DEVILS
A dishwasher detergent soap mixed with water in a spray bottle will kill earwigs upon contact. Use 1 ounce per spray bottle of water. To find them go looking after dark with a flashlight and the spray bottle in your holster.

TRAPS WORK GREAT
If you plan on trapping the earwigs, place a shallow dish or tuna can that is buried so that it is level with the ground, they are real lazy and will not work too hard for a meal. Place some honey and peanut butter laced with borax in the dish. You can also use food-grade DE if you have some handy.

STICKY-SIDE UP
Earwigs will not cross a piece of tape with the sticky side up or Vaseline®.

HEAVY DRINKERS
Earwigs love beer and if you leave a shallow dish around in the evening where they frequent, you will find the dish full of earwigs in the morning.

HERE LITTLE EARWIG
Chickens love to eat earwigs and will snoop all over the place looking for them. If you have a few chickens you will never have an earwig problem.

GRUBS

GARLIC VS GRUBS
Finely mince 5 garlic cloves and allow it to dry then crush into a powder. Place the powder in 2 teaspoons of water and allow it to stand for 2 hours. Add 2 quarts of water mix well, strain and place into sprayer. Test an area first in case the mixture is too potent for plant leaves. Spray the area where the grubs have been found. Use only glass spray jars, never metal since metal may react with the chemicals in garlic.

HEAD LICE

This is a wingless blood, sucking parasite that is only about 1/10th of an inch long. It bites and will suck blood from the scalp of the person it gets attached to. It causes itching, swelling and lays eggs called "nits" on strands of hair. There are thousands of species worldwide in both the sucking and biting types. These bugs can only live for a few days when they are away from a human body. A female louse can lay about 8-10 eggs a day and only lives for a month.

Lice are able to take on the color of the hair that they infest. If you are a blond, the lice will be light-colored and if you are a brunette they will be darker. A growing louse will keep feeding over and over every 2-3 hours and making a new puncture every time. This results in itching and discomfort. Its specialized anticoagulant saliva is what causes the itching and burning, which tends to force you to scratch your head. The scratching will then cause more bleeding and possibly and infection.

If you get a bad cold with a fever it will kill the lice since they cannot tolerate high temperatures.

KILL THE BUGGERS
Use a coconut-based shampoo specifically designed for head lice. Drug stores sell lice combs that will comb out the nits. Shampoos with pyrethrums also work very well. Check with the pharmacist for any new treatments. Keep repeating the process daily until the lice and their nits are 100% gone.

SEE THE DOC OR PHARMACIST
If you feel that you have contracted lice it would be best to see your doctor of pharmacist for medication that will remove them safely. There are a number of shampoos and medications that work well.

LEAFHOPPER

Identification:
These are slender wedge-shaped bugs that suck juices from the plants and kill the leaves as well as spreading viruses and bacteria to other plants. Some are green, while other are green with some red and white markings. They will fly off when disturbed and will usually be found on the underneath side of the leaf.

General Information:
Leafhoppers tend to frequent apple trees, beet plants and potatoes. The dragonfly will eat them, when they can find them. The most common leafhopper is the "aster," which has six spots over a greenish-yellow area on its back, the beet leafhopper, the potato leafhopper and the red-banded leafhopper.

KILL THEM IN THE MORNINGS
The best method of killing them is to spray them early in the morning with an insecticidal soap solution. The leafhoppers are less active in the mornings. The only bug that seems to like these insects is the lacewing, which will eat their eggs. Of course, the lacewings will eat almost any insect eggs.

A GOLDEN CURE
Marigolds will eliminate the leafhoppers. Just crush 6 ounces of the leaves, roots and flowers then pour 4 cups of boiling water over it and allow it to soak for 24 hours. Add 4 more cups of cold water, strain and use as a spray.

THEY HATE PETUNIAS
If you plant petunias or geraniums in areas where you suspect trouble it will repel the bugs.

SPRAY THEM
Any liquid soap spray will eliminate the bugs in short order. Also Diatomaceous earth (DE) will also work great at keeping them at bay.

GRAPE LEAFHOPPER
Both the adults and nymphs feed on the underneath side of the leaves resulting in spots that will turn brown. If there is a bad infestation the fruit will be affected.

LEAFHOPPERS KILLED BY WASPS
The grape leafhopper: can be controlled by releasing the parasitic wasp called *Anagrus epos* in the early part of the growing season. These wasps are capable of producing three generations in one summer.

During the early part of the summer the wasp prefers to feed on leafhoppers that frequent blackberries and it would be wise to plant some around the edges of the grape vineyard. When summer arrives the wasps will head for the vineyard and eat the grape leafhoppers.

ZAP, BLUE-LIGHT SPECIAL
A special blue-light insect electrocuting light trap is available that will make short work of theses pests.

POTATO LEAFHOPPER
In the southern states this bug is called the "bean jassid." It is a small wedge-shaped green leafhopper with white spots on its head and thorax. The nymphs have an odd habit of crawling sideways like a crab. The leafhopper causes a condition on the potato plants known as "hopperburn" in which the tips and sides of the potato leaf will curl upward, then turn yellow or brown and become brittle. They will lay their eggs in the main veins of the leaves.

CANOPIES WORK
Leafhoppers prefer open areas where they can easily move on if necessary. If you plant the potato plants in a sheltered area they will probably not come around. If this is not practical then you may need to protect the plants with a netting of cheesecloth, muslin or other type of netting material.

KILLS THE BUGS AND INCREASES GROWTH
A dusting of pyrethrum will eliminate the leafhoppers as well as act as a growth stimulant for the plants.

LEAFMINER

Identification:
These maggots are green or black and about 1/8th of an inch long. They actually tunnel between the upper and lower leaf surfaces and leave a white trail behind for you to follow. The adults are flies that are half the size of a housefly, black with yellow markings and hairy.

General Information:
Three or four generations of the fly can hatch every year. They prefer to feed on spinach, berries, potatoes, peppers and cabbage. They will also feed on columbine, roses, nasturtiums and chrysanthemums.

DINNERTIME
Ladybugs and lacewings are an excellent deterrent to these maggots. If you can't get them try purchasing other parasites such as *Diglyphus begini* or *Diglyphus isaea*.

PEPPER THEM GOOD
Pepper spray is highly recommended as a spray treatment that usually works every time. When the plants are wet try dusting them with lime and this will repel the flies and stop them from laying their eggs.

CROP ROTATION WORKS
It is best to rotate your crops so that the leafminers in the soil gets confused and are unable to find the plants every year in the same spot. If you till in the fall it will also destroy the pupae.

THESE LEAVE YOUR PLANTS TIPSY
The arborvitae leafminer causes browning at the tips of the leaves. Spray plants and trees in late June or early July if you have the problem with a soap spray. Shaded plants are usually more heavily infested.

LYGUS BUG

These bugs are not too fussy what they eat but do prefer beans, strawberries and most orchard crops. The adults may be green, yellow or brown with a yellow or green triangle on their backs. When they are on beans they attack the buds and flowers causing them to fall off. If they attack tomatoes and fruit they will cause discoloration, bumps or depressions. If you disc or rototill the area and especially the weeds, it will reduce the infestation.

DAISY'S TO THE RESCUE
If you border your strawberry patch with Shasta daisies it will keep the lygus out of the strawberry patch. They will eat the daisies as long as they are flowering and leave the strawberries alone.

MEALYBUGS

They are elliptically-shaped and have short spines. The females do not have wings. They prefer soft-stemmed plants and suck out their juices. Mealybugs love orchids and other exotic plants. They are a problem for citrus crops and a number of solutions will kill them and their relatives. They excrete honeydew, which makes them a friend of the ants. They can usually be picked off the plants with a long tweezers and look like small tufts of cotton on the underneath sides of leaves. In the northeastern United States mealybugs are indoor pests as well.

THE DOUBLE WHAMMY
You can make a spray that is two killers in one by mixing 1 gallon of cool water with 2 tablespoons of canola oil and 2 tablespoons of dishwasher liquid soap. Place the mixture in a power sprayer and spray your plants in the area where the problem exists. The dishwasher liquid soap will kill most of them on contact and the oil will penetrate their skins and eventually suffocate them.

THE MEALY MASSAGE
If you only have a small number of mealy bugs, just keep a spray bottle around with rubbing alcohol in it and give them a squirt. You can also dip a paintbrush in the alcohol or use nail polish remover and paint them; however, be very careful not to touch the plant or the alcohol will cause damage.

PARASITES TO THE RESCUE
There are two parasites that are very effective in controlling mealybugs. They are *Cryptolaemus ladybug* (not the one we are used to) and *Pauridia*. Both of these should be available through a garden supply or agricultural house.

MEALYBUG KILLER SPRAY
The following ingredients will be needed:

3	Tablespoons of light corn oil
2	Tablespoons of liquid dish soap
2	Gallon of cold tap water

Place all the ingredients in a medium bucket and mix well. Place a small amount in a sprayer and spray the plants that have the mealybugs on them. Give the bugs a good squirt or two.

GET OUT THE MAGNIFYING GLASS
When you get new potted plants it is very important to quarantine the plants for about 30 days and be sure and examine them frequently for mealybugs.

POKE THEM WITH A TOOTHPICK
Use a toothpick or the point of a knife to pick off mealybugs and scale from a plant. These tools should easily dislodge them without damaging the plant.

PINEAPPLE MEALYBUG

The bug is a whitish/gray insect that is covered with a white, waxy excretion. This bug is the number one pest of pineapple plants. However, the insect has also been known to infest nutgrass, panic grass, Spanish needle, caladium, avocado, citrus, mulberry, royal palm, hibiscus, sugarcane and some ferns. They are known to be the cause of pineapple wilt disease, which results in stunted plants that have leaves of reddish yellow with light green spots.

The leaf tips of the plants will look dead or are in the process of dying. Fire ants are a real friend of these bugs and will even carry them from wilted plants to healthy plants to get the honeydew they excrete.

PARASITES DO THE JOB
A tiny wasp called *Habletonia pseudoccina* will sting the mealybug and lay her eggs in them. Using a dormant oil spray or sprinkling crushed bone meal around will also help do the job.

MITES

Identification:
These bugs are very tiny and about the size of a grain of salt. Their color will change depending on their diet; however, they are usually found red, yellow or green. They have eight pairs of legs and have no wings or antennae. Mites range in size from almost invisible to about ½ inch and can be found in water, on land and in the air.

General Information:
There are over 40,000 species worldwide and 50% of them live as parasites on animals. The most common ones we encounter is the house dust mite who usually inhabits the folds in mattresses waiting for a meal of dead skin to munch on. They cause numerous allergies and may even cause asthmatic attacks. Mites are distant relatives of spiders.

VACUUM, VACUUM, VACUUM
The best method of reducing the mite population or eliminating the problem it is to vacuum regularly.

NOT TOO MITEY AFTER THIS

Mix 2 tablespoons of cayenne pepper or a very hot, spicy sauce with 3-4 drop of Ivory Liquid Soap™ in 1 quart of tap water. Mix well, then place into a spray bottle and spray plants making sure that you spray the underneath sides of the leaves well. Make sure that the mixture stays in solution by shaking the bottle frequently.

HIT THEM WITH A SYRINGA

Soak 2 ounces of fresh syringa leaves in 4 cups of cold water for about 24 hours then strain and use in a sprayer. Test a few leaves and leave overnight. If the mixture is too strong it can burn your plants. **The fruit is very poisonous.**

USE SULFUR POWDER

One of the best insecticides for mites is to use sulfur powder from your drug store. There are a number of different preparations that contain sulfur.

MITES LIKE MARIGOLDS

Unlike most bugs, spider mites love marigolds and are not repelled by the plants.

SQUIRT THE BOXWOODS

The boxwood plant; can be damaged by boxwood mites. The leaves will become withered, bronzed and may drop to the ground making the plant look scraggly. The best method of eliminating the problem is to squirt the plant with water several times during the spring and summer months.

BULB MITES MAY RIDE A MOUSE OR FLY

These mites love bulbs and can do significant damage. They are whitish and have a few brown spots and grow up on onions and potatoes and then go on to the bulbs. While the mites will not do a lot of damage they allow decay organisms to enter and damage the plant. When the mite enters a stage where it develops a hard shell it will stop eating and look for a free ride aboard a mouse or fly looking for its next location. If you have a problem, just dip the bulbs in hot water for 20 minutes and make sure that you clean up any rotting or old bulb material.

PILLBUGS

These bugs are actually related to lobsters and crayfish and have seven pairs of legs and segmented bodies. They are sometimes called "rolly-polies" since they will roll up in a ball when disturbed. They like moisture and will normally be found in moist areas. If the area becomes dry they will move on. They like to eat ground cover, especially if the ground cover has a good amount of moisture in it.

Their favorite home is a corncob and they are also fond of potatoes.

THE BARKING PILLBUG

Pillbugs love dry dog food and if you sprinkle some dry dog food around the base of the plants they are bothering they will eat the dog food and stay away from the plants. Cat food may work as well.

ONION SPRAY

3	Onions
1/4	Cup Ivory Liquid Soap™
4	Cups of cool tap water

Slice and peel the onions then place them in a food processor and cover them with water. Blend very well then allow them to stand for 24 hours before straining and adding the liquid soap.

THE POTATO TRAP

Cut a raw potato in half and scoop out part of the insides then place it just below the surface of the ground where the pillbugs frequent. The pillbugs will congregate in the potato and can be discarded very easily.

ROOT MAGGOTS

Identification:
These look like houseflies and will lay their eggs in the soil. When they hatch the white maggots emerge looking like a grub with a pointed head. They will burrow down to the roots of the plants and feed until the plant dies and wilts. They lay about 200 eggs at the base of the host plant.

General Information:
If you think that root maggots are your problem, just pull up the plant and see if there are little white maggots on the roots. The two most common root maggots are the cabbage and onion root maggots. They prefer young seedlings. Their pupae spend the winter 1-6 inches into the soil then the flies come out in the spring and lay their eggs, immediately producing white maggots.

SERVE THEM TEA

Save all your used tea bags and place the loose tea in your planting mix or mulch. This acts as an excellent deterrent for maggots. Coffee grounds may work almost as well as the tea.

ITS DARK IN HERE

Place old pieces of carpeting or pieces of tar paper with slits cut around the base of the plants to stop the root maggots from getting to the roots. Cover the slits with a good waterproof tape. Maggots do not like the smell of tar, which is an excellent repellent.

MAKE A BARRIER

Try and acquire large quantities of eggshells from a local restaurant. Crush the eggshells and mix it in with the soil. You can also use DE or plain sawdust mixed in with the soil. This will stop them from burrowing in. Wood ashes can also be sprinkled around the base of the plant with good results.

REPELS 100% OF THE TIME
Prepare a mixture of equal parts of lime, rock phosphate and bone meal. Mix well then add an equal measure of wood ash. Place some of this mixture in the hole that you are planting in.

PARASITE KILLERS
You can order Nc nematodes or Chalcid and trichogramma wasps and release them as well as rove beetles.

ONION MAGGOTS

These maggots are more common in coastal areas. The maggot tapers to the head similar to the cabbage maggot. They damage the onions by feeding on the lower areas of the stem or bulb. A single maggot is capable of destroying a number of seedlings by eating their underground parts. Several maggots will ruin a large onion by attacking the onion through its base where they enter the root and burrow upwards. If the damaged onions are placed into storage they will readily decay.

THEY LOVE ONIONS
These bugs love onions with the exception of yellow onions. Yellow onions will usually repel the bugs, however, red and white ones will not.

SPACE OUT THE PLANTS
Since home gardens are arranged in rows the maggots find it easy to go from one plant to another. You can stop this pest by scattering the onion plants all over the garden. Every maggot needs several young seedlings to survive or they will die after they eat one. If they can't find the next seedling, they literally starve to death after their first meal.

ASHES TO ASHES
If you add sand or wood ashes to the top layer in planting rows it will stop the maggots and kill them.

SCALE

Scales have similar biology to mealybugs but with a white waxy covering and a hard shell of a variety of colors. There are about 1,700 species. Most do not lay eggs but bear live nymphs. They will reproduce faster indoors, which may be as little as a month while outdoor scales may take up to a year. There are soft scales and hard scales and it takes different methods to get rid of them so identification is a must.

SOFT SCALE VS HARD SCALE
To get rid of soft scales or black scales a wasp parasite, *Metaphycus helvolus* will solve the problem. To get rid of the hard, red scales call in the parasite *Aphytis melinus* to kill off the scale. Another very good scale eradicator is the ladybug *Chilococorus nigritis*. Actually, almost any ladybug beetle will be glad to eat your scales.

SWAB THEM
Scales can be removed from the infected plants if the areas where they reside are swabbed with isopropyl alcohol. This application must be repeated on the affected areas every 3-4 days until the scales die.

THE EARLY SPRING SOLUTION
In the early spring before the buds of the plants open, try spraying the plants with a solution of soap and lime, as long as the particular plant will tolerate the spray. Most plant will tolerate this spray very well and it will eliminate the scale problem.

DON'T CRY FOR ME...............
To get rid of scale, just crush up 1 pound of white onions and place them in 3 pints of water then allow it to stand for 24 hours. Strain the mixture and use in a sprayer in areas where you have a scale problem. Test a leaf first to be sure that you will not damage any plants.

A STICKY WICKET

    3   Cups of warm tap water
    1   Tablespoon of liquid paper glue

Mix the two items together and place in a sprayer. This will make the plant leaves inedible and the glue will coat the bug's bodies and suffocate them. The spray will flake off the plant. Do not use a spray-on adhesive from an aerosol can since this will work but is not environmentally safe.

GET OUT THE OIL CAN
In the late winter before any new growth starts you will need to spray the plants with horticultural oil spray. This will suffocate any scale that is on the plants.

LADYBUG, LADYBUG WHERE HAVE YOU BEEN......
Ladybugs are one of the best methods of controlling scale.

BLACK SCALE

The female is a dark brown or black color and will have ridges on her back that form the letter "H." It is usually found on twigs or leaves and occasionally fruit. Black scale; can be controlled by using the parasite *Metaphycus helvolus*, which is commercially available. Good identification is a must so call on your local gardening or agricultural supply house to assist you. They prefer citrus and olive trees.

BROWN SCALE

These scales will attack avocados and citrus and are soft brown oval scales. They are usually found on leaves and young twigs and will rarely bother the fruit. Heavy infestations will leave honeydew, sooty mold and ants that are attracted to the sweet honeydew.

BEETLES AND PARASITES DO THE JOB

The parasite *Metaphycus luteolus* and the lady beetle *Chilcorus cacti* will make short work of this brown scale.

CALIFORNIA RED SCALE

This is an armored scale with no visible egg stage. Crawlers are usually light yellow and the adult is a tiny yellow-winged bug. It is almost always found on fruit and fruit should be inspected at regular intervals.

PARASITES AND PREDATORS

There are a number of parasites and predators that will easily take care of any California Red Scale problem. These include the wasps *Aphytis melinus, Aphytis lingnanensis, Encarsia perniciosi* and *Comperiella bifasciata*. The predators are the small black ladybeetle *Lindorus lophanthae*.

CITRICOLA SCALE

This scale can produce honeydew, which will cause a sooty mold to grow on fruit and plants. Specific parasites are very effective and it is best to check with your garden supply store. They prefer citrus, walnuts and pomegranate and luckily only produce one generation each year. The parasites *Metaphycus luteolus* and *Metaphycus helvolus* should take care of the pests.

COTTONY CUSHION SCALE

This scale prefers citrus trees and excretes a large amount of honeydew, which pleases the ants to no end. They will be found mainly on twigs and leaves and rarely on the fruit. The nymphs are red and have black legs and antennae. The females lay a cottony-looking egg sac, which will remain attached to their bodies.

NATURAL ENEMIES TO THE RESCUE
The natural enemies include the vedelia beetle and the parasite fly *Cryptochetum iceryae*. The beetle will usually be hanging around if you have any cottony cushion scale in the area.

PURPLE SCALE

This scale is found on leaves, twigs and some fruit. The scale produces a toxic substance that can kill the more heavily infested areas of trees and plants. You will easily be able to spot the dead areas. The female has an oyster shell shape that is purple.

OYSTERSHELL SCALE

This armored scale attacks most fruit and nut trees and is shaped like a mussel or oystershell. It only feeds on bark and will leave the leaves and fruit alone. It will be more of a pest if the fruit trees are located near a poplar, willow or walnut tree, which are the preferred host trees. Dormant sprays are not affective since it winters in the egg stage and is protected by the old female covers. Best to locate the scale and prune the limbs or twigs.

RED SCALE

Found on twigs, leaves and fruit and will produce a toxic substance that will kill the leaves, twigs and fruit it inhabits. The scale is reddish-brown and round. If it is found on green fruit is will appear as a yellow spot that will go through to both sides of leaves. Most chalcid wasps will eliminate this pest.

SAN JOSE SCALE

Attacks most fruit and nut trees. The adults are gray-brown with a tiny white bump in the center of their bodies. These scales should be found during the dormant season and destroyed. They will be found on the top of trees as well as the limbs and twigs.

ELIMINATING THE PROBLEM
Pheromone traps work very well on this scale as well as releasing a natural enemy the twice-stabbed lady beetle *Chilocorus orbus*.

WALNUT SCALE

This is an armored scale that lays tiny eggs all together on a chain. They hatch into yellow worms within 3-4 days. The adult males are very small yellow-winged bugs. This bug will blend in very well with tree bark and are hard to locate. Best to spray a supreme or superior-type oil: at the end of the dormant season to control the walnut scale.

WASP FOR CONTROL

The tiny parasitic wasp called *Aphytis melinus;* does an excellent job of locating and destroying the walnut scale.

SCALES FOUND IN ORCHARDS

SCALE	PRINCIPAL HOST
Brown Soft Scale	Citrus, avocado, stone fruit
Calico Scale	Walnuts, pear, stone fruit
California Red Scale	Citrus, grape & olive
Citricola Scale	Citrus,walnuts,pomegranate
Cottony Cushion Scale	Citrus, other trees
European Fruit Lecanium	Walnuts,almonds,stone fruit pears , grapes
Frosted Scale	Walnuts
Italian Pear Scale	Walnuts, apples, pears
Olive Scale	Olive trees, almond trees
Oystershell Scale	Apples, nuts & pears
Purple Scale	Citrus
San Jose Scale	Fruit & nut trees
Soft Scale	Citrus, olives, nut trees, fig, apple, pear
Walnut Scale	Walnut trees

SCORPIONS

HIRE A CHICKEN

Chickens like to dine on scorpions and will hunt them out. However, I don't think you want a bunch of chickens walking through the living room so best to let them remove the scorpions that are outside.

HERE KITTY, KITTY

Cats are very effective in catching and removing scorpions, especially ones that do not like catching mice. We haven't figured out the reasoning for this one yet.

LIGHT 'EM UP
Scorpions tend to fluoresce under ultraviolet or black light and can easily be found at night. They are unable to jump and can easily be killed or captured. If you carry a hand vacuum with you, you can just vacuum them up and dispose of the bag.

BAIT THEM
A shallow plate with water and boric acid will work great at getting rid of them and their relatives. Be sure that there are no pets or children around.

TRAP THEM
If you dampen an old burlap bag or any heavy piece of cloth and leave it on the ground at night, the scorpions will crawl under making it easy for you to find and kill them.

SILVERFISH

These bugs have silvery overlapping scales, which tend to rub off very easily. They scavenge for food at night and like moist flour and especially love glue and the sizing in books. For dessert they will eat wallpaper glue if you have a piece of wallpaper that has pulled away or the glue from a postage stamp. If you see silverfish it would be best to clean and vacuum the area well, since any minute food particle will attract them. They would prefer to live in a damp, warm condition, usually in kitchens and bathrooms. You may also find them munching on the starch in shirts if they are real hungry.

These bugs have no odor and will not harm you. They also love to eat very young termites if there is a nest in the vicinity.

SETTING A STICKY TRAP
Take a piece of light cardboard and place some Tanglefoot™ on it, then place some oatmeal in the center. The Tanglefoot™ is very sticky and they can't escape. They will never even make it to the oatmeal.

BE SWEET TO SILVERFISH
To get rid of silverfish, try mixing 1 part of molasses in 2 parts of white vinegar, then apply the mixture to any cracks or holes where they tend to reside. Make sure that you treat the baseboards and the table legs as well.

THEY LIKE HIGH HUMIDITY
If you keep the humidity low in the house with a dehumidifier chances are that you will never have to worry about silverfish. You can also keep packets of silica gel around your bookshelf. These gel packets are available in most hardware stores.

PROTECT YOUR BOOKS
If you set out some of the herb santolina (lavender cotton) around your bookshelves it will repel silverfish. You can also sprinkle some diatomaceous earth (DE) around the books. If you use DE be sure and wear a mask and eye protection.

THE GLASS TRAP WORKS GREAT
Use a jar and butter the inside 1-2 inches. Wrap the outside with masking tape and give them a tongue depressor ramp. Bait the trap with some wheat flour or sugar and in the morning it should be filled with silverfish. Pour soapy water in to drown them.

SYMPHYLAN

This bug is often confused with the centipede and is called the "garden centipede." It is not a good bug to have in the garden. It has a body that is broken up into 14 segments and moves around on 12 pairs of legs. They will eat young plant roots and are voracious eaters. To check to see if you have this pest doing damage, just dunk a root ball in a bucket of water and wait for the pest to rise to the top.

THEY DON'T CARRY FLOOD INSURANCE
If you have a field that is infested the best method is to flood the area and drown them. This is not a good method if all you have is a small garden.

INVITE THEM TO TEA
Preparing a tea with garlic and tobacco will do in the bugs in short order. Just drench the area to kill them.

TARNISHED PLANT BUG

These are brown and black bugs with nymphs that love to suck up plant juices. The areas on the affected plants will be a dark color. They lay their eggs on the leaves and will also feed on weeds and grass. They will hibernate in the winter in cracks or in trash.

TOUGH CRITTERS
There are no known good controls for these bugs. You can try the typical bug removal methods of picking them off and using Nc nematode mulch around the base of the plants. The soap and lime spray will irritate them and they may move on.

CHAPTER 15

DEER

DEER

On the average a deer consumes about 5 pounds of greenery every day. Their diet consists of stems, leaves and buds of woody plants, however, their diet will vary depending on the food source available. They are creatures of habit and will return to the same general vicinity every day. Deer especially like to eat roses, but will settle for corn or grains and will usually not eat grasses.

There are a number of methods of deterring deer without harming them. It is best to use a non-toxic method that does not have to be applied after every rain. However, if the rain is very heavy it will be necessary to re-apply a deterrent. Once a deterrent is used the deer will go to another area to forage and you may not have to spray again.

DEER DETERRENT

The following ingredients will be needed:

1	Tablespoon of cayenne pepper
3	Tablespoons of kelp
3	Tablespoons of liquid hand soap
½	Teaspoon of oil of peppermint
1	Pint of warm water

Place all the ingredients into a medium bowl and mix well. Be careful not to get the cayenne pepper in your eyes. Place the mixture into a spray bottle and spray the areas where the deer frequent. **Do not use on plants that you will be consuming.**

SAVE THE USED SOAP

Small bars of used soap can be hung from trees and bushes that deer eat. The human smell on the bar of soap tends to keep them away. Small bags of blood meal hung on the trees will accomplish the same thing. You can also use soap flakes instead of bars of soap placed in old stockings.

SOUNDS FISHY

I'll NEVER COME HERE AGAIN

This is a sure-fire deer deterrent if you want to go through the trouble. For a small area it really works well but is mainly used on large flower farms or by people with really big areas near a national forest. Mix together 3 tablespoons of finely ground kelp with 1 cup of smelly fish emulsion and throw in 3 tablespoons of Ivory Liquid Soap™. Add enough water to make it easy to spray, then spray directly on the plants or trees.

STICKY SOLUTION
Mix 1 large egg in a quarter cup of tap water and mix well. The mixture is placed into a spray bottle and sprayed on the tree or plants. This is fine for a small area and the egg mixture is sticky enough to withstand a light rain without being re-applied.

MAKE THEM AN OMELET
For a large area mix 1 cup of whole milk, 2 large eggs 2 tablespoons of canola oil, 2 tablespoons of Ivory Liquid Soap™ into 2 gallons of cool water. This mixture is very effective and is normally used in a spray bottle.

HAIR, HERE
Offer to sweep up the hair for your local beauty or barbershop, keep the hair and spread a small amount around the areas you are having trouble in. The human scent will keep deer away for some time or at least until it rains 2-3 times. You can place the hair into old socks and hang them from the tree. Using dirty gym socks works really great and will probably keep the neighbors away as well.

A REAL STINKER
The smell of rotten eggs is very offensive to many animals, especially deer. When eggs go bad they give off hydrogen sulfide and that really stinks bad. Deer will never come anywhere near an area that smells that bad. This is not a good deterrent to use too near your home.

A BLOODY DETERRENT
The following ingredients will be needed:

1	Tablespoons of dried blood (garden supply house)
4	Cloves of powdered garlic
2	Gallons of cool tap water

Place the water into a bucket and add the dried blood, then mix well. Place a portion into a sprayer and spray the area that the deer frequent. Use sparingly, since this formula is high in nitrogen and may burn plants. Works great to keep rabbits away as well.

OLD DOGGIE BLANKET WORKS GREAT
If you change your dog's blanket, don't throw it away if you have a deer or other small critter problem. Just cut up the blanket and leave pieces anywhere you have a problem with the critters.

PLANT SMELLY PLANTS
There are a number of plants that when planted in an area where deer frequent will deter them from munching on your trees and plants. These include rotunda Chinese holly, foxglove, Mexican oregano, mint, wormwood, spearmint, lemon thyme, Madagascar periwinkle and artemisias. Also planting thorny bushes such as blackberry or raspberry will act as a deterrent.

DEER-RESISTANT PLANTS

Ageratum	Daffodil	Myrtle
Ash	Daphne	Narcissus
Astilbe	Daylily	Nightshade
Black-eyed Susan	Devil's Poker	Oleander
Black Locust	Dogwood	Pampas Grass
Bleeding-heart	Dusty Miller	Peony
Blue Lily-of-the-Nile	English Ivy	Persimmon
Bottle Brush	English Lavender	Pine
Boxwood	Foxglove	Peppermint
Butterfly Bush	Giant Reed	Red Elderberry
Calla Lily	Hazelnut	Rosemary
Canterberry Bells	Holly	Scotch Broom
Carolina Cherry Laurel	Iceland Poppy	Solomon's Seal
Chives	Iris	Silvery Aremesia
Clematis	Japanese Rose	Spearmint
Columbine	Jasmine	Spruce
Coreopsis	Lamb's Ear	Tulip
Cransebill Gernaium	Larkspur	Yarrow

GIVE THEM THE SHOCK OF THEIR LIVES

Fences are usually not a good solution since deer can jump over most fences. An electrically charged fence, however, is a different story if built right. An electric fence only needs to be 5-feet high to be effective. The fence needs to have 6 strands of wire with each strand starting at the bottom and is further away from the garden area than the one below it. This means that the fence must be at a 45^0 angle. When the deer sees the wire they will usually only see the top wire at the 5-foot level since the other wires are further away. When they try and go under the 5-foot wire they hit the lower wire and get the shock. Purchase the electric charger at any hardware store.

NOT AT ALL STICKY

If you plant molasses grass around your property it will repel deer and even trap their ticks in the sticky plant hairs.

CACKLEBERRY DETERRENT

4	Large raw eggs
1	Gallon of cool tap water

Place the eggs in the water and mix well, be sure that the water is not warm or the eggs will not mix well. Allow it to stand for 1 hour before straining and placing in a sprayer.

I TAUGHT I SAW A PUTTY TAT, SMELLED LIKE ONE!

This will keep deer far away from your property. If all else fails, go to your local zoo and ask them if you can have manure from the big cats cages. I do mean the BIG cats including lions, tigers, leopards and panthers. This is guaranteed to keep deer away as long as the aroma lasts.

BUILD A MOAT

This is used quite a bit around small areas. Just place human hair in a shallow trench around the entire perimeter of the garden or trees you want to protect. This keeps the deer away and the birds have a ball using the hair for their nest. The hair is rich in nitrogen and can be worked into the soil after the deer season is over.

ATTACK OF THE CREEPING VINE

Deer will shy away from an area that has tomato and squash vines along the ground. If they are planted early before other plants so that they have some time to mature they will act as an excellent deer deterrent.

SPRINKLE SOME BLOOD

There are two excellent items that you can sprinkle around the areas to deter deer. They are blood meal or beef liver that has been processed. The blood meal can be purchased in any garden supply store. The raw liver (about ½ pound) needs to be placed in a food processor with 1 quart or less of water and then finely processed.

HIRE A DEER DOG

Dogs are excellent deer deterrents. Deer will never come near a property that has a dog that is able to get to them.

NOT A PIPE DREAM

You can purchase thin plastic pipe and cut the pipe with a saw do that it will go around the trunk of the tree. This makes an excellent barrier not only for deer but other animals as well.

CHAPTER 16

RODENTS

RODENTS

GOPHERS

Gophers enjoy feasting on your plants, vegetables, tree roots and anything else they can get their teeth into that grows with roots. Their teeth can grow up to 14 inches per year. They just wear down and keep on growing back. To tell the difference all you have to look at their mounds. Gopher's mounds have dirt pushed off to one side while moles build a volcano-shaped with their entrance in the center. The moles entrance is usually plugged up.

The biggest pest gopher is the pocket gopher; who has fur-lined pockets in their cheeks, which they utilize to carry food back to their nest for storage. Their favorite food is alfalfa.

SMELLY SOLUTION
The following ingredients will be need:

1	Teaspoon of oil of peppermint
1	Teaspoon of chili powder
½	Ounce of Tabasco Sauce™
1	Pint of cold tap water
	Cotton balls

Place all the ingredients into a medium bowl and mix well. Place about 10 drops of the solution on a cotton ball and place the cotton ball anywhere a rodent problem exists or drop the cotton ball down a gopher or mole hole.

DOWN SOUTH REMEDY
Gophers and moles do not like hominy grits. Place the grits down the hole and it will act as a stomach irritant. Any instant grain will also make them very ill and wanting to leave your property and head for the nearest rodent emergency room.

HAIR RAISING
If you want to get rid of gophers without killing them, just drop human hair down their tunnels. Keep placing the hair in all their new tunnels until they get tired of digging them in your yard and head for your neighbors yard.

THE OLD SMELLY HERB TRICK
Place 3-4 drops of oil of peppermint (not the extract) on cotton balls and drop the cotton ball down all the entrances to the gopher or mole holes. They are allergic to peppermint and will leave your property or sneeze themselves to death. Citronella works well too if you can't find oil of peppermint. You can also place the product "Deer Off™" on the cotton balls to irritate them. Other oils work well too, such as pennyroyal, citronella and lavender.

GERMAN GOPHER ROCKS

These are lava rocks that have been soaked in a garlic and onion solution that will smell up tunnels to such a degree that the gophers and moles pack their bags and head for the neighbors yard. The rocks are buried about 6-inches deep in areas where you have plants that they are feeding on. Depending on the amount of rain or watering in the area the rocks will remain effective for 4-12 months. They are sold as "Rodent Rocks™."

MARK THEIR TERRITORY

When you find gopher or mole holes the first step is to place a small flag at every entrance. Purchase an injector tool from your garden supply house to be used with a mixture that will be sprayed into their holes. Hopefully you have found all the holes. The mixture is as follows:

1	Pound of cayenne pepper or ground very hot chilies
¼	Pound of garlic powder

Place the mixture into the injector and spray into every tunnel and cover with a rock or brick. Best to cover all holes before you start spraying, then open them up one at a time and spray them then replace the cover. Try not to water the area for 24 hours after the treatment.

SMELLY CACKLEBERRIES

If you leave some eggs out of the refrigerator for about 2-3 weeks, they will have a high hydrogen sulfide content from the chemicals that break down. The smell of rotten eggs is very offensive to gophers and moles and they will not appreciate your dropping these eggs into their living quarters or tunnels.

PLANT WIRE IN YOUR GARDEN

If you have a problem with gophers every season, it may be best to lay a layer of aviary wire (about ¼ inch mesh) about 6-inches underground. You can also bury ½ inch galvanized wire fencing mesh about 2 feet underground as a barrier. The wire must come all the way to the surface to be effective.

A SCARY SIGHT
Colored wine bottles have been used very effectively when placed underground around the garden. The gophers and moles see their reflection and get scared and run away.

NATURAL PLANT BARRIERS
If you plant a number of garlic and onion plants around the garden it will repel the gophers and moles. They prefer areas that do not contain plants that are offensive to them.

RENT-A-SNAKE
Gopher snakes love to chase and eat gophers and moles. They are not poisonous and many people keep them as pets. Your local pet store should have a gopher snake that you can just drop down the gopher or mole hole. You will probably not have another problem for a long time.

GOPHER-PROOF HEDGE
Gopher purge (uphorbia lathyrus) is a plant that contains pods each containing three seeds. The plant is a natural repellant to gophers and moles and all other burrowing animals. The roots are so poisonous to them as well as humans that it will eliminate the problem in short order. Do not get the white milky substance on your hands or face: if you do best to wash it off immediately. It is usually planted as a hedge around gardens and used mainly on the east coast of the United States.

BUY A BLACK HOLE
A Black Hole™ is a circular trap with a hole in the end. An apple attached to a piece of string is used and is very effective for catching gophers. There are a number of traps made to trap gophers and moles but the Black Hole™ seems to be the best.

POWERFUL NATURAL SUPPLEMENT
One of the most effective gopher and mole killers is vitamin D or actually D_3. D_3 is a form of vitamin D that's upsets calcium metabolism in burrowing animals and eventually kills them. D_3 is safe for humans and animals making it an excellent gopher and mole killer.

WATCH 'EM RUN
The following ingredients will be needed:

1	Ounce of peppermint oil
¼	Ounce of cayenne pepper

Place the ingredients in a small bowl and mix. Dip a cotton ball in the mixture and drop the cotton ball down the gopher or mole hole. You will never see those critters again.

SMOKE 'EM OUT
Just purchase a pack of non-filter cigarettes and shred them. Drop the pieces of tobacco down all the holes and the nicotine in the leaves will kill gophers and moles. Keep nicotine away from roses and fishes. Nicotine is a poison.

THIS WILL GIVE THEM THE RUNS
Mix one cup of castor oil and 3 tablespoons of ivory liquid soap in 1 gallon of water and pour some down every hole and around their areas. You can use a sprayer if you wish. Apply this mixture early in the morning of a real hot day for the best results.

AYE CHIHUAHUA
Drop a habanero or Serrano chili down the gopher of mole hole and you will never see them again. They will dig to China to get away from it.

BOMBS AWAY
There are few commercial products that can be used if all else fails. Commercial mole smoke bombs are available through garden supply houses. The mole, however, if it gets away will return since the tunnels have not been destroyed and take up housekeeping again.

THEY WON'T HAVE ANY MOTHS IN THEIR HOME
Dropping mothballs works great, they hate the smell and immediately leave their happy home. **Mothballs are also very poisonous to humans as well as all animals.** This would be a very last resort.

POISONOUS PLANT
If you plant a few castor bean plants *Euphobia lathyris* around your garden it will either kill the gopher or mole or for them to move to another location. The leaves and stems are poisonous and you need to keep pets and children away from these plants.

A POWERFUL THREESOME
There are oils that will eliminate all rodents. Just add 1 cup of castor oil, tea tree oil, cinnamon oil, garlic oil or mineral oil to 1 gallon of warm water. Place a small amount of a natural liquid soap to the mixture and spray the area where they frequent. This is a pretty potent spray. If you want to just scare them away use only 4 drops of the oils in the gallon of water and don't spray directly on them.

GOPHER & MOLE KILLER
The following ingredients will be needed:

4	Ounce of powdered seaweed
2	Ounces of powdered vitamin D_3
2	Ounces of any vegetable powder

Place all the ingredients in a small plastic container and mix well. Rodents have difficulty regulating their calcium absorption and the vitamin will eventually kill them off. Just place a small amount of the mixture inside a small piece of any vegetable (potato,etc.) by

THIS WILL NOT DOUBLE THEIR PLEASURE
Gophers love Juicy Fruit gum. Just drop a stick or two down the gopher hole and they will eat it and plug up their intestinal tract. Best to use gloves when unwrapping and handling the gum to avoid the smell of humans.

CHASE THEM AWAY WITH STATIC
Purchase a small, cheap portable radio and put a long-life battery in it. Wrap the radio in plastic and put on static, then drop it down the gopher hole. If he doesn't change the station you will never see him again.

SOUNDS FISHY
This will drive out moles and gophers immediately. They can't stand the smell of fish and especially rotting fish. Grandpa had an old trick that worked every time he saw a gopher or mole hole. He would drop a fish head down the hole and never saw the gopher again. This irritates them into an instant move on to less odoriferous areas.

SKIP THE FLOODING
I remember cartoons where the gopher was flooded out with a hose poked into his tunnel. While this may work it may also collapse the tunnels in your yard and make a big mess to re-do the yard.

LIGHT 'EM UP
This one really makes them mad. Close off all their tunnel openings and just leave one open for a few minutes. Drop a lighted highway flare down the tunnel and no more gophers or moles.

RATTLE THEM
Place a stick into the ground near one of their tunnels and attach a rattling pinwheel to the stick. The vibrations from the pinwheel will drive them batty. Gophers are extremely sensitive to ground vibrations.

BUY A GO'PHER™
The Go'pher™ is sold in garden shops and emits an ultrasonic noise. It is a battery, operated unit and the sound: cannot be heard by humans and most animals. It will also keep moles and voles away. The device is advertised to keep areas up to 1000 square feet clear of these varmints.

SQUILLS TO THE RESCUE
Gophers hate areas where there are scilla bulbs (squills) planted. These flowering bulb-type ornamentals have grassy leaves and clusters of flowers on the top of long stems. They are easy to grow and if you border you garden it will keep all gophers away.

MICE/RATS

Mice, while looking cute can cause damage to electrical wiring, clothing and food stores. The U.S. Environmental Protection Agency estimates that one pair of mice in a six month period can consume about four pounds of foodstuffs and contaminate another 40 pounds while leaving 20,000 droppings along the way. A pair of mice can produce up to 50 young in a one-year period. Trapping them is still one of the best methods.

A rat can fall 50 feet and land on its feet with no injury and squeeze through a hole that is the size of a quarter. They can also tread water for 3 days without a life vest and survive an atomic blast if they are not at ground zero.

RODENT POISON THAT IS HARMLESS TO HUMANS
The following ingredients will be needed:

2	Ounces of barium carbonate
½	Ounce of granulated sugar
½	Pound of bread crumbs

Place All the ingredients into a bowl and mix well, then add a small amount of water to dampen and allow the mixture to be made into small balls that can be placed out for the rodents.

DON'T BE A MISER WITH THE TRAPS
Trapping is the best method of getting rid of mice and rats. If you have decided to trap the mice, use plenty of traps: just keep them away from pets and children. You can bait the traps with cotton balls, which attract the females who are nest building or peanut butter, which they really like. If you want to give them a real treat mix the peanut butter with rolled oats and add a raisin. Remember, mice travel along the edges of the wall. Don't set the traps for a day or two, just set them out, this really fakes them out and you will get instant results when you do set them with bait.

Other foods that work well in traps are gumdrops and dried fruit. If you are bothered by Norway rats just feed them hot dogs in the trap.

BORDERING ON THE INSANE

In Cleveland, Ohio there is still an old law on the books that prohibits catching mice without a license.

THE MOUSE ALLERGY
Rodents and especially mice are allergic to oil of peppermint and will not frequent a property where they can smell it. If you place a few drops of oil of peppermint on a piece of cotton and place it anywhere you feel that there is a mouse problem you will never see them again. Use only the "real" oil of peppermint not peppermint extract for the best results. You can also plant peppermint in your garden to keep all types of rodents away from the plants. They are also repelled by camphor and pine tar.

SOUND OFF
Devices that emit ultrasonic sound waves have not been found to work very efficiently on rodents.

KILLER MASHED POTATOES
If you leave a bowl of potato flakes and a small bowl of water where the mice can get to them, they will eat the flakes and drink the water. The flakes will expand in their stomachs and their stomach will burst killing them.

WILL NOT WORK ON MEXICAN MICE
Mice tend to damage plant bulbs, especially in the spring. To reduce the amount of damage mix together ½ ounce of Tabasco Sauce™ or other hot sauce in 1 pint of water, add ½ teaspoon of Ivory Liquid Soap™ and 1 teaspoon of cayenne pepper. Place the mixture into a spray bottle and spray around the base of the plants.

IT'S BARBECUE TIME
If you are lucky enough to locate an active rodent burrow, drop some lighted barbecue charcoal briquettes down the burrow. The carbon monoxide should kill the rodents. You can also drop a few pieces of dry ice in the burrow and the carbon dioxide given off will kill the rodents.

REPEL WITH GROUND COVERS
There are a few ground covers that rodents do not like to live in or be around. These include adjuga, carpet bugle, cape weed, chamomile, Indian rock strawberry and creeping speedwell.

DOGS ARE GREAT RATTERS
Dogs are better at catching rats than most cats. In fact, the rat terrier was named for the fact that it was a great rat catcher.

HIRE SOME BARN OWLS
New York City had such a rat problem that they actually built special nesting boxes for barn owls to attract them. A family of 6 barn owls can consume as many as 16 or more rats in one night. This didn't work too well because the nesting boxes were stolen.

CATCHING THE FAMILY PET MOUSE OR HAMSTER
Take a large bowl and butter the inside to make it real slippery. Place a piece of cheese in the bottom and set up a ramp with a piece of wood, tongue depressor or ? The mouse will go for the bait and will not be able to get out.

PLANTS TO THE RESCUE
Rodents will avoid certain plants that give off repulsive scents. These include daffodils, hyancinths and scillia.

THE CAT'S MEOW
A sure fire method of getting rid of rodents is to place a few drops of "Nepeta" or catnip oil on a cotton ball and place it anywhere you have a problem.

HIRE A RAT TO CHASE MICE
Rats hate mice and given the chance will run them down and kill them for you. If you don't mind a few rats around you will not have any mice. This is not a great way to get rid of mice.

CEMENT THEM IN
A non-toxic poison for rats and mice is to place a dish containing cornmeal and dry cement mixed together in an easy location for them to find. If you place a bowl of water near the dish it will make the rodents stomachs set up faster and turn to solid cement.

MOLES/VOLES

A TUNNELING NUISANCE
Moles are great at tunneling with their powerful claws on their front feet. Moles: are actually not a member of the rodent family, however, they are included in this chapter since all the deterrents used for gophers apply to them as well. They normally prefer to live on insects, but when the insects are intermingled with the root system of a plant, they will eat both the insect and the plant's roots. Their favorite bug is the grub and if you can control the grub population you will probably be able to control the mole population in you're yard.

Spraying your yard in early spring for fleas will eliminate the majority of the grub population and reduce the overall number of insects for moles to feed on. Many different types of methods have been tried to remove moles including; smoke bombs, high-pressure water, poisons, rat bait, hand grenades and dynamite.

Because moles expend a high degree of energy they cannot survive more than a few hours without food.

MUSIC TO GOPHER BY
Gophers and moles do not like loud sounds. If you place a cheap transistor radio playing hard rock into their domain you will never see them again. They are very sensitive to sound waves.

GRUB CONTROL
If you control the grubs on your property, chances are that you will never have a mole around.

WHERE'S THE CAT
Used kitty litter placed into the mole's tunnel will cause them to move on to your neighbors' property very quickly.

YUK.........................
Place an ear of fresh corn painted with roofing tar in their tunnel. They hate the odor of tar and will look for a new home in your neighbors yard.

GET 'EM ON THE RUN
Drop a few Ex-Lax™ squares down their hole. You will never see them again!

PORCUPINE

The porcupine is also known as the "quill pig" and is a member of the rodent family. It has about 30,000 spiny quills, which are barbed at the head. The quills cover the entire body with the exception of the underneath side and the head. They like thin tree bark, leaves and buds but have a sweet tooth and will eat corn, melon and berries if they can get them. They have been known to ruin berry bushes by stripping the bark off the stems and trunks. If your dog has a run in with a porcupine it would be best to get the dog to the vet as soon as possible. If shocking doesn't work you will have to trap them.

SHOCK THEM
Porcupines are good climbers and you will need a chicken wire fence about 2 feet high with an electric wire on top just a few inches above it. Angle the fence at a 65^0 angle away from the garden for the best results.

SHREWS

SHREWS ARE SHREWD
You have to be crafty to catch a shrew, but the best method is a mousetrap. The bait needs to be peanut butter and rolled oats and if you add just a hint of bacon grease or hamburger it will increase the effectiveness.

SQUIRRELS

STOP TULIP DECAPITATING

If you mix up a batch of squirrel deterrent spray, it will keep the cute little critters away from your budding plants, which they enjoy munching on. Boil 1 quart of water and remove from the heat as soon as it starts to boil, then add 2 tablespoons of cayenne pepper and ½ teaspoon of Tabasco Sauce. Allow it to stand for about 2-3 hours making sure it is very cool before placing the mixture into a sprayer and spraying the stems of the plants as soon as the buds appear.

STOP THE FURNITURE CHEWER

Some squirrels like to chew on legs of wooden garden furniture. To stop them, just paint the legs with a watery solution of hot sauce, then wipe clean. This will leave enough hot residue to discourage them.

PROVIDING YOU HAVE A PUTTY TAT

Place a very small amount of used cat litter around the base of the budding plants. This will deter squirrels and chipmunks from digging up bulbs. Also works well on all flowering plants in areas where you have a rodent problem. They think that there is a cat nearby waiting to pounce on them.

WRAP YOUR TRUNKS

Placing a metal band around tree trunks works great as long as there are no other trees for the squirrel to go from one tree to the other. The band should be a smooth metal and at least 2-feet wide and 6-8 feet off the ground.

USE STEEL WOOL

If you have any openings into the attic from the outside it would be best to place steel wool to keep the squirrel and other critters from setting up housekeeping there. If they are already in the attic then place a heavy piece of rubber to block the opening only allowing them to exit and not enter.

TRAPPING SQUIRELS

Traps can be purchased in most hardware stores or garden supply centers. The bait needs to be peanut butter, nuts, seeds or their favorite, vanilla extract.

PETER PIPER'S PLATES

When squirrels become a pest and get into your fruit trees, try tying some "real" aluminum pie plates to the tree to scare them off. Place them on the lower limbs of all trees.

WHOOOOPS

If you place a layer of lubricating gel around the trunk of the tree about one-foot wide the squirrels will not be able to climb the tree. The only problem here is if you have another tree that you have not done this too in close proximity to the tree you wan to protect. Best to do this on all trees.

TANGLE THEM UP

If you want to discourage them, just place some Tanglefoot™ around the trunk of the tree. This sticky substance will deter them from climbing the tree.

WEIRD BARRACADE
If you can get a bunch of 1 quart plastic milk bottles, ones with the little handles, just place a string through the handles and hang them around the trunk of the trees you are having a problem with. If you can't find enough quart ones use the gallon size and just cut off the tops and nail them on with the open side down around the trunk of the tree touching each other.

A BLOODY GOOD IDEA
If you sprinkle blood meal around the borders of your garden where you are having a squirrel problem it will deter them.

HOT PEPPER SPRAY
If you prepare a spray made from pureed hot peppers and dilute it with water, then add a few drops of Ivory liquid soap and spray it on plants that the squirrels are frequenting it will keep them away.

THIS WILL GIVE THEM THE RUNS
If you puree some red hot peppers and add a tablespoon of mineral oil to it then apply it to ears of corn that you are having a problem with to deter squirrels. Just apply the solution to the silk end of the corn.

BAFFLE THEM
Baffles can be placed on trees to stop the squirrels from climbing the tree, however, if other trees are not baffled near the tree they will just jump across.

WOODCHUCKS

These rodents are also known as "**groundhogs**" and can really do a lot of damage in a garden or farm. They are usually found in farms near a wooded area and build burrows that can cause damage to farm vehicles. They hibernate in the winter months. Live off their fat layer and their respiration can fall to only one breath every 5 minutes. Woodchucks only live through 4-5 winters. They burrow 2-5 feet deep and are continually improving their den or building a new one. Horses and other farm animals have often been injured stepping in a woodchuck hole.

Be careful around woodchucks since they can carry rabies and you do not want to be bitten by them. If you do get bitten go to the doctor immediately. If you have a big problem with woodchucks, trapping is the only answer.

THEY DON'T LIKE THE ALLIUM FAMILY
Woodchucks do not like certain plants of the allium family. These include garlic and onions.

PEPPER SPRAY WORKS
Puree a number of very hot peppers, strain the mixture and add water and a few drops of liquid soap then spray the area where you are having a problem with woodchucks. They hate hot peppers and will leave very quickly.

THE OLD WATER IN GLASS JUG TRICK

Farmer's in the mid-west have a solution to woodchuck problems! They place clear glass jugs filled ¾ full with clear water and seal the top. They leave the jugs around the areas where the woodchucks like to frequent. Woodchucks are scared of their own reflection and will shy away from these areas.

A LITTLE HERE AND THERE

Just sprinkle blood meal or even talcum powder around a burrow to force the woodchuck to find another location to reside in.

FOR A SERIOUS PROBLEM

If you have a serious problem the best way to solve it if the area is not too big is with a fence. The fence needs to be 3-4 feet high and at least 18 inches deep. If you can electrify the top strand it would help as well as angling the fence 65^0 away from your garden so that they can't climb it easily.

BRRRRRRRRRRRRRRR

If you place dry ice in their tunnel it will cause them to move rather quickly. They do not like the increase of carbon dioxide gas that is released.

CHAPTER 17

NEIGHBOR'S PETS

NEIGHBOR'S PETS

DIGGER THE CAT
The cat formula for keeping kitty out of the soft garden beds and using it as a latrine is a little different than for dogs. Mix together 2 tablespoons of cayenne pepper, 3 tablespoons of powdered Chinese mustard, 4 tablespoons of all-purpose flour in 2 quarts of warm tap water. Allow it to stand for 1 hour before straining and placing the mixture into a spray bottle. This will repel a mountain lion as well.

KEEP CATS AT BAY OR USE AS A SALAD DRESSING
If you want to keep cats away from your property and especially the birdbath that Tweety uses, just mix 2 ounces of white vinegar in a small sprayer bottle and give the area a squirt or two, but not in the bird bath water. Cats hate the smell of vinegar.

SCARE 'EM HALF TO DEATH
Cats are afraid of snakes! If you have a feline problem, just place an old piece of garden hose around your garden.

NOT VERY CATTY
Cats do not like to see their reflection in a plastic bottle. Try filling plastic soda bottles half full with water and leave them around the garden where they frequent. They will go looking for another area to use as a bathroom.

GET THE CATS WIRED
If you plant chicken wire just under the surface around the garden the cats have too much trouble digging and go find an easier area.

DRIVE THEM CRAZY
To keep cats away from your flowerbed or garden, just plant some catnip far way from the areas that you wan to keep them away from. Cats will stay near the catnip plants. Be sure that the catnip plants are good healthy plants before you plant them so that they will have a good chance of surviving the cats.

THEY WILL RUE THE DAY
Cats do not like the herb "rue." If you scatter the rue leaves around the areas that they frequent they will leave very quickly. If you plant the herb near your garden that they are bothering they will not go there.

DOGS

DIGGER THE DOG
To stop dogs from digging your garden or flowerbed, just prepare a mixture of:

1	Finely chopped garlic clove
1	Really smelly onion chopped fine
1	Teaspoon of Tabasco Sauce™
1	Teaspoon of cayenne pepper

Place all the ingredients into 1 quart of warm tap water and allow it to stand overnight. Strain through a piece of cheesecloth or use a fine strainer and place the mixture into a spray bottle and spray around the areas. This should stop all critters, not just the dog.

REPELLENT SPRAY

2	Cups of rubbing alcohol
2	Teaspoons of lemon grass oil

Place the mixture into a sprayer and spray any areas that you would like the dog to stay away from.

KEEP THEIR LEGS ON THE GROUND
To eliminate your dog (male) urinating on a post or somewhere that they shouldn't, just grind up a few "cheap" cigars or several cigarettes and soak them in a bowl of tap water overnight. Spray or dribble the mixture in areas that you want them to avoid. This is a toxic mixture and you don't want them to drink it. Dispose of the leftovers safely. Leave them someplace to go, however, so they don't run around with their legs crossed trying to find a spot to relieve themselves.

GOOD USE FOR THE OLD ROSE STEMS

When you trim the rose bushes down in the fall save the stems with the prickly thorns on them. Place them around the garden and the cats and dogs will not dig there. They will only try it once to get the idea.

BARRIER FOR NEIGHBORS DOGS

If you are having a serious problem with a neighbor's dog digging under your fence you can plant a prickly hedge or shrub such as Pyracantha. It is fast growing, looks nice and stops the problem.

HAVING A PROBLEM WITH YOUR CAN?

Dogs love to get into garbage cans! However, if you just sprinkle some ammonia around the base of the can they will steer clear.

CHAPTER 18

SNAILS & SLUGS

SNAILS & SLUGS

SOLUTIONS TO THE PROBLEM

SLUGGING IT OUT WITH SNAILS

The preferred meal for a slug is a succulent plant, especially their favorite, pansies. They feed different from any other insect in that they eat the leaf from the middle to the end, leaving you half a leaf. They do not like dry, cold weather and daylight and will hide under boards or debris. They feed at night and they are easy to track since they leave a trail of slime.

Snails are hermaphrodites, which means that they contain both the male and female sex organs and do not need another snail to mate. Snails are capable of producing over 300 eggs per day, which can lie dormant in the soil for up to 10 years.

Their breeding seasons are spring and fall. They love moisture and the dark, which is where they will nest. Plain "cheap" beer seems to attract them and when they consume it, it has the ability to dry them out thus killing them.

JUNGLE RAIN WORKS GREAT

The following ingredients will be needed:

1¼	Tablespoons of brewers yeast
1	Quart of very cheap beer
1	Quart of apple cider vinegar
1	Tablespoon of Jungle Rain™
1	Cup of warm tap water
2	Tablespoons of granulated sugar
1	One-gallon bottle

Place the cheap beer and vinegar in the gallon bottle and shake. Add the brewers yeast and the water with the sugar dissolved, to the beer and vinegar solution and mix. Add the Jungle Rain™, mix well and pour into small lids or holders that can easily be placed where the snails frequent. This will attract every snail in the neighborhood and do them all in.

Snails and slugs prefer a near beer and go crazy for Kingsbury Malt Beverage®

HAVE A SNAIL-PICKING PARTY

One of the best methods of eliminating or at least reducing the snail population in your garden is to pay a neighbors kid anywhere from a penny to a nickel per snail. They need a flashlight and prowl your garden after dark and pick the snails up by hand. Have rubber gloves available for the pickers and a bucket with salt, soapy water to drop them into.

ESCARGO FOR CHICKENS

If you don't want to kill the snails immediately and you or your neighbor has chickens, just feed the snails to the chickens. Chickens love to feast on snails.

HAPPY HOUR FOR SNAILS & SLUGS

Place a mixture of 1 quart of cheap beer, 1 teaspoon of powdered sugar and 1 teaspoon of white vinegar into wide jar lids or other similar container and leave out in the garden. Baker's yeast may be substituted for the vinegar if you prefer. This mixture will kill off hundreds of snails and slugs in short order. The slugs will really appreciate it if you place a small tent over the beer so that they will have some shade while they are dining.

SEASONING YOUR SNAILS

Use a saltshaker and mix together 1 part iodized salt and 1 part cayenne pepper. Shake the mixture on the snails and slugs to cause them to dehydrate and quietly pass away.

SLIPPERY GUNK FOR SNAILS

The following ingredients will be needed:

7	Ounces Vaseline®
8	Ounces castor oil
1	Ounce cayenne pepper
1	Ounce Tabasco Sauce™

Place the Vaseline® and the castor oil in a medium plastic container and mix. Add the pepper and Tabasco Sauce™ to give it a real boost. This mixture works great if placed on the trunk of a plant.

SHOWER THEM WITH AMMONIA

Fill a 1-quart spray bottle with warm tap water and add 1 tablespoon of household ammonia them shake and spray the snails and slugs.

USE SALAD DRESSING ON THEM
Mix up 2 tablespoons of white vinegar, 2 tablespoons of Ivory liquid soap and 1 tablespoon of red Tabasco Sauce™. Place the mixture in a spray bottle and spray the dressing on them. You can also just place 8-10 drops of Tabasco Sauce™ in 1 quart of water and spray them with this mixture. Actually any hot sauce will do, it doesn't have to be Tabasco Sauce™.

POWDER THEIR NOSE
Snails and slugs will not cross baby powder, flour or rock dust. Placing these powders around your plant beds will discourage them from entering.

PROTECT YOUR TREES
Place Tanglefoot™ around the base of trees to keep snails off the tree. Tanglefoot™ is made from castor oil and wax and works great as a natural barrier. If you want to increase the effectiveness add a small amount of cayenne pepper to it. The barrier should be about 1-foot wide to have maximum effectiveness.

CACKLEBERRY SHELLS WORK GREAT
Snails and slugs will not cross an area that is covered with eggshells. It is too difficult for them to navigate across and they will avoid the area.

CLOG THOSE PORES
If you sprinkle diatomaceous earth (DE) around it will clog the pores and the snails and slugs will suffocate. You can mix a solution of DE, a small amount of Ivory Liquid Soap™ and water and spray your plants in areas that are frequented by snails and slugs. DE will irritate your lungs so try not to breathe it in. DE also prevents snails from laying eggs, which will reduce the population over the years.

GOOD FOR PLANTS, BAD FOR SNAILS
Alfalfa meal is a high nitrogen plant food that if sprinkled around plants will supply the plant with nutrients and will provide a barrier against snails and slugs. If you do use alfalfa meal, make sure that you do not water the plants for 24 hours after the treatment.

SNAIL BARRIER FROM THE SEA
Kelp or dried seaweed will provide a barrier for snails and slugs while providing your plants with an excellent source of trace minerals. Kelp is high in salt content, which the snails try to avoid at all costs.

HORSE POO, POO
Horse manure added to mulch and spread around the garden when you are fertilizing is another natural barrier for snails and slugs. There are also other ingredients that can be added to mulch such as pine needles, kelp and rock dust that will keep the little critters at bay.

Formula to paint on tree trunks:

1	Bucket of old horse manure
2	Pounds of all-purpose flour
4	Ounces of cayenne pepper
2	Pounds powdered seaweed

Add enough water to prepare a paste that can be used as paint, ask a neighbors kid to do the chore.

BAKE THEM A HOT CAKE
Mix together 1 cup of all-purpose flour, 1 tablespoon of cayenne pepper and just enough water to prepare a mixture that can be used in a spray bottle. Spray around tree trunks or the base of plants.

CALL FOR THE COPPER
Copper bands can be purchased from a gardening supply house or hardware store and provide a non-lethal method of keeping the snails and slugs from damaging your trees and plants.

SKINNED SLUGS ANYONE?
If you mix 1½ cups of household ammonia with 1½ cups of water you can prepare a mixture that will literally fry the skin off a slug and kill them. Just place the mixture in a spray bottle and when you see the very small slugs, just spray them and ZAP!

CALL IN THE WORMS
A common snail and slug deterrent is to use Nc nematodes to kill the pests. Nc nematodes can be purchased through most garden shops or agricultural supply houses. They will track down and infect the snail or slug causing them to develop a swollen mantle and they quietly pass away within 2-3 days.

FORMULA FOR STICKY STUFF

Place the following mixture around the base or on the stems of plants and trees to keep off the snails and slugs.

8	Ounces of Vaseline®
1	Tablespoon of cayenne pepper
10	Ounces of castor oil
½	Ounce of any red-hot sauce

LIKE BEES TO HONEY

If you don't mind picking up the little creatures, just attract them with any kind of citrus fruit into any container you have that they can easily climb into.

GIVE THEM A TREAT

Snails and slugs prefer cabbage before any other vegetable or plant. If you don't like cabbage, just plant a few in your garden and that is where you will always find them hanging out.

CHILI PODS WILL FIX THEM

Grind up 8 ounces of ripe chili pods then soak them in 1 quart of water for 24 hours. Mix well and strain then add 3 quarts of water and ½ teaspoon of liquid soap. Use as a spray; wherever the snails and slugs hideout.

GRIND UP YOUR OLD MARBLES

There are a number of barriers that can be placed in the garden to keep snails and slugs at bay. The barrier must be at least 3 inches wide to be effective. You can use marble dust, hydrated lime, ammonium sulfate, crushed oyster shells or wood ash.

SPECIAL MULCH

If your mulch is high in oak leaves or seaweed it will stop the snails and slugs from coming into the garden.

SNAIL-RESISTANT PLANTS

The following are plants that snails do not like and tend to shy away from: corn, grape, bean, basil, azalea, sage ginger, hibiscus, parsley, rose, poppy, sunflower, fuschia and rhododendrum.

REPELLENT PLANTS

There are two plants that will actually repel snails and slugs. These are prostrate rosemary (*Rosemarinus officionalis*) and wormwood (*Artemisia absinthium*). If you prepare a tea with either of these herbs and use it as a spray it will deter the snails and slugs as well.

THE KILLER HAIR

Hair can be used very effectively to kill snails. Either human or horse works great, the coarser the better. Just scatter the hair around areas that the snails or slugs frequent and you can eliminate most of them. The horse hair especially will irritate their soft, moist skin to such a degree that they dehydrate themselves trying to get rid of the hairs that cling to them.

TURTLES ON THE LOOKOUT

Turtles like snails and slugs and will go after them every chance they get. If you place a turtle in your yard you will never see another snail or slug.

PROTECTIVE BARRIER

If you border an area with sand, lime or ashes it will protect the area from snails.

NEVER USE ANY POISONS TO GET RID OF SNAILS AND SLUGS. MOST OF THE COMMERCIAL POISONS MADE TO KILL THEM WILL KILL THE BIRDS IF THE BIRDS EAT THEM.

CHAPTER 19

WORMS

WORMS

ARMYWORM

Identification:
This is a 2-inch long caterpillar that is green with yellow-orange stripes down its back. It is a type of cutworm and usually feeds close to the ground, usually on plant stalks. They lay their eggs on leaves and their larvae eat grass stems. They tend to travel in mass like an army and will invade your garden with extreme prejudice. They will feed at night and lay low during the day. The females may lay as many as 700 eggs.

SPRAY THEM OR TRAP THEM
Prepare a mixture of a soapy solution with ¼ cup of lime and spray the caterpillars. If you want to trap them use a commercial pheromone trap. Nc nematodes and Bt also work very well.

SOUTH OF THE BORDER, DOWN MEXICO WAY
To get rid of armyworms, just remove the seeds from Mexican poppies and grind them into a powder. Us the powder to dust the plants you are having a worm problem with. This is an excellent method of control.

BAGWORM

Identification:
These are real pests that hide inside a rolled up leaf and eat away from the inside out. It is very hard to find the worm inside their spindle-shaped bags. They are a brownish color and seal up their bag they live in with silk. They will drag the bag along to different locations and stay hidden as they eat. A large number of bagworms can defoliate and kill a tree in short order. Their eggs are laid in the winter months and hatch in the early spring. Most of the bagworms are found on the east coast.

234

SNEAKY LITTLE EAST COAST BUGS
If you have a bad infestation the best method of eliminating the problem is to spray Bt on all the foliage. If the infestation is light, just handpick the little devils.

GIVE THEM A SQUIRT OR TWO
The soap and lime spray works great. Just mix together ¼ cup of lime and 4 drops of liquid soap in 1 gallon of water. If you prefer you can use garlic, onion juice or hot pepper sauce in place of the lime.

MEALWORMS

These little creatures reside in your flour or other grains and can survive in all conditions from very dry to moist. They love areas with poor sanitation, especially if grains or flour has fallen to the floor. Pet stores sell mealworms for people to feed to their pets such as turtles, fish and birds.

DOUBLE YOUR PLEASURE
Mealworms will avoid your grain products (macaroni, spaghetti, etc) if you keep a wrapped slice of spearmint gum near or in the products. The bugs do not like spearmint gum but love Juicy Fruit.

NEMATODES

Identification:
The small worms are only 1/125th of an inch and you will need a microscope to see them. They are tapered on both ends and their egg masses look like small, pearly lumps.

General Information:
These roundworms are the bad relative of the good Nc nematode and can cause wilting, yellowing and stunting of plants. The root-knot nematode causes galls or swellings on the roots of plants. They lay their eggs near the roots so that their offspring does not have far to go for a meal and can live their whole life underground. They can damage 2,000 different plants, which include almost any vegetable you can think of. They can be found everywhere in the United States, but like coarse soil the best.

Nematodes prefer soil that is lacking in organic matter. If you use mulch that is high in organic matter you should not have a problem with nematodes. There are over 500,000 species of this worm. They go from microscopic in size to a 20 footer that is found in whales.

LEMON CONTROL

There are beneficial nematodes that destroy other bug eggs as well as the bad nematodes. If you have the bad ones and you want to get rid of them, just grow lemon grass in the areas where you want to reduce or eliminate a population. This is one of the most effective methods of control.

HOW SWEET IT IS

2	Cup of granulated sugar
2	Cups of boiling water
1	Gallon of cool tap water

Dissolve the sugar into the boiling water, remove from the heat and add the cool water, then pour on the soil area that is infested. Sugar has the ability to draw moisture from the worms and dries them out.

TURN UP THE HEAT

If the weather is hot you can get rid of the nematode pests by giving them a steam bath. Make sure that there is no chance of rain and prepare the soil for cultivation first. Water the area thoroughly until the ground is well saturated, then cover the ground with a heavy-duty clear plastic sheet. Secure the plastic sheet to the ground on all sides. If the temperature is hot it will make the ground about 140°F and kill off the nematodes. This process will take about 5 weeks to accomplish. You will also eliminate many other pests as well as weed seeds.

GO FOR THE GOLD

There are two varieties of marigolds that when planted in an area that harbors nematodes will get rid of them. The French or African marigold releases a chemical from their roots that can kill nematodes. After the marigolds have finished blooming grind them into the soil or add them to your compost. Other plants that will repel nematodes are mustard, watercress, rutabaga and radishes.

THE GREEN KILLER

Next time you cook asparagus, save the cooking water. The water will contain a chemical that will kill nematodes. Pour or spray the cooking water in areas that are infested. Other plants that will repel nematodes include garlic, calendula, salvia, dahlias and velvet beans.

SEAWEED COMPOST

If you are able to acquire some seaweed, either place it on the soil or add it to your compost for a great nematode killer.

SUFFOCATE THEM

If you prepare a solution of corn oil mixed with water and sprinkle the solution near the roots it will kill off the nematodes. To make it easier to mix oil and water add 2 ampoules of lecithin to the mixture.

FERTILIZE THEM TO DEATH

If you use a fertilizer composed of 70% fish emulsion and 30% yucca extract (Pent-A-Vate™) nematodes will leave the plants alone.

GLUB, GLUB

If you flood an area where you are having a serious nematode problem, it will have to be under water for two years to get rid of the pest and all the egg masses.

ROOT-KNOT NEMATODE

This is not the good Nc nematode. This one thrives on infecting plants causing cell decay and root galls to form. It will release toxins and bacteria as it feeds on the plant roots. The galls are large, round formations on the roots. The galls will split open and cause the plant tissue to decay. The plants will wilt and be stunted.

THE FRENCH CONNECTION

Root-knot nematodes will not go near a garden or plants in an area where there are French marigolds *Tagetes patula*. If you plant a whole area with the marigolds foe a season and then plow them under you will never have these destructive nematodes. The marigolds actually release a toxin that is very poisonous to the nematodes.

TIE 'EM TIGHT, REAL TIGHT

PICKLEWORM AKA MELONWORM

The moths lay their eggs on the underneath sides of leaves on cucumbers, melons, pumpkins and squash. Squash is their number one favorite if it is available and will feed on the flowers and leaf buds. The caterpillars will feed on vegetation but a large number tend to find fruit and bore holes in them. The pickleworm is usually only found east of the Rockies and may also be found in New York State. The south is where the worst infestations are found, mainly in Florida and Texas.

SMELL THEM OUT
If you plant strong smelling herbs within your garden it will keep these pests out. They do not like onion and garlic plants.

WIREWORMS (CLICK BEETLES)

Identification:
The adults are called **"click beetles,"** which is the name they were given since when they right themselves after being turned over they hit the ground and it sounds like a "click." The larvae are very thin worms that have a leathery skin and three pairs of legs close to their head. They are yellow to dark red in color and can grow to 1½-inches long. They lay their eggs in the soil and will live for 3-4 years.

General Information:
The beetle got the name click beetle since it makes a clicking sound when it rights itself after being placed on its back. It loves to consume corn, peas, potato tubers, sweet potatoes, carrots and rutabaga. It also likes to munch on the roots of cabbage, onions, watermelon, cucumber and tomatoes.

SKEWER THEM
To trap wireworms you will need some wooden skewers, carrots and apples. Cut the apples and carrots into small pieces and place the skewer through a piece. Bury the food leaving the skewer where you can see it. The wireworms will eat the fruit or vegetable since it an easier meal and then you can remove the skewer and destroy them with extreme prejudice. They also love potatoes and they can be used to trap them as well by just placing pieces of potatoes into the soil and digging them up in a few days.

WORMS WILL KILL WORMS
If you apply Nc nematodes about two months before you plant, it should eliminate the problem. This is one of the best methods of control.

THEY DON'T LIKE BUCKWHEAT
Wireworms do not like to be around buckwheat or white mustard. If you plant these around the plants that they do like they will stay far away. Natural plants used as repellants work very well with a number of insects.

CHAPTER 20

MISCELLANEOUS ANIMALS

Miscellaneous Animals

OPOSSOMS

JUST HANGING AROUND

This is one of the more intelligent critters that will invade your premises looking for food and a safe location to raise their family. They can have as many as 25 babies in every litter but only 7-8 babies survive. The possum is not a good climber and tends to fall out of trees. Their favorite food is roadkill and they will wait by the side of the road until you hit an animal so that they can have dinner.

They are not fussy eaters and will also indulge in your compost pile and all types of vegetables. They love fruit when it is handy and will invade a trashcan if you leave it where they can get to it. When trapping possums be sure and wear heavy gloves since they are know to carry rabies.

EASILY TRAPPED

Possums are easily trapped, even though they are considered smart. When they see food as bait they tend to enter almost any trap to get at the food. Relocation is possible if you call the local animal control officer.

RABBITS

Rabbits and hares can have as many as 4-6 litters per year. Rabbits in the wild only live for 1-3 years and usually only 3-4 years in captivity. They love vegetables and prefer carrots, peas, lettuce, beans, beets and flowers but will a variety of foods. If they have trouble finding wild food they will visit your garden regularly. There are a few crops that rabbits don't like and will stay away from. These include squash, tomatoes, corn, cucumbers, peppers and potatoes. If these are bothered it will not be from rabbits.

POOR BUGS, NO CARROTS TODAY

A galvanized chicken wire fence works great providing it is sturdy and is placed about 1 foot underground and 3 feet above ground. Best to angle the bottom 6 inches outward to stop the rabbit from digging under the fence. Chicken wire also works around the bottom of trees since rabbits like to munch on the bark.

PUT UP A BARRIER

A very effective method of keeping rabbits away from your vegetable garden is to build a cylindrical barrier enclosure. It should be about 3 feet high around all trees and plants and use ¼ inch hardware cloth then bury the bottom of the enclosure 3 inches below the ground. Make sure there is 1-2 feet between the barrier and the plants. You can also build a 3-foot high fence of chicken wire since rabbits are not good climbers.

GET SPICY WITH THEM

A mixture of ground black pepper with a dash of cayenne pepper and some bone meal sprinkled around the areas should repel the rabbits. This may upset any pets you have as well but it does work on rabbits. Best to apply just after the sun goes down since rabbits prefer evening dining.

THE RABBIT TRAPPER

Trapping rabbits is easy; the problem is what to do with them once you trap them. It is against the law to release them where they will become someone else's pest so you have to come up with a good idea. They also tend to injure themselves trying to escape, which means now you have an injured animal to contend with. If you live in the country you may try and make rabbit stew, however, wild rabbit is a little tough to chew.

PLANT A DETERRENT

If you plant a border of wormwood around the area you wan to keep rabbits out of it should work great. Rabbits hate wormwood and will avoid it at all costs. Another deterrent is to just plant a row of lettuce where they can easily get to it. Many farmers find that this works great. They may even allow you to take some occasionally.

WOOD ASHES WORK GREAT

If you sprinkle wood ashes around your plants the rabbits will leave them alone. The only problem is that when it rains the wood ashes will lose their effectiveness and you will need to add more.

TALK RADIO

If you purchase an inexpensive small portable radio and place it in the garden covered with a protective plastic bag it will keep almost all the critters away. Animals that invade the garden are afraid that there is a human around.

GET A SNAKE

Rabbits are deathly afraid of snakes and will stay away, far away from your property if they see anything that resembles a snake. Rubber fake snakes are easy to purchase and tend to be an effective deterrent.

RABBITS LOVE SAPLINGS
Rabbits love to nibble on tender saplings and one of the best ways to stop them is to wrap the sapling with a piece of plastic pipe. Be sure and leave enough room for growth. There are also a number of commercial products that can be used to wrap the saplings. Most garden supply stores carry the wraps.

A LITTLE SHMEAR WILL DO YA
A very effective method of keeping rabbits and mice away from young trees and their tender bark is to smear some bacon grease or any other animal fat on the trunk of the tree to deter them.

SPACE AGE TECHNOLOGY
If you hang aluminum strips on string tied to wooden stakes that are 3 feet high it will scare the critters away.

RACCOONS

These night raiders attack during the night and love garbage cans. They can pry open most cans and are capable of springing traps and taking the bait without being caught in them. They are not fussy about what they will eat and consume insects, snails, vegetables, eggs, mice and even crayfish. Their favorite food is sweet corn with melons coming in a close second. They can even be found under chicken coops looking for grubs. They will eat chickens by biting off their heads and pulling the body's apart.

A LITTLE BIT WILL GO A LONG WAY
Raccoons tend to look for an easy meal before they have to work for one. If you sprinkle some hydrated lime around the garbage cans it will keep them away. A little ammonia, Lysol™ or any hot sauce placed on the lids works great too.

PHEEEW, WHAT WILL THE NEIGHBORS THINK
If you hang some old smelly clothes on your fence or on a post that is staked near their entry point it will repel them. Raccoons do not like the human smell and will avoid it at all costs.

CORN IS THEIR FAVORITE FOOD
If you are growing corn the raccoons will find it. One of the best methods of keeping them away from your corn is to sprinkle the corn with water and then dust the corn with cayenne pepper. You can also spray the corn with a solution of ½ cup of cayenne, 1 pint of water and 1 tablespoon of Ivory Liquid Soap™. Allow the mixture to stand overnight before straining and spraying.

ONLY IF YOU HAVE THE TENDER TOUCH
If you rub your hand over each ear of corn it will keep the animals away. They do not like the smell of humans. If you have a big field of corn this may not be practical unless you have plenty of time and nothing else to do.

PEEK-A-BOO
Raccoons like to look up from their meal occasionally especially if they hear a strange sound. They stand up on their hind legs for a quick peek. They prefer not to dine in areas where they cannot do this easily. Some farmers will plant pumpkin seeds among the corn. Which results in large leaves. This stops the raccoons from seeing if one of their predators is coming and they will stay out of the cornfield.

SAVE YOUR POOCH'S HAIR
Raccoons do not like to be around dogs. If you have a dog groomer near you, try and get the clippings from them. If you even offer to pay them a few dollars for hair they throw away they will probably be delighted. Spread the hair around the areas where you have problems and you will never see another raccoon or rabbit.

TRAPS WILL DO THE JOB
Traps to capture the raccoons can be purchased through many mail order houses or borrowed from your local animal control agency. There are two popular traps the Havahart Trap™ and the Safe-N-Sound™ trap. Since raccoons have a sweet tooth the best bait is honey-soaked bread, marshmallows and peanut butter is another favorite.

NOISES WORK GREAT
Any item that makes noise will scare raccoons off. This can be a noisy windmill or pinwheel device or a portable radio. Many farmers place a portable radio in their fields with the volume turned all the way up. Hopefully your home and your neighbor's home is not too close to the field. The only cost is for batteries.

WIRE MESH YOUR PLANTS
If you have a serious problem: just place wire mesh around your plants. They don't like walking on the mesh and will not come near the plants.

SKUNKS

Skunks really are not much trouble to most gardeners since they feed mainly on insects and small animal pests, which account for about 50% of their diet. They will, however, eat the lower ears of corn. Skunks love grubs and will dig for them in your lawn or garden making them a pest. They will eat pet food if you leave it out, which is not a bad idea since they will leave your garden alone.

A PROBLEM SKUNK
Trapping a skunk should probably be left to professionals or animal control since some do carry rabies. They can be trapped; by placing the trap inside a large plastic bag, keeping it open and baiting the trap with dry cat food. Skunks are usually found in pairs and if you trap one the other will surely be around to see where their partner is.

OUTSMELLING A SKUNK

If you take some old clothes that have been worn and not washed and pour some household ammonia on them then leave them out where you expect the skunk to enter or around your garden it will repel them and they will never come back. Skunks will remember the smell of ammonia and rarely come back to a location where they smelled the odor.

THE GARDENER'S FRIEND

They may be smelly when threatened, but these animals are one of the gardener's best friends. Hopefully they will not become a resident under your home or in a shed. They are great rodent hunters and can live on a variety of insects such as grasshoppers, cutworms, tobacco worms, potato beetles, grubs and armyworms.

SNAKES

There are only four poisonous snakes in the United States. These are the rattlesnake, copperhead, coral snake and the water moccasin. Snakes are one of the best controllers of rodents and should be tolerated unless you have the poisonous type on your property. Bull snakes, king snakes, boas, rat snakes and gopher snakes help keep the gopher and mole population down, which is very beneficial. Garter snakes love snails and slugs and king snakes will kill the poisonous snakes as well as rodents.

Garter, brown and green snakes will eat snails, slugs and small varmints, however, they do like a tasty earthworm occasionally, which is not good for the garden.

REPELLANTS DON'T REPEL

There are no snake repellants that have been tried that will work to keep snakes away from your property. A number have been tried commercially and they end up killing the snakes.

SNAKE-PROOF FENCE

Best to use a very heavy galvanized screen about 36 inches wide and use ¼ inch mesh. You will need to bury the lower edges 2-3 inches in the ground and then slant it outward from the bottom to the top at a 30-degree angle. Your supporting stakes should be inside the fence and the gates must be tightly fitted. This is an expensive method if you have a large yard. Best to just fence in your children's play area.

CHAPTER 21

BIRDS

BIRDS

Because of the number of insects birds consume, they are considered very beneficial to your yard and especially the garden. There are many birds that you should try and attract to your property. However, to attract the right birds you will need to feed them foods that they prefer and build them houses that they can reside in. Some of the foods recommended are for indoor bird pets as well as outdoor wild birds.

BIRD FOOD

CANARY FOOD
The following ingredients will be needed:

1	Ounces of dried egg yolk
1	Ounce of powdered poppy heads
1	Ounce of powdered cuttlefish bone
2	Ounces of granulated sugar

Place all the ingredients into a small bowl and mix well. Store the feed in a well-sealed container in a cool dry location.

PARROT GRIT
The following ingredients will be needed:

1	Teaspoon of coarse, sharp sand
1	Teaspoon of powdered charcoal (fine)
1	Teaspoon of ashes (filtered and clean)
1	Teaspoon of flowers of sulfur

Place all the ingredients into a sifter and sift together, then keep a portion of the mixture in the parrot's cage at all times.

MAKING MIXED BIRDSEED
The following ingredients will be needed:

6	Ounces of canary seed
2	Ounces of rapeseed
1	Ounces of Maw seed
2	Ounces of millet seed

Place all the seeds in a jar and shake well. This formula is mainly for wild birds.

MAKING MOCKINGBIRD FOOD

The following ingredients will be needed:

2	Ounces of cayenne pepper
8	Ounces of rapeseed
16	Ounces of hemp seed
2	Ounces of corn meal
2	Ounces of rice
8	Ounces of crushed cracker
2	Ounces of lard oil

Place the first 6 ingredients into a bowl and crush into a powder, then add the oil and blend well.

MAKING CARDINAL FOOD

The following ingredients will be needed:

8	Ounces of sunflower seed
16	Ounces of hemp seed
10	Ounces of canary seed
8	Ounces of wheat
6	Ounces of rice

Place all the ingredients into a bowl and grind into a powder.

HOW TO ATTRACT BIRDS

BARN SWALLOW

These birds like an area where there is available water and mud and you must provide straw for their nests. They like a 6"X6" shelve for their nesting support and it needs to be 8-12 feet above the ground. They like eaves and well-protected areas.

BLUEBIRD

These birds like a birdbath that is high enough off the ground so that cats can't get to it. They prefer mulberry, holly, blueberry, wild cherry and Virginia creeper plants to munch on. They are fussy about their birdhouses and they would prefer a 5"X5"X8" birdhouse with 1½" entry holes about 6 inches above the floor. If you place the nest 5 feet off the ground it will discourage the sparrows; who prefer nest that are higher up.

CHICKADEE

They prefer a diet of peanut butter, suet, sunflower seeds and some breadcrumbs. Their birdhouse should be 4"X4"X8" with the holes 1 1/8th inches and should be 6 inches above the floor. The house needs to be 8-15 feet high.

KESTREL

Wild birdseed is their favorite, a good mix will do. Their birdhouse should be 8"X8"X12" with a 3 inch hole that is 9-12 inches above the floor. It should be at least 10 feet above the ground but not more than 30 feet.

KINGLET

Prefers to eat suet, wild birdseed, cracked nuts and raw peanuts. Likes to nest in conifers preferably near the northern gardens.

MOCKINGBIRD (from the hill)

These birds are fussy and insist on a nice birdbath and attractive surroundings. They prefer to eat crab apples, cherry, blueberries, grapes and blackberries. However, they won't turn down a meal of dogwood, pasture rose, red cedar, elderberry, mulberry, manzanita and Virginia creeper.

OWL (old hooty)

Prefers to nest in large shade trees, oak trees or conifers. If they find a dead tree with a hollow hole they will reside there before almost any other location. They are night hunters and eat rodents and prefer a grassy area to hunt in.

OWL (barn)

They are fussy and require that you build them a nesting box 10"X18"X16" that has a 6 inch opening and about 4 inches from the floor. They dine on rodents and small animals and like an open field or pasture nearby.

OWL (saw-whet)

You will need to build a nesting box that is 6"X6"X10" that has a 2½" entry hole that is 8 inches above the floor. The house needs to be securely fastened 15-20 feet above the ground.

OWL (screecher)

Their home must be 8"X8"X14" and have a 3 inch hole. The house must be about 12-30 feet off the ground and must be in a secluded area since they like their privacy.

PHOEBE

These birds require a nesting platform that is about 6-8 inches square and 8-12 feet off the ground. They would prefer to be under an eave or in any protected area.

PURPLE MARTIN

These are apartment dwellers but don't put the apartment house up until the Martin's arrive or the starlings will move in. You will need 15-20 small apartments measuring 6"X6"X6" with the entry hole about 2½ inches and 1 inch from the floor. The birdhouse should be 15-20 feet off the ground. They eat wild birdseed and insects with a worm or two for dessert.

TITMOUSE

This bird will do anything for a doughnut but also loves to eat suet, nuts, sunflower seeds, peanut butter and breadcrumbs. The bird likes to be around elderberry, wild strawberry, pine, beech, mulberry and pine. The birdhouse needs to be 4"X4"X8" and have a 1¼ inch entry hole about 6 inches off the floor. The house ideally needs to be 8-15 feet off the ground.

WARBLER

Prefers nice landscaping and pleasant surroundings (fussy bird). They will go crazy for mulberry and especially raspberries but also like wild rose, barberry, hedge, privet, grapevines, current, elder, which provide additional nesting sites.

WREN

The birdhouse must be 4"X4"X6" with 1 inch holes for entry and the holes should be about 4 inches off the floor. The birdhouse should be 8-10 feet high.

Hints About Building A Birdhouse

- Don't bother with a perch since they are rarely used.
- Drill some ventilation holes just under the roofline and a few in the floor for drainage.
- The house should blend in with the scenery and not be frilly.
- The inside should be rough and even if bark is showing it is best.
- Use screws not nails to insure the stability and quality.
- Hollowing out a small log works great as a birdhouse.
- The roof must be waterproof.
- The dimensions should be for the bird for which you are building it.
- Never use screw eyes to hang the house up since they will loosen in time.
- Hinge the bottom so that it will be easy to clean. The house needs to be cleaned after the birds leave.
- You can be creative as long as the house does not look out-of-place in its surroundings.
- If you are not handy, buy one in your garden shop.

PROBLEM BIRDS

If birds are a problem it is best to identify which bird is really causing the problem. Only three birds are really bad pests that will damage a garden enough to warrant going after them. They are crows, starlings, woodpeckers and blackbirds. However, damage that looks like birds are doing it may be from raccoons or other animals.

BUZZ AROUND, BUZZ AROUND

If you want to keep all birds away from your garden and plants, try using a piece of commercial buzzing or humming tape. This tape is stretched across an area near the garden and will make noise when the wind blows to scare away the birds.

ORDER A CAT SCARECROW
Make a cutout of a cat and decorate it to look like the real thing. If birds are a problem this works great.

THE OLD HOOTY OWL
This really works better than almost any other means of keeping all birds away. Make sure that you purchase an owl with a movable head. When the wind blows the head moves around the body.

PANTYHOSE FOR SQUASH????????
If you want to keep the birds away from melons and squash, just place the squash or melon in an old pantyhose leg.

GET A SNEAKY SNAKE
Not all but most birds are afraid of snakes so you may want to purchase a realistic rubber snake or use a piece of garden hose.

PORCUPINE WIRE
There are a number of tactile repellants made to keep birds away. They are called porcupine wires and are sold under the names of Nixalite™ and Cat Claw™. These are permanent repellants that are usually placed on windowsills, eaves, ledges and anywhere that the birds will roost. The prongs extend outward and they can be fastened to any surface. These will cause some discomfort to the bird but will not do serious damage.

VENTS ARE PROBLEMS
Many birds tend to nest in vents, especially dryer vents. It is best to cover these vents with a netting to prevent the problem. Special plastic bird netting is available through a garden supply house or from InterNet, Inc. at (800) 328-8456.

RING-A-DING-DING
If you have a good view of your garden most of the time when at home during the day, just rig a long string to a bell and have the string where you can get to it from the house. When you see birds bothering your garden pull the string and the bell will ring and they will leave the premises.

BUILD A HOUSE FOR MARTINS
One of the best insect eaters is the purple martin. If you have them in your area and you build them a house, they will assist you in keeping your garden insect-free. Best to obtain a book on birdhouses and build one for their special needs.

SET UP A BIRD DINER
One of the best methods of attracting birds is to place a number of feeders around your property. A good variety of different seeds will attract different birds and they will have your insects for dessert.

ARE BIRDS EATING YOUR CHERRIES?
Birds can be kept from eating your cherries by spraying the cherries with salt water. The birds may also be eating the cherries because they are thirsty and the cherries are an excellent source of water for them.

BIRDS PREFER TART BERRIES
If you are having a problem with birds eating your sweet berries, just plant some tart berries near the sweet ones and the bird will only eat the tart ones.

POPCORN FOR THE BIRDS
If you are having a problem with birds bothering your corn, they may just be after the corn earworms. However, to be on the safe side, just soak some popcorn corn overnight and throw it on the ground around you ears of corn. They prefer the easy meal instead of bothering your corn.

SAVE THOSE STRAWBERRIES
One of only ways to stop birds from consuming your strawberries is to throw some netting over the patch. Birds get scared off and think that they may get tangled up in the netting.

SAVING THE FRUIT TREES
There are a number of items that can be hung in trees to discourage birds from feeding on the fruit. Try using, a ball of crumpled up aluminum foil, empty milk cartons, fake snake, owl or a paper plate with strips of fabric attached. Best to alternate these items since the birds are smart and if they see the same item in the tree all the time they will be back eating the fruit.

PLANT FOOD FOR THE BIRDS
If you plant some of the bird's favorite foods they will leave the rest of the garden and trees alone. These include bayberry, honeysuckle, wild grape, juniper berry, yews, verbena, crab apple, persimmon trees, California poppy, columbine tree, cotoneaster and Virginia creeper.

SPARROWS LOVE APHIDS
If you have a lot of sparrows round your property they should easily take care of any aphid problems you have. Aphids are one of their favorite food sources.

BLACKBIRDS

Blackbirds include 21 different species of bird with the most common being the red-winged blackbird. They are found throughout the United States and tend to frequent the suburban areas. They are most damaging to cornfields just before harvest time and also love to feast on sunflower heads. While 30% of their diet is insects, which does help, the balance of their diet is usually your corn or berry patch.

ROOSTING CONTROL
All trees should be thinned out that are near your garden to reduce their nesting locations. The birds do not feel safe unless they have adequate cover.

AIR-SOCK PEOPLE
The tall air-socks in the shape of people that you can see around car dealerships will work great to keep blackbirds away. Check with your local car dealership to find out where to purchase them.

DECOYS WORK GREAT
Owl and hawk decoys will deter these birds without a problem. They are deathly afraid of these birds and will not go near your garden.

SCARE THEM WITH TAPE
You can purchase a bird scare reflecting tape in garden supply stores. Place long strips of the reflecting tape on poles around your garden. When the breezes blow the tape moves and the reflection scares the birds away. Twist the tape before attaching it to the poles to be more effective. It also makes a weird humming noise that scares them off.

BALLOONS TO THE RESCUE
Place some balloons with helium in them and a face painted on the balloon to scare the blackbirds away.

TRY A TAPE RECORDER
If you tape the sounds of human voices or a tractor, etc. and place it in your garden it will scare the birds off.

NYLON NETTING WILL BOTHER THEM
There is special thin nylon netting that can be placed over your garden to deter birds that works very well. Check with your local garden supply or hardware store.

CROWS

These are one of the smartest birds around and you may have to try a few different methods mentioned for blackbirds to keep them at bay. Crows have even been seen using a stick as a tool to dislodge seeds instead of getting their beaks in the dirt. Crows will eat 600 different types of crops, insects and foods of every kind imaginable, even roadkill. Corn, however, is their favorite food and crows will ignore scarecrows so don't even bother with them. Try all the methods mentioned for blackbirds, but alternate methods since they catch on fast.

PIGEONS

HOO! ME THAT'S HOO
This is sure-fire and I use it myself with 100% results. Place a plastic owl with a moveable head so that it moves in the wind and you will never have another pigeon problem. Pigeons are deathly afraid of owls.

SCARED OF THEIR REFLECTION
Almost all birds and especially pigeons hate to see their reflection in a mirror. If you glue down some mirrors so that when a bird or pigeon lands on a flat surface they will see themselves, they will leave immediately.

STARLINGS

These are real pests and will chase away the good birds and even take over their nests and birdhouses. A flock of starlings can devastate a garden in a short period of time before you even know what happened. Their favorite foods are cherries, blueberries and grapes. However, they will eat fruits and seeds if the berries are not available. They can be found all over the United States and Southern Canada.

Starlings will fly 10-15 miles away from their roosting areas in their daily hunt for food. They are also attracted to livestock areas and will eat their feed and water. Many of the same methods used for blackbirds will also work very well.

STICK-'EM-UP

There is a product called Roost No More™, which can be placed on ledges and other areas that they will make their nest on. Tanglefoot™ also works well as a deterrent if you smear it along areas that they may roost on.

THEY WILL GET BOARD

If you place a board at a 45⁰ angle on any ledges it will stop them from making a nest. If you keep a bright light in areas where they may nest it will also discourage them.

ATTACK OF THE BERRY EATERS

If you have a serious problem in your area, you will have to place netting over all berry bushes on poles, held down with rocks around the edges. They will go to extreme lengths to get berries.

WOODPECKERS

Woodpeckers can do a lot of damage and can be a real pest. They are usually after carpenter bees and tend to look for their tunnels.

VINEGAR DOES THE TRICK

To discourage the woodpeckers from digging into the holes looking for bugs, just spray a solution of 2 tablespoons of white vinegar mixed in 1 quart of water into the holes or around the areas they frequent.

CHAPTER 22

PROBLEMS AND SOLUTIONS
FRUITS & VEGETABLES

PROBLEMS AND SOLUTIONS
FRUITS & VEGETABLES

GET THE LEAD OUT

If your garden is near a road and you are worried about auto emissions getting on your plants, just spray them with a solution of 2½ teaspoons of white vinegar in 1-gallon of tap water.

ARTICHOKES

ARTICHOKE PEST PROBLEM SOLVERS

THE PROBLEM	CAUSED BY
Holes bored in stems, discoloration of choke	Artichoke plume moth
Sticky substance on chokes or black mold	Aphids
Holes in leaves and stem, blackening of choke	Snails & slugs
Curled leaves, small plants, misshapen chokes	Curly dwarf virus
Grey or brown fungus growth	Botrytis fungus

ASPARAGUS

ASPARAGUS PEST PROBLEM SOLVERS

THE PROBLEM	CAUSED BY
New spears are chewed on	Snails & slugs
Growing tips chewed with black blemishes	Asparagus beetle
Rust-colored spots on spears	Fungus damage
Weak spears with discoloration	Fusarium wilt
Whitish or yellowish stippling on shoots	Spider mites
Plants stunted and rosetted	European asparagus aphid
Small holes eaten out of new spears	Cutworms

AVOCADO

AVOCADO PEST PROBLEM SOLVERS

THE PROBLEM	CAUSED BY
Leaves skeletonized and sometimes webbed	Amorbia caterpillar
Leaves skeletonized, no webbing, scars on fruit	Omnivorous looper
Leaves smaller than normal, yellowish, feeder root blackened	Avocado root rot
Purple discoloration around leaf veins	Six-spotted mite
Leaves spotted, yellow mites with webbing	Persea mite
Leaves turn brown	Avocado brown mite
Brown discoloration on fruit, tiny brown varnish spots	Greenhouse thrips

BEANS

THE EARLY BIRD GETS THE BEAN

If you want your snap beans to produce over a longer period of time, just pick them when the beans are about pencil width. Make sure that the seeds are just visible. If you wait too long the plant will make the seeds larger instead of the meat of the bean and use up all its energy.

IS IT A BEANSTALK OR A CORNSTALK?

If you plant pole beans next to corn stalks, the beans will use the corn stalk and wind its way up making it easier to grow them without putting up pole for them.

BEAN PEST PROBLEM SOLVERS

THE PROBLEM	CAUSED BY
Seedlings collapse after they come up	Seedcorn maggot
Plants weak, leaves yellow or dying	Stem rot
Plants wilt and turn yellow, fine webbing on underneath side of leaves	Spider mite
Leaves curled and deformed, may have shiny appearance from honeydew and blackened	Aphids

White strippling on upper surface of leaves	Leafhoppers
Leaves turn yellow, slightly curled, cloud of tiny white insects fly up when plant disturbed	Whiteflies
Stunted seedlings with misshapen leaves	Thrips
Holes or leaves skeletonized	Cucumber beetle
Buds and flowers drop off. Beans pitted	Lygus bug
Blossoms drop off	Low soil moisture, smog
Stunted plants, roots have knots or beads	Nematodes
Tiny white grubs inside pod, round holes	Bean weevil
Holes in pods, seed hollow and eaten	Lycaenid pod borer
Chewing damage on pods or flowers	Corn earworm

BEETS

IF YOU LIKE THEM YOUNG AND TENDER
Try sowing the beets in a short row about every two weeks and begin four weeks before the last frost during spring.

HOW SWEET IT IS
Beets grown in the spring and fall are usually sweeter than the beets grown in the summer. The cool temperatures tend to cause the beet to store more sugar. If you must grow beets in the summer and would like them sweet, then mulch them to keep the ground as cool as possible.

BERRIES

PLANT THEM OR CHILL THEM
Strawberries need to be planted as soon as possible after being purchased. If you can't plant them, then you need to store them in a refrigerator at 40ºF to keep them dormant. When you remove them, they must be planted immediately or the yield will be reduced.

THE SOUTH WINS THIS ONE
If you plant strawberries on a south-facing slope instead of a north-facing slope, they will bear fruit at least a week earlier.

DON'T WANT THOSE SUNSHADES

If you plant strawberries in narrow rows you will produce more berries. When you plant in wide rows, the plants in the middle of the rows will receive too much shade.

MATURE STRAWBERRIES IN 8 WEEKS??????????

The secret to harvesting mature strawberries in only 8 weeks will depend on the following:

- Plants should be spaced 4 inches apart in rows of 12 inches wide and allow enough room to walk between rows.
- Make sure you mulch the plants and allow them to flower.
- Remove all runners.
- The first year's crop will ripen about 2 months later. The second year's crop will be larger and will come in earlier.
- Forget the old matted row system of planting.

BRRRRRRRRRRRRRRRRRRR

Place about a 2-inch layer of straw over strawberry plants to protect them during the winter. More than 2 inches tends to allow water to percolate through the straw and suffocate the plants. This results in the soil being unable to breathe and allowing carbon dioxide to build up and kill the roots.

DON'T GET BLUE OVER BLUEBERRIES

Blueberries are one of the berry families that do not need a lot of feeding. If you have mature bushes, you should only feed them about 1 pound of a quality cottonseed meal every year to provide you with an excellent yield.

SOME BERRIES DON'T NEED AN OLD CANE

Blackberries, dewberries and most raspberry varieties produce the fruit on "canes" that grew the year before. After harvest pruning is essential in order to grow a good crop the following year. Cut the canes at ground level and do not allow them to remain in the garden. Take care not to damage the new canes that are growing since these will provide you with next years crop.

BERRY PEST PROBLEM SOLVERS

THE PROBLEM	CAUSED BY
Blackberries don't turn black enough, become red and sour	Redberry mite
Leaves stippled and yellow, dried out and brown, underside of leaves with strands of webbing	Spider mites
Tips of young shoots wilt in sprung, thick white worm in cane	Raspberry horntail
New shoots wilt in spring, grub burrowing in cane	Raspberry cane borer
Plants stunted, cane dies, worm tunneling in cane	Crown borers
White winding trails on canes in spring or summer	Bushberry cane miner
Young stems wilt, partially chewed canes	Cutworm
Buds and new growth eaten in spring, webbed together	Leafroller, orange tortrix
Tiny holes in leaves and skeletonized	Raspberry sawfly
Canes covered with white crust or brownish bumps	Scale
Tiny green insects along stems or on new growth	Raspberry aphid
Tiny white spots on leaves in spring, underneath sides of leaves inhabited by whitish bugs	Rose leafhopper
Berries deformed or scarred, thin insects on berries	Flower thrips

CARROTS

ARE YOU SUFFERING FROM CRUSTY SOIL?

Crust tends to form on the ground and causes patchy carrot growth. The seedlings are not strong enough to break through in some areas. Never cover carrot seeds with soil, instead use peat, compost or vermiculite.

CARROT PEST PROBLEM SOLVERS

THE PROBLEM	CAUSED BY
Carrots do not break soil	Seedling pest
Roots hairy or misshapen	Root knot nematode

Carrots curled around each other	Planted too close together
Roots have surface tunnels with rusty excrement	Carrot rust fly
White growth on leaves	Powdery mildew

RADISHES TO THE RESCUE
Radishes have stronger sprouts and can break through the soil easier than carrot sprouts. If you plant radishes with the carrots they will break through the soil crust and allow the carrots to sprout more easily.

CAULIFLOWER

BROWN OUT
It is a common practice to tie the leaves up around a cauliflower plant as it grows to bleach the heads. Instead of the old method, try gathering up the leaves and then place a brown bag over the head. The air will still be able to circulate and will prevent rotting that is common when the leaves are tied.

COLE CROP PEST PROBLEM SOLVERS
(Broccoli, Brussels sprouts, Cabbage, Cauliflower)

THE PROBLEM	CAUSED BY
Irregular holes in leaves, seedlings damaged	Caterpillars
Small holes in leaves, stunted plant growth	Diamondback moth caterpillar
Deformed, curled leaves, gray-green insects on leaves, possibly honeydew	Aphids
Plants wilted, with misshapen leaves, browning	Harlequin bug
Tunnels through roots of seedlings, wilting	Cabbage maggot
Stunted plants, wilting, yellowish leaves	Cyst nematode
Heads split prematurely	Heavy watering after dry spell

CHIVES

A WARM CHIVE IS A HEALTHY CHIVE
If you start seeds in the late summer and keep them inside where they can get adequate sun, you will have a nice supply of chives during the winter months.

CORN

DON'T HURT THOSE LITTLE SUCKERS

Corn suckers are the small shoots that grow out from the stalk at ground level. Many people remove them, but the latest research shows that they will not reduce yield and if there is a drought they will send nutrients to the main stalk. If you do remove them and don't remove them properly you may cause diseases to enter the stalk.

CORN PEST PROBLEM SOLVERS

THE PROBLEM	CAUSED BY
Worms eating kernels or tassels	Corn earworm
Holes in leaves	Armyworm, corn earworm, beetles
Ears only partially developed	Earwigs
Sticky or shiny leaves, small plants stunted	Aphids

FIGS

PUT A PLASTIC BAG ON JACK FROST

Figs do not like frost and the best method to protect them is to cover the branches that will bear fruit with a plastic bag before a frost appears. If you tie small cans filled with a few stones each to the bottom of the bags they cannot blow off.

GRAPES

GRAPE PEST PROBLEM SOLVERS

THE PROBLEM	CAUSED BY
Pale-colored stippling on top of leaves, leaf may die and turn brown, older leaves die first	Grape leafhopper
Yellow stippling on top of leaves spreading through main veins, webbing-underside of leaf	Spider mites
Pale reddish swelling on young leaves upper surfaces, underneath has plant hairs	Grape erineum mite
Honeydew and black sooty mold, black speckling of grapes, flies fly up when disturbed	Grape whitefly
Honeydew drips from clusters, black mold	Grape mealybug

Scarring and redu... grapes have dark...	...Western flower thrips
Brown bumps on...	European fruit lecanium
Whitish bumps...	Grape scale
Lower leaves f... berries webbe...	Omnivorous leafroller
Pencil-sized le... summer, redu...	Grape leaffolder
Leaves and b...	Orange tortrix
Underneath s...	Western grapeleaf skeletonizer
Buds eaten...	Cutworms
Tiny round... ...n	Achemon sphinx moth
Large amo...	Grasshoppers
Young lea... shoots a...	Hoplia beetle
New sho... crotch, ... in	Branch & twig borer
Premat... owth	Grape phylloxera
Slower then normal... s	Nematodes

LETTUCE

LETTUCE PEST PROBLEM SOLVERS

THE PROBLEM	CAUSED BY
Curled, distorted leaves, honeydew present	Aphids
Damaged seedlings, crowns chewed	Armyworms, corn earworms
Ragged holes in leaves, holes in head	Loopers
Skeletonized leaves	Armyworms
Small holes in leaves or skeletonization	Vegetable weevil

| Black areas on borders of inner leaves | Hot weather |
| Torn areas on leaves, small pieces missing | Birds, rabbits, kids |

OKRA

GET OUT THE HAMMER AND CHISEL

Okra seeds have a very hard outer coat, which can hamper germination resulting in an uneven patchy garden. There a number of ways to avoid the potential problem:

- Barely nick the seed coating with a sharp knife.
- Place the seeds on a piece of fine sandpaper and rub them with another sheet.
- The seeds can be soaked in tepid water at room temperature for 24 hours.
- The seeds can be placed in the freezer for about 12 hours, and then soaked in hot tap water for 30 minutes just before planting.

ONIONS

ONION & GARLIC PEST PROBLEM SOLVERS

THE PROBLEM	CAUSED BY
Tunnels and cavities in bulbs & stems, wilting and yellowing	Onion maggot
Leaves turning silvery	Onion thrips
Seedlings are pale, thickened, deformed, bulbs swollen at base, leaftips dying	Stem & bulb nematode

PEAS

PEA PEST PROBLEM SOLVERS

THE PROBLEM	CAUSED BY
Surface scarring of pods or deformed pods	Thrips
Leaves and stems covered with honeydew and black sooty mold	Aphids
Holes in leaves, greenish-yellow beetle	Cucumber beetle
Leaves are skeletonized	Armyworm
Off white stippling on upper leaf surface and fine webbing on underneath side of leaf	Spider mite

Curving white trails in leaves, stems or pods	Leafminers
Half-moon chewed notches on edges of leaves	Pea leaf weevil adults
Pods partially damaged or removed	Birds, rabbits, kids
White grubs with brown heads in peas and round holes on pods	Pea weevil

PEPPERS

GIVE THEM SOMETHING TO READ

Next time you plant peppers, try wrapping each plant stem in 6X6-inch square of newspaper. Dip the newspaper in cool tap water before wrapping each pepper plant. When the roots are kept moist it keep away the cutworms.

PEPPERS & EGGPLANT

PEPPERS & EGGPLANT PEST PROBLEM SOLVERS

THE PROBLEM	CAUSED BY
Buds or fruit turns yellow or drop from plant, pods that remain may turn yellow or be misshapen	Pepper weevil
Curled and distorted leaves or stunted plants	Aphids
Small holes in leaves worse at lower levels	Flea beetle
White frothy foam on eggplant stems	Spittle beetle
Peppers have small worm holes	Corn earworm or leafroller
Leaves wilt and turn yellow	Whiteflies

POTATOES

POTATO PEST PROBLEM SOLVERS

THE PROBLEM	CAUSED BY
Tunneling in tubers, pink eyes with silk	Potato tuberworm
Curled and distorted leaves, stunted plant	Aphids
Leaves curled upward, older leaves yellow, edges of younger leaves turn purple	Potato psyllid
White stippling on upper leaf surface, leaf edges yellow or brown	Leafhopper
Leaves have many holes, tubers have bumps, shallow winding trails on upper surface of leaf	Flea beetle
Bumps on tubers, swelling on roots, brown spots	Nematodes
Leaves missing, yellow-striped beetle visible	Colorodo potato beetle

PUMPKIN

BOARD UP YOUR PUMPKINS

When your pumpkins or squash start to mature, try placing a small board under each fruit. This will protect the fruit from soil-borne bacteria and fungus.

CUCURBIT CROP PEST PROBLEM SOLVERS
(Cantaloupe, Cucumber, Pumpkin, Squash, Watermelon)

THE PROBLEM	CAUSED BY
Deformed or curled leaves, tiny, soft bodied insects on underneath side of leaves. Honeydew or black sooty mold present	Aphids
Fine strippling on leaves, yellowing or browning of leaves, orange or red dots	Spider mites
Yellowish leaves, honeydew present, clouds of tiny white bugs	Whiteflies
White strippling on upper leaf surface	Leafhopper
Holes in leaves, wilting, scarred runners	Cucumber beetle
Leaves have small yellow specs that turn brown, vines wilt	Squash bug

Swelling or beads on roots, low yield	Nematodes

RADISHES

FRIENDS FOREVER

Radish seeds develop strong sprouts that are capable of breaking through the ground. Parsnips do not have very strong sprouts and need the radish sprouts to open up the soil for them.

RADISH PEST PROBLEM SOLVERS

THE PROBLEM	CAUSED BY
Small plants wilt and die, grooves on root surfaces, tunnels in roots	Cabbage maggot
Foliage deformed with whitish-yellow spots	Harlequin bug
Tiny holes in leaves	Flea beetle

SPINACH

SPINACH PEST PROBLEM SOLVERS

THE PROBLEM	CAUSED BY
Leaves partially eaten and green caterpillar hanging around	Loopers
Leaves yellowing	Aphids
Leaves have green or yellow spots with maggots in them	Leafminers

STRAWBERRIES

STRAWBERRY PEST PROBLEM SOLVERS

THE PROBLEM	CAUSED BY
New growth becomes stunted and crinkled, flowers wither and die	Cyclamen mite
Dry brown areas on lower leaf surface in spring, leaves get brown and die	Spider mites
Leaves rolled up and webbed together with silk, small holes, look for tiny caterpillar	Leafroller

Ripe fruit has large holes, some leaves eaten	Cutworms
Deep holes in berries with dried slime around	Snails & slugs
Holes in fruit with oval bugs in them	Sowbugs
Tiny holes in ripening fruit, no slime around	Earwigs
Plant wilting and dying in spring or fall, whitish caterpillar in crowns	Strawberry crown moth
Leaves have scalloped look, smaller roots eaten	Otiorhynchus root weevil
Honeydew and black sooty mold	Strawberry aphid
Berries have deep furrows or twisted shape, deformed areas, large hollowed seeds	Lygus bug
Plants wilt in warm weather even when watered, cottony deposit on roots	Ground mealybug

TOMATOES

TO FLOWER OR NOT TO FLOWER
If you would like early tomatoes, purchase plants with flowers. Don't be upset if the flowers fall off while you are planting them. They are in their reproductive stage and more flowers will appear shortly. If the plants are young and without flowers they will bear fruit later but will give a better harvest,

SPEEDY PLANTING
The easiest method of planting tomatoes plants is to use a bulb planter. It will result in a deep hole and will not take a lot of work.

MOOOOOOO
Dry cow manure is the best fertilizer for tomato plants. It will give you a higher yield. Use about 100 pounds per square feet in plants that are spaced about 3 feet apart.

TOMATO PEST PROBLEM SOLVERS

THE PROBLEM	CAUSED BY
Worms in ripe tomatoes	Tomato fruitworm
Worms tunneling in fruit	Potato tuberworm
Leaves mined and folded, tiny worms tunneling	Tomato pinworm
Leaves eaten and only stems remain, fruit small	Hornworms

Fruit surface eaten or hollowed out	Snails & slugs
Yellowish cloudy spots on ripe tomatoes, soft spots	Stink bugs
Leaves totally eaten off young plants	Vegetable weevil
Lower leaves and stems are bronze color, plants losing leaves	Tomato russet mite
Leaves yellow and slightly curled, insects fly when disturbed, greenish scales on underneath side of leaves	Whiteflies
Leaves curled downward, fruit with shiny spots	Aphids
Seedlings or transplants with holes in leaves	Flea beetle
Poor yield plants, yellow leaves, swelling or beads on roots	Root knot nematodes
Irregular yellow blotches on leaves	Powdery mildew

TURNIPS

TURNIP PEST PROBLEMS

THE PROBLEM	CAUSED BY
Distorted plants, curling, wilting, insects on underneath sides of leaves	Aphids
Holes in leaves, chewing on buds and roots	Vegetable weevil
Irregular holes in leaves, seedlings destroyed	Caterpillars
Deformed leaves with yellow spotting, possible wilting	Harlequin bug
Tunneling in roots of seedlings, wilting	Cabbage maggot

FIGHTING PLANT DISEASES

HELP! MY BLOSSOMS ARE ROTTING

Blossom-end rotting, is usually caused by too little water or too much water. This problem is common on tomato, peppers and melon plants. If drought is the problem the plants will need at least 1-inch of water per week and keep the plants well mulched. The other cause of blossom-end rot is lack of calcium in the soil. The soil Ph should be about 6-6.5, which can be controlled by using limestone.

MY POTATOES ARE SCABING

To stop potatoes from developing scab, you will need to plant a new breed of potato called the scab-free potato or rotate your crop. If you rotate your crop, do not plant them in a field that has been growing turnips, carrots or beets since these vegetables tend to develop scab as well.

FIRE BLIGHT – CALL THE FIRE DEPARTMENT

Blight in an apple orchard is not uncommon. The best method to combat the problem is to spray with a 50:50 solution of apple cider vinegar and water. Make sure you spray after each rainfall, especially if you see burnt leaves.

BLIGHT PREVENTION

Celery is very susceptible to blight and the best method of avoiding the problem is to soak the seeds in very warm (120°F) water for about 20-25 minutes before you plant the seeds.

GENERAL VEGETABLE SEEDLING PEST PROBLEMS

THE PROBLEM	CAUSED BY
Seeds will not germinate or emerge	Birds, seedcorn maggots, wireworms, garden symphylan, seedrot, damping off disease, seeds planted too deep or too shallow
New seedlings emerge dead or fall over	Damping-off disease, summer high Heat
Seedling stems chewed off at soil line	Cutworms
Both seedling leaves & stem chewed off	Earwigs, snails and slugs, sowbugs, pillbugs, caterpillars, darkling beetles, vegetable weevils, rabbits
Roots of seedlings chewed off	Wireworms, maggots, gophers
Leaves have small round holes	Flea beetles
Yellow spots on leaves with tiny black spots	Thrips

Twisting white lines in leaves	Leafminers
Pear-shaped insects on leaves	Aphids
Plant has disappeared	Gopher or rabbit
Thin, spindly plants	Competition from weeds or other plants too close

CHAPTER 23

PLANTS FOR PEST CONTROL

PLANTS FOR PEST CONTROL

AGAVE
Crush the plant leaves and stems in water and use 1 part of the crushed up plant material to 5 parts water. Allow the mixture to sit for 1 hour before straining and placing in a sprayer. This is a general insect killer. If you prefer the plant parts can be dried and ground into a powder to dust the plants.

ANISE
This herb is best made into an infusion, which should remain for about 1 hour before adding a dash of hot sauce and ½ teaspoon of Dr. Bronner's Peppermint Soap™. This solution works on most caterpillars and leaf-eating insects. It will, however, remove many beneficial insects as well. Start with anise oil from a health food store.

AZALEA
Dry azalea flowers and crush them into a dust. This will kill many harmful insects by poisoning them, however, it is best not to use it on vegetable gardens.

BALM
Balm oil is the form to use. It will repel aphids, all ants and many other insects. Only use one capful to 1 quart of tap water. Should be available in most drug stores.

BASIL
Best to purchase it as sweet basil oil. It is more effective when added to pyrethrum or tobacco leaves. The basil extracts are very powerful and it doesn't take much to eliminate mosquitoes, their larvae and even houseflies. Use only 1 ounce per gallon of water in a sprayer. Basil has also been shown effective on a number of fungi. If you do use tobacco, remember it is a poison and keep it away from roses and fishes.

BEER
Beer can be an excellent bug killer, however, since there are 72 different chemicals it would be best to make your own beer if you plan on using it as a bug deterrent in your garden or even on your plants.

BEET JUICE
Flying insects hate beet juice especially if you add a small amount of Tabasco Sauce™ or other hot sauce to it. Effective as a spray, that will control a variety of plant diseases. Easy and inexpensive to make providing you have a juicer.

BLACK PEPPER
If you sprinkle a small amount of black pepper around squash vines it will repel squash vine borers.

BORAGE OIL
Prepare as an infusion to control most leaf-eating insects. Borage oil is very effective in repelling them as well.

CABBAGER LEAVES

These leaves are very attractive to aphids and are used to attract the bug into aphid traps. If you want to make an infusion for a spray, just allow some cabbage leaves to simmer in boiling water and add a dash of Tabasco Sauce™. Allow it to remain overnight before using it in the sprayer.

CHAMOMILE

Prepare as a tea and allow the tea to cool before spraying on plants. Commonly used by landscape supply houses, sprayed on flats and flowerpots. Also commonly used on cucumber seedlings to prevent mildew.

CHIVES

Use very fresh chives and prepare a tea that has steeped for about 15 minutes. Cool before using on plants and spray gooseberries and cucumbers to prevent mildew.

CAMPHOR

This is a whitish, crystalline substance that is produced from the gum of an Asian tree. The odor is very pungent and it will repel a number of insect pests. Moths, especially hate camphor. Dilution with alcohol is recommended if you plan on using it for a spray. The natural sources for camphor include sage, tansy, feverfew and plants from the artemesia family.

COCONUT OIL

The oil can be diluted depending on the strength needed and will kill most soft-bodied insects. Can kill beneficial insects, so you need to use sparingly. The leaves can also be used as well as the sap. Make sure the label reads 100% pure coconut oil. Works great against most hard-shelled insects.

CARAWAY

Works great on chewing insects when prepared as an infusion with a small amount of Ivory Liquid Soap™ added. You can also add a dash or two of Tabasco Sauce™ to give it a kick.

CASTOR OIL

Made from the castor bean it works better when added to pyrethrum or any other natural insecticide. Best to purchase the concentrated oil and use 1 ounce per gallon of water with pyrethrum added. It is not recommended for use on vegetables or fruit.

CATNIP

When a solution of catnip is sprayed on plants it will prevent insects from setting up housekeeping and it will even work on caterpillars and some worms. Best to make a tea that is not too strong so that you don't damage the plant while killing the bugs. Don't use if you have a cat or one visits your garden.

CAYENNE PEPPER

Tabasco Sauce™ is a good source of cayenne pepper, however, you can use the ground pepper with an equally good result. A weak tea can be prepared from the powder, which will kill most insect pests. Don't make the tea too strong or it may kill all the insects that are sprayed. Make sure you purchase only cayenne or hot sauce that does not contain any preservatives.

CHAMOMILE

Chamomile tea with a dash of Tabasco Sauce™ will eliminate most beetles and chewing insects. Has the ability to eliminate many plant diseases as well.

CITRONELLA OIL

Famous for its role as a mosquito repellant: as well as a base for many insect sprays. Do not use on oil-based trees such as a pine tree. Best to use the essential oil from a health food store.

CITRUS OIL

Contains an extract derived for citrus peels called "limonene." Very effective: when combined with any number of natural pest remedies. Do not use more than 10 drops per gallon of water, if using the extract. The weak strength is very effective against most soft-bodied insects. The spray can be used on most plants and vegetable gardens. The spray will control flies, larvae and many chewing insects. May kill some of the beneficial insects as well. Can be purchased as Citra Solv™ in most garden stores.

CORIANDER

The seeds are powdered and made into an infusion, then used in a sprayer to repel many chewing insects.

CUCUMBER

Cucumber and cucumber peelings have been used for hundreds of years as an insect repellant. The seeds are the most potent part and should be ground into a powder and used to make an infusion. They will repel worms, fleas, ants and some beetles.

CURRY

In some countries curry is made into a paste and painted on the trunk of plants and trees. When made into a liquid it is used in a sprayer. Place the curry into a blender to liquefy then use 1 tablespoon to 1 gallon of water.

DILL

Purchase dill oil for the best results and mix it with water to be used in a sprayer to repel flying insects.

EUCALYPTUS OIL

Best to add a small amount to almost any infusion to be used in a sprayer. It is capable of killing numerous soft-bodied insects on contact or will at least repel them. Works best when used with Dr. Bronner's Peppermint Soap™.

FENNEL
Purchase as an extract and make a spray adding 1 drop of fennel, a dash of a very hot sauce into 1 gallon of water. Effective: on almost all chewing insects.

FIREMIST SPRAY
This is a spray composed of a very hot sauce and is very effective on many insects. It is sold in many garden supply houses.

GARLIC
All parts of the plants can be juiced and used as a concentrate to be added to water. For a potent spray use 1 cup of garlic juice to 1 gallon of water and allow to remain for about 45 minutes before using, then use immediately and discard the balance. If you are purchasing the extract only use 1 ounce per 1 gallon of water. Garlic pellets can be purchase and placed in the ground around plants and trees to keep animals from damaging them.

HORSERADISH
This is one plant that very few insects or burrowing animals will eat. If you can purchase an extract made from the roots, place 1 ounce in 1 gallon of water and use as a spray against most insects.

HYSSOP
Hyssop has been used for centuries and is about as powerful as pyrethrum. Best to try using it as an infusion to get rid of most insect pests.

LETTUCE LEAVES
Best to simmer them and make an infusion to repel aphids and especially whiteflies. If you add a dash of a very hot sauce to the infusion it will be more effective.

MUSTARD SEED
The seeds need to be crushed and made into an infusion. Best to just purchase a strong Chinese mustard and place 1 tablespoon into 1 gallon of water. Allow the mixture to settle then strain well and add a drop or two of Ivory Liquid Soap™ to the mixture before placing it into a sprayer. This mixture can also be painted on tree trunks to keep critters and insects away.

NEEM TREE TEA OIL
This is one of the best anti-fungal oils that will also repel a number of insects. It tends to kill many insects on contact including the beneficial ones. This is one of the more commonly used natural pesticides.

ONION
Very effective in controlling many insects and critters! Best to use strong onions and juice them. Use ½ cup of onion juice in 1 gallon of water.

PEANUT SAUCE
Produced in Thailand and is sold as Hot Peanut Sauce™ in many garden shops. Used mainly to repel deer, rabbits and raccoons.

PENNYROYAL
Purchase as an extract and add only 1-2 drops per gallon of water that has already been made into a spray. Has the ability to kill most insects and when used in herbal powder form will repel spiders. Works synergistically with almost all other herbs to make them more effective.

PEPPERMINT OIL
Mix 5 tablespoons in 1 gallon of water for the best results. Will kill most insects on contact.

PEPPERS
This is one of the best methods of natural pest control. It will repel the insects as well as the critters. Chili peppers are the best source of insect repellant and can be used as a powder; however, concentrates are available in health food stores. Chili pepper oil can be purchased in Asian markets and only 5 drops are needed in 1 gallon of water to be effective.

PEPPERCORNS
Peppercorns from India are usually the hottest and can repel most critters that will frequent your garden. Grind them into a dust and dust you garden to keep most insects and pest away.

PINE OIL
Best used only on ant. Will kill on contact, just place 1 drop of the concentrate into 1 quart of water.

POTATO SOUP
Make up a pot of potato soup, strain it well and add 3-4 drops of Tabasco Sauce™ to it. Spray the plants to control chewing insects and beetles.

PYRETHRUM
Produced from the pyrethrum flower and considered a very strong insecticide. However, it will kill all insects even the beneficial ones. Try and find natural insecticides that will not kill all bugs. When small amounts are added as a synergistic it improves the effectiveness.

QUASSIA
The bark and chips have an excellent level of insecticidal properties when used as an extract. Do not use on fruits and vegetables. The chips need to simmer for about 3-4 hours then add a small amount of a very hot sauce and place in a sprayer.

RADISH
Use the leaves and make an infusion adding a small amount of a very hot sauce like Tabasco Sauce™. This will repel most chewing insects, ant and whiteflies when sprayed on the plants and may also keep rabbits away.

SABADILLA
A plant related to the lily family. The seeds need to be ground up and made into a tea. After the tea cools, strain the mixture and add a dash of Tabasco Sauce™, mix thoroughly and use in a spray. The powder can be used and is very toxic to insects since it affects their nervous systems.

SUGAR APPLE
The roots and seeds can be made into a very effective toxin to many insects. The roots especially are more effective than the seeds and can be dried and powdered. Place ½ cup of the dried preparation into 4 cups of boiling water, then allow the mixture to remain standing for about 8 hours before using it.

TOBACCO
Works great on gophers and moles. The extracts have high nicotine content and should only be used by professionals since they are **very toxic to humans, fish and all animals.** Never use nicotine on roses.

TOMATO LEAVES
The leaves are dried and made into a tea that can be placed in a sprayer and is very effective in controlling most chewing insects.

CHAPTER 24

CARNIVOROUS PLANTS

CARNIVOROUS PLANTS

GENERAL INFORMATION:
Carnivorous plants should not be used to keep the insect population down in your garden or around the house or barn. They require a lot of tender care and plenty of water. While some will catch houseflies they do not have a big enough appetite to do a big job. They will eat flies, moths, butterflies and most small insects by attracting them with a sugary substance. To be called a carnivorous plant, the plant has to be able to attract, capture and kill life forms. It must also have the ability to digest and absorb the nutrients.

GOURMET BUGS FOR THE DISCRIMINATING PLANT

Your animals and small children are safe, the plants are harmless to people and animals and only produce a very weak digestive enzyme. These enzymes are not the acids we are aware of in the human stomach and are just weak enzymes that will digest small insect juices and soft tissue. Many of the plants utilize bacteria to do the work of breaking down the bugs into a "bug-soup" so that they can utilize the nutrients. While others wait until the bug meal rots and then absorbs the food molecules.

The assassin bugs like the sweet substance excreted by the carnivorous plants and will eat the substance without being bothered by the plants and leave a pile of excrement for the plant to consume.

The largest carnivorous plant is the *Nepenthes*, which may occasionally catch a small frog and has large vines that will extend10-20 feet from the plant base.

THE MORE COMMON CARNIVOROUS PLANTS FOUND IN THE UNITED STATES

BLADDERWORTS (Utricularia)
There are over 210 species of this plant worldwide and the species is found in every state, even Hawaii, where it is considered a non-native weed. The largest number can be found in Florida and New Jersey. It lives above and below water; however, the carnivorous action only takes place under water. Each plant develops a number of bladders, which are the mouths of the plant.

When a bug bumps into long hair-like organs, a trapdoor catches the bug and they are sucked in when a vacuum is formed. The trapdoor shuts in 1/30th of a second and the plant digests the bug.

BUTTERWORTS (Pinguicula)
These plants are only found in the lower 48 states and there are only eight species. The plant has leaves similar to the artichoke plant. The leaves have small glands that capture tiny insects like gnats and even have limited movement capabilities. The flowers look very much like a violet but there is no relation to the violet plant. The plant is grown mainly on trees in Mexico.

PITCHER PLANTS (Darlingtonia & Sarracenia)
The *Darlingtonia* species is found on the far west coast usually California and Oregon and is usually located near serpentine outcrops. The *Sarracenia* species are found in the southeastern United States with the largest plant population around Mobile, Alabama and are trumpet-shaped plants.

The pitcher plant secretes a number of chemicals to attract and digest their prey. Some use an insect narcotic, wetting agents or sweet substances to attract the bug and then use bacterial action to digest it. This plant will eliminate a number of insects but does not discriminate between good and bad bugs.

SUNDEWS (Drosera)
These plants are worldwide with only seven species found in the United States. The plant has long whip-like leaves that are covered with short tentacles that contain an adhesive substance, which allows the plant to hold on to its bug prey. The prey is covered with a mucous coating and the more it struggles the more it is trapped and eventually drowns in the mucous coating. In some species the entire leaf will encircle the bug.

VENUS FLYTRAP (Dionaea)
Only found in specific areas of North and South Carolina with the colonies in South Carolina about gone. Human activity has all but eliminated this species in the United States. The plant captures insects by attracting the insect with nectar to bilobed leaves, which then snap shut trapping the bug. The plants are green with areas of red on the inside surfaces of the leaves.

CHAPTER 25

FRUIT, VEGETABLES, FLOWERS & SHRUBS AND THEIR MOST COMMON PESTS

| FRUITS, VEGETABLES, FLOWERS & SHRUBS |
| AND THEIR MOST COMMON PESTS |

FRUIT/VEGETABLE/FLOWERS/SHRUBS	DAMAGING INSECTS
Apples	Coddling moth, tent caterpillars, cankerworm, apple maggot, European red mite
Artichoke, globe	Aphids
Artichoke, Jeruselum	None
Apricot	Pear borer, Oriental fruit moth
Asparagus	Asparagus beetles
Aster	Root aphids, flea beetles
Beans, fava	Black fly
Beans, green & pole	Been weevil, Mexican bean beetle
Beans, Lima	Mexican bean beetle, black fly
Beets	Leaf miner
Blackberries	Aphids, cutworms, Japanese beetles, cane borer, galls
Blueberries	Blueberry maggot, Japanese beetles, galls
Broccoli	Cabbage worm, aphids
Brussels Sprouts	Cutworm, slugs, cabbage worm, root maggot, harlequin bug
Cabbage	Cabbage root maggot, slugs, cutworm
Calendula	Cutworm, climbing cutworm
Cantaloupe	Squash bug, striped cucumber beetle
Carrots	Root aphids, carrot worm, root fly, wire worm, harlequin bug
Cauliflower	Cutworm, cabbage worm, root maggot
Celeriac	Celery hopper
Celery	Tarnished plant bug, celery hopper
Cherries	Plum curculio, tent caterpillar
Chicory	None
Chinese Cabbage	Cabbage root maggot, slugs, cutworm
Chives	Almost none
Chrysanthemum	Cabbage loopers, flea beetle, gall
Collard Greens	Cutworm, slugs, root maggots
Columbine	Columbine leaf miner
Corn, sweet	European corn borer, corn earworm

Cucumber	Cucumber beetle, aphids, root maggot fly
Current	Current aphid, current worm, gooseberry caterpillar
Dahlia	Corn ear worms, burdock borer, earwigs
Dandelion	None
Dill	Carrot worm
Eggplant	Flea beetle, Colorado potato beetle, Cutworm
Elderberry	None or very few
Endive	None
Garlic	Onion maggot, gray fly larvae
Geranium	Cabbage loopers, leaf tier, fall web worm, tussock moth caterpillar
Gooseberry	Aphids, gooseberry caterpillar
Grapes	Leaf hoppers, Japanese beetles, rose chafer, grape curculio, leaf tier, mealybug
Hollyhock	Burdock borer, slugs, iris borer
Horseradish	Flea beetle
Hydrangea	Woolly bear caterpillar
Kale	Cutworm, slugs, cabbage worm, cabbage root maggot, harlequin bug
Kohlrabi	Same as for kale
Larkspur	Burdock borer, leaf miner
Laurel	European leaf roller
Leek	Onion maggot, gray fly larvae
Lilac	European leaf roller, greenhouse whitefly, leaf miner
Marigold	Greenhouse whitefly, Japanese beetle, earwigs
Muskmelon	Striped cucumber beetle, squash bug, squash vine borer
Mustard greens	Cutworm, harlequin bug, cabbage worm, slugs, cabbage root maggot
Nasturtium	Aphids
Okra	Green stink bug, cabbage loopers
Onion	Onion fly, onion maggot, thrips
Pansy	Leaf miner, cutworm
Parsley	Carrot worm
Peach	Peach borer, Oriental fruit moth
Peanut	None
Pear	Plum curculio, pear psylla, coddling moth, rose slug

Peas..Pea aphid, red spider mite, bean weevil
Peony...Leaf roller
Peppermint..Greenhouse whitefly
Peppers, hot..Cutworms
Peppers, sweet..Cutworms
Petunia..Flea beetle
Potato..Potato beetle, flea beetle, Colorado potato beetle, wireworm, potato stem borer
Pumpkin...Squash bug, squash vine borer
Radish..Radish root maggot, flea beetle, harlequin beetle
Rose...European leaf roller, leaf tier, burdock borer, tent caterpillar, rose flea beetle, June bugs, earwigs, leaf gall
Quince..Coddling moth
Raspberries..Raspberry fruit worm, cane borer, white grub, red spider mite, grasshopper
Rhubarb...None, leaves are poisonous
Rutabaga..Same as cabbage
Sage...Hawk moth caterpillar
Salsify..Carrot worm
Snapdragons..Stink bugs
Soybeans...None or very few
Spearmint...Hawk moth caterpillar
Spinach..Leaf miner, flea beetle
Squash, summer...Squash bug, squash vine borer
Squash, winter..Squash bug, squash vine borer
Strawberry..Cane borer, cutworm, crown borer, sawfly, strawberry weevil
Sweet basil..Asiatic garden beetle
Sweet peas..Pea aphids, corn ear worm, red spider mite
Sweet potato...None or very few
Swiss chard...Leaf miner, grasshoppers
Tomato...Cutworm, flea beetle, tomato horn worm

Watercress..None
Watermelon..Cucumber beetle, squash bug, squash vine borer
White daisy...Thrips, earwigs
Zinnia..Tarnished plant bug, Japanese beetle

CHAPTER 26

INSECT-RESISTANT VEGETABLES & FRUITS

INSECT-RESISTANT: VEGETABLES & FRUITS

The following fruits and vegetables will provide additional information regarding which fruits and vegetables are more or less resistant to insect infestations and subsequent damage by them. Remember, even the resistant varieties may not be 100% resistant in some areas of the world. If you plant the following fruits and vegetables it would be wise to plant the most resistant varieties for the best results.

FRUIT OR VEGETABLE	BUG		VARIETY
Alfalfa	Aphid	Resistant:	Cody, Lahontan, Zia
		Susceptible:	Buffalo
Barley	Greenbug	Resistant:	Omugi, Dictoo, Will
		Susceptible	Rogers, Reno
Bean	Cutworm	Resistant Beans:	Snap Wade, Idaho Refugee, Gold Crop, Regal
		Resistant Limas:	Black Valentine, Baby Fordhook, Baby White
	Mexican Bean Beetle	Resistant:	Wade, Logan, Black Valentine (Limas)
		Susceptible:	State, Bountiful, Dwarf Horticultural
Broccoli	Diamondback Moth	Resistant:	Coastal, Italian Green Atlantic
		Susceptible:	De Cicco
	Harlequin Bug	Resistant:	Grande, Atlantic, Coastal
		Susceptible:	Gem
	Striped Flea Beetle	Resistant:	De Cicco, Coastal, Italian Green
		Susceptible:	Gem
Cabbage	Cabbage Looper	Resistant:	Mammoth, Red Rock,
	Cabbageworm		Savory Chieftain, Savory Perfection, Drumhead
		Moderately Resistant:	Penn State Ball Head. Early Flat Dutch, Badger Ball, Globe, Bugner, All Seasons, Wisconsin Ball Head
		Susceptible:	Golden Acre, Elite

FRUIT OR VEGETABLE	BUG		VARIETY
			Copenhagen Market 86, Stein's Flat Dutch
	Diamondback Moth	Resistant:	Michihli Chinese, Mammoth Red Rock
		Moderately Resistant:	Stein's Early Flat Dutch, Savory Perfection Drumhead, Early Jersey Wakefield
		Susceptible:	Copenhagen Market 86
	Harlequin Bug	Resistant:	Copenhagen Market 86, Headstart, Savory Perfection Drumhead, Stein's Flat Dutch
		Susceptible:	Michihli Chinese
Cantaloupe	Mexican Bean Beetle		All cantaloupe is resistant to this bug
	Spotted Cucumber Beetle	Resistant: (foliage)	Edisto 47, Edisto, Harper Hybrid
		Susceptible: (seedlings)	Edisto 47, Edisto, Harper Hybrid, Honey dew
		Susceptible: (foliage)	Honey Dew
Cauliflower	Diamondback Moth	Moderately Resistant:	Snowball A
	Harlequin Bug	Resistant:	Early Snowball X, Snowball Y
	Striped Flea Beetle	Resistant:	Snowball A & X
Collard	Diamondback Moth	Resistant:	Green Glaze
		Moderately Resistant:	Morris Heading, Vates Georgia Southern
	Harlequin Bug	Resistant:	Vates, Morris Improved Heading, Green Glaze
		Moderately Resistant:	Georgia LS, Georgia

FRUIT OR VEGETABLE	BUG		VARIETY
Sweet Corn	Corn Earworm	Resistant:	Dixie 18, Calumet, Country Gentleman, Staygold, Victory Golden, Silvergent, Aristogold, Ioana
		Susceptible:	Spancross, Seneca Chief, North Star, Evertender
	Fall Armyworm	Resistant:	Golden Market, Ioana Golden Beauty, Silver & Golden Cross Bantam, Triplegold, Deep Gold
	Sap Beetle	Resistant:	Country Gentleman, Deligold, Gold Pack, Tender Joy, Victory Golden, Tucker's Favorite
		Moderately Resistant:	Atlas, Duet, Eastern Market, Gold Strike, Golden Grain, Merit, Spring Gold, Merit
		Susceptible:	Aristogold, Gold Mine, Corona, Sixty Pak, Spring Bounty, Northern Belle, Titan
Cucumber	Mexican Bean Beetle	Susceptible:	Arkansas Hybrid 4, Colorado, Crispy, Hokus, Nappa 63, Piccadilly, Packer, Table Green
	Pickleworm	Resistant:	Arkansas Hybrid 4, Cubit, Gemini, Nappa 63, Princess Spartan Dawn, Stono, Ashley, Colorado, Hokus, Long Ashley, Packer, Table Green

FRUIT OR VEGETABLE	BUG	VARIETY	
	Spotted Cucumber Beetle	Resistant: (seedlings)	Ashley, Chipper, Crispy, Explorer, Jet, Gemini, Frontier, White Wonder
		Resistant: (foliage)	Ashley, Chipper, Cherokee, Gemini, High Mark II, Stono, Southern Cross, Pontsett
		Susceptible: (seedlings)	Cherokee, Coolgreen, Model, Nappa 61, Packer, Pioneer, Southern Cross, Table Green
		Susceptible: (foliage)	Coolgreen, Cubit, Hokus, Jet, Model, Nappa 63, Packer, Pioneer, Spartan Dawn, SMR 58
Kale	*Diamond Back Moth*	Resistant:	Vates
		Susceptible:	Early and Dwarf Siberian
	Harlequin Bug	Resistant:	Vale
		Susceptible:	Dwarf Siberian
	Mexican Bean Beetle	Resistant:	Dwarf Siberian
	Striped Flea Beetle	Resistant:	Vates, Dwarf Siberian Dwarf Green, Curled Scotch
Lettuce	*Lettuce Root Aphid*	Resistant:	Avondefiance, Avon Crisp
Muskmelon	*Striped & Spotted Cucumber Beetle*	Resistant:	Hearts of Gold
		Susceptible:	Crenshaw, Smith Perfect
Potato	*Aphids*	Resistant:	British Queen, DeSota, Houma, Early Pinkeye, Irish Daisy, LaSalle

FRUIT OR VEGETABLE	BUG	VARIETY	
		Susceptible:	Katahdin, Irish, Cobbler, Idaho Russet, Sebago Sequoia
	Colorado Potato Beetle	Resistant:	Sequoia, Katahdin
		Susceptible:	Fundy, Plymouth, Catoosa
	Potato Leafhopper	Resistant:	Delus
		Susceptible:	Cobbler, Plymouth
Pumpkin	Serpentine Leafminer	Resistant:	Mammoth Chili, Small Sugar
		Susceptible:	Green Striped Cushaw, King of the Mammoth
	Spotted Cucumber Beetle	Resistant:	King of the Mammoth
		(foliage)	Mammoth Chili, Dickenson Field
		Susceptible: (seedlings)	Green Striped, Cushaw, King of the Mammoth, Mammoth Chili, Small Sugar
		Susceptible: (foliage)	Connecticut Field, Green Striped Cushaw, Small Sugar
Radish	Cabbage Webworm	Resistant:	Cherry Belle
		Moderately Resistant:	Globemaster
		Susceptible:	White Icicle, Red Devil, Champion
	Diamondback Moth	Resistant:	Cherry Belle, White Icicle, Globemaster, Champion
	Harlequin Bug	Resistant:	Red Devil, White Icicle, Globemaster, Cherry Belle, Red Prince, Champion
		Moderately Resistant:	Crimson Sweet
	Mexican Bean Beetle	Susceptible:	Sparkler, Champion, White Icicle

FRUIT OR VEGETABLE	BUG	VARIETY	
	Striped Flea Beetle	Moderately Resistant:	Champion, Sparkler
		Susceptible:	Globemaster, Cherry Belle, White Icicle
Squash	*Mexican Bean Beetle*	Susceptible:	White Bush Scallop
	Pickleworm	Resistant:	Summer Crookneck, Butternut 23, Boston Marrow, Buttercup, Blue Hubbard
		Susceptible:	Black Beauty, Seneca Zucchini, Zucchini, Cozini, Cozella Hybrid, U Conn
	Serpentine Leafminer	Resistant:	Butternut 23, Cozella
		Moderately Resistant:	Blue Hubbard, Pink Banana, Zucchini, Boston Marrow,
		Susceptible:	Seneca Prolific, Long Cozella, Summer Crookneck, Green Hubbard, Zucchini
	Spotted Cucumber Beetle	Resistant: (seedlings)	Blue Hubbard, Green Hubbard, Summer Crookneck, Long Cozella, Seneca Prolific
		Resistant: (foliage)	Black Zucchini, Blue Hubbard, Royal Acorn, Early Golden Bush Scallop
		Susceptible: (seedlings)	Black Zucchini, Cozella, Cozini, Seneca Zucchini
		Susceptible: (foliage)	Boston Marrow, Buttercup, Cozini, Zucchini, Seneca Prolific

294

FRUIT OR VEGETABLE	BUG	VARIETY	
	Squash Bug	Resistant:	Butternut, Table Queen, Royal Acorn, Early Summer Crook-neck, Straightneck, Improved Green Hubbard
		Susceptible:	Striped Green Cushaw, Pink Banana, Black Zucchini
	Squash Vine Borer	Resistant:	Butternut, Butternut23
	Striped Cucumber Beetle	Resistant:	U Conn, Early Prolific Straightneck, White Bush Scallop, Cozella Hybrid, Black Zucchini
		Susceptible:	Cozini, Caserta, Black Beauty
Sweet Potato	*Southern Potato Wireworm*	Resistant:	Nugget, All Gold
		Moderately Resistant:	Centennial, Georgia Red, Porto Rico, Gem
		Susceptible:	Red Jewel, Georgia 41 Nemagold, Jullian
Tomato	*Twospotted Mite*	Resistant:	Campbell 135 & 146
		Susceptible:	Homestead 24
Watermelon	*Spotted Cucumber Beetle*	Resistant: (foliage)	Crimson Sweet, Sweet Princess
		Susceptible: (seedlings)	Blue Ribbon
		Susceptible: (foliage)	Charleston Gray, Blue Ribbon, Sugar Baby
Wheat	*Hessian Fly*	Resistant:	Ottawa, Ponca, Big Club 43, Pawnee, Rus, Dual

CHAPTER 27

GRANDMA'S
SECRET GARDENING TIPS

GRANDMA'S SECRET GRARDENING TIPS

BOG & POND GARDENING

A bog garden is basically a marshy area with plants that will survive in a year-round moist climate. It is not necessarily a pond. A pond is usually made using a ready-made shell or plastic liner. In a bog it is essential that the soil is kept very moist all through the year. The best is one that will be low-lying and collects surface drainage. It doesn't take very much water to keep a bog garden moist, and just a trickle will do.

YOU WON'T NEED A HEAVY EQUIPMENT OPERATER
Ideally: to make a bog just dig out about 2 feet of the topsoil. Place this aside and place about 5 inches of smooth rocks on the bottom. Prepare a mixture of half peat and half loam and fill the hole to the top, keeping it level with the surrounding area. Two feet is the maximum depth for a successful bog garden.

OLD POOL LINERS WORK GREAT
Just place the pool liner on the bottom instead of the rocks and puncture it to allow for drainage. This can be used for a bog garden or a pond.

TRICKLE, TRICKLE
If you have a natural flow of water, no problem! If not, you will have to provide a small artificial trickle, which must be just enough to keep the bog garden well saturated.

OPEN THE FLOOD GATES
During the summer, it would be best to allow the bog garden to flood and become heavily saturated for at least 4-6 weeks. This depends on your climate and the rain during that period.

HOW DRY I AM
To allow a bog garden to suffer from drought will probably kill all the plants in a short period of time. Bogs are not recommended for the southwestern United States.

GETTING THE PICK OF THE LITTER
Most landscape or gardening businesses will have a selection of plants that will do well in a bog garden and provide you with planting and feeding tips for the plants you choose. Color of the plants, planting location and height selection is important.
The following are some of the more common plants for a bog garden:

- Lysichitum (yellow skunk cabbage.) 18-36 inches
- Flag iris versicolor 36-48 inches
- Osmunda 24-48 inches
- Hosta 12-36 inches
- Astilbe 18-48 inches
- Primula 6-18 inches

DON'T DROWN THE LITTLE CREATURES
Be sure that your bog garden has a shallow end to allow any small amphibians to enter and leave without drowning and getting trapped.

THE EDIBLE BOG GARDEN

Many plants are edible and have been very successful in bog gardens for centuries. The following are a few of the more common varieties:

- *WATERCRESS* will grow very nicely in areas were the water is about 2 inches deep. The seeds can be used as a mustard substitute. It should be started by seed or a cutting which will take root easily.
- *BROOKWEED* prefers shallow water and very wet soil. Only the young leaves can be eaten either cooked or raw.
- *CREEPING DOGWOOD* will grow better on the outer edges of the bog, but does not do well if the soil is too chalky. The fruit is edible.
- *CAPE PONDWEED* grows well in bogs when the water is between 6 inches and 2 feet. Prefers a highly fertilized soil and the tubers are edible as well as the flowering spikes. The tubers are often substituted for spinach.
- *GALINGALE* likes a marshy soil. The root can be eaten or powdered and used as a spice.
- *YELLOW WATER LILY* prefers water of 1-2 feet in depth and full sun. The roots and stalks can be eaten either cooked or raw. The flowers can be used to make a tea.
- *WHITE WATER LILY* prefers the deepest area of the bog garden and likes the sun and a rich soil diet. The seeds may be roasted and used as you would coffee.
- *ARROW HEAD* likes water levels of about 1-2 feet in depth. The tuber can be cooked and mashed and is a very popular starch in China.
- *WATER CHESTNUT* likes water 1-2 feet deep. The seeds can be consumed raw, dried or cooked. When dried the seeds can be powdered and used as a flour.
- *SMALL CRANBERRY* does best grown in an acidic soil. The fruit is edible and a tea can be prepared from the leaves.
- *FLOAT GRASS* is best grown in the shallow areas of the bog garden. The seeds are edible and commonly used in puddings.

HAVE A BUG FOR DINNER

Carnivorous plants do very well in a bog garden especially when planted in sphagnum moss. The ones that do best are:
- *Sundews*
- *Venus Flytrap*
- *Pitcher Plants*

PLANT A PRETTY

Orchids do well in most bog gardens. The most desirable ones are the white or orange fringed, grass pink, rose pogonia and the pink lady slipper. Best to purchase the orchids from a nursery.

STAYING IN CONTROL

Some bog plants tend to do too well and need to be controlled. These include cranberry plants, rosemary, bog laurel, bog bean, horsetails and cotton grass. Be firm with these and don't let them get out of hand.

GETTING POTTED IN A POND
Deep-water aquatic plants can be planted in plastic pots with soil as long as you place small rocks or gravel around the top of the soil. Metal pots may disintegrate and rust. The gravel will stop any fish from bothering the soil. The best soil will be rotted turf. Don't use soil rich in organic matter such as manure.

BULBS

Bulbs are actually storage tanks for nutrients. They are normally planted in the early spring, but certain varieties can be planted at various times of the year depending on when you want the flowers to bloom.

HOPE YOU CAN DIG IT!
Many bulbs are very tender and should be removed from the ground before freezing winter temperatures. Bulbs will remain healthier if removed from the ground in almost any climate. If the foliage begins to turn yellow and the plant falls over, it is time to remove it from the ground.

HELP! I'M GETTING WATERLOGGED
The biggest problem that ruins bulbs and bulb plants is over-watering. If the water is left standing around the plant, the bulb will be worthless for the next season.

ROOM TO BREATHE
Planting bulbs in a small pot, then burying the pot is a favorite method of growing flowers from bulbs and makes it easier to remove the bulbs for the next season. When storing the pots be sure that the soil is very dry or the bulbs will rot during the winter storage.

IT'S GETTING DARK DOWN HERE
Be careful not to plant bulbs upside down. The narrow end goes up, which should not have any sign of roots. However sometimes the roots do not show.

FOOD, I NEED FOOD
After you dig a hole to plant the bulbs in, be sure and add a handful of a fertilizer that contains about 9% phosphorus, 9% nitrogen and about 6% potassium. If the bulbs are not removed just add some fertilizer to the topsoil every year.

I NEED A COMFORTABLE BED
Bulbs should be stored in a brown paper bag that has been filled with peat. This will control the level of moisture during the winter months.

Bulbs that are removed from the ground need to be stored in a cool, dry location. Ideally, the temperature should be around 50°F. When they are removed from the ground cut the tops back and only allow about 2 inches of the stem to remain. Be sure and remove any traces of soil.

DON'T STORE ME NEAR THE HEATER

I'M NEVER BLUE
Begonias will bloom all summer until the first frost. They can be any color except blue, even two-toned ones. Remember to always stalk begonias. If they get more than 3 hours of morning sun they may burn, so check the area carefully before you plant them.

HEY BUD, I JUST GOT PINCHED
To grow the largest flowers from a begonia plant, just pinch off the smaller buds on either side of the larger one.

HO HUM, TIME TO SLEEP
Begonias will start to go dormant usually in August and should not be fertilized or you will interfere with their dormancy period. They need to have time to store up food for the next season.

I'M REALLY A LATE BLOOMER
Crocuses will usually bloom in the spring but are not as pretty. If you wait until the early fall you will see nicer flowers appearing. Best to plant the bulbs in late summer and allow them to bloom in the early fall initially.

I'M BEST IF YOU CONTAIN ME
Dahlias tend to do better if planted in a container. Add mulch around the bulb to keep the moisture contained, especially if the weather is very hot.

OPEN WIDE
Gladiolas are excellent for flower arrangements. Make sure when they are cut that at least half the flowers have not opened since they will open shortly.

LEAVE MY FOOD ALONE
Daffodils must be left alone and the yellow leaves allowed to remain until they equal about 1/3 of the leaves on the plant. If they are removed too soon you will remove too much of the food supply and the plants will not have stored enough energy.

RING-A-DING DING
Spanish bluebells should always be planted in the shade. They require no special care and will do just fine on their own.

TRYING, BUT STILL CAN'T MAKE BLUE
Tulips can be grown in every color except blue. They like full sun if you live in a northern climate. Late fall or early December is the best time to plant tulips. If the ground warms up before they are ready, they will not do well.

TAKE CARE WHEN POTTING BULBS
Bulbs should never be placed on the bottom of a pot. Always plant them about 2 inches deep for the best results.

COMPOSTING

Composting is layering natural ingredients in a pile in certain mixed proportions. It is also necessary to provide the pile with adequate air and moisture so that bacterial action will decay the material releasing fertilization components for plants. Composting can be done in a specific wooden bin built for that purpose or just placed in an unused location away from your house.

An effective compost pile is usually about 6 feet high about 4 feet wide and about 20 feet long.

WORD TO THE WISE
Always compost sawdust before you place any in the garden. Sawdust is a low nitrogen and high carbon substance. If placed in the garden without going through composting it may cause a nitrogen deficiency in the soil as it decays. If you do decide to use fresh sawdust, be sure and add some manure to increase the soil nitrogen content.

SOWBUGS AWAY
Sowbugs need to be part of your compost workers. They prefer decaying material to healthy growing plants. Gather up all the sowbugs you can find and make a deep hole in the compost pile and drop them in. The sowbugs will tunnel into the compost and aerate the compost. To increase the number of sowbugs, just place a flat piece of wood on top of the compost so that they will have a place to reproduce on the underneath side.

GREAT MIXTURE
Manure and sawdust: the compost of champion composters. Manure has a high enough nitrogen content to activate the compost pile and help create the heat needed for the decaying reaction to take place efficiently. If you cover the pile with a plastic sheet it will help to retain the moisture.

THE SECRET COMPONENTS

- Leaves are great since they are high in mineral content, but make sure they are shredded. They can include any plant or lawn clippings.
- Shredded hay can be of almost any type.
- Paper and cardboard is OK if it doesn't contain printing. Both must be shredded for the best effect.
- Grass clippings.
- Any type of plant or garden residue will do, especially vegetable residues.
- Garbage from the kitchen is OK, especially anything green or vegetables.
- Animal manure is a great addition.
- Miscellaneous residues of many types can be included such as wood shavings, peanut hulls, sawdust and even coffee grounds.

THE DEVIL MADE ME DO IT

The compost pile should be turned every 2-3 weeks using a pitchfork. The outer material should be placed on the inside of the pile every time you turn it. The inside of the pile will heat up to 140°-150°F but after about 3 months it should be finished and the heat level will probably level off to about 130°F.

NATURAL SUBSTITUTE

If you don't have any animal manure, grass clipping will be a good substitute. However, one or the other must be part of the compost pile.

MEASURING YOUR COMPOST

When using compost to fertilize your garden area, be sure to only use about 2 bushels per 100 square feet and only once a year.

ORGANIC FERTILIZERS

There are two schools of thought regarding organic fertilizers versus inorganic fertilizers. Most organic farmers do claim that their produce tastes better, however, most will admit that the produce tends to lose a certain amount of eye appeal. Chemically, plants cannot discern between a nutrient coming from an organic source or one coming from a chemically prepared concoction. The following is general information regarding organic fertilizers, which do provide well-balanced nutrients needed by the plants.

FEED ME, FEED ME

- *ANIMAL MANURE (dried)* – Not the best source of nutrients but does contain a good level of trace minerals. Should be mixed with peat for the best results. The nitrogen, phosphorus and potassium content are about 1% for each.
- *ANIMAL MANURE (liquid)* – Most contain the major nutrients but not in high amounts. It is high in trace minerals. The nitrogen, phosphorus and potassium content are about 1% each.
- *FISH MEAL* – Normally sold as semi-organic since certain nutrients are usually added. Contains about 9% nitrogen and 2-3% phosphorus. Best if potash has been added on the label.

- *BONE MEAL* – This is one of the more popular fertilizers and has the ability to activate root growth better than most. If you purchase bone meal the label must state that it is "steamed." Raw bone meal may carry anthrax virus, however, it is safe if steamed. **Best to wear gloves and a quality mask** when using bone meal as an extra precaution. Contains about 3-4& nitrogen and 22% phosphorus.
- *DRIED BLOOD* – One of the fastest acting nitrogen fertilizers, usually used when a farmer feels that the plants need a "nitrogen boost." Best not to use dried blood if you expect frost or are in a rainy period. Tends to wash into the soil too easily. Mid-summer is the latest this fertilizer is usually recommended. The nitrogen content is about 12-14% and the phosphorus content is less than 1%.
- *GENERAL ALL-PURPOSE* – Should be composed of animal manure, seaweed, minerals and plant residues. This combination supplies the best all around nutrition for your plants. The nitrogen and phosphorus content will vary but should be in very adequate supply.
- *HOOF & HORN* – These are very good sources of slow-release nitrogen fertilizer components. The horns and hoofs are high-heat processed to 140ºF before they are packaged making them safe to use. Needs to be broken down by soil bacteria and should be applied at least 2 weeks before it is needed. Best used in the spring on cruciferous plants. The nitrogen content is about 12-13% and the phosphorus content is about 2%.
- *POTASH (rock)* – Excellent source of potassium: which is missing from most fertilizers. Has poor solubility so it will remain on the soil and not be absorbed when it rains that easily. This allows the plants to use the fertilizer as needed.
- *SEAWEED (liquid)* – Contains excellent source of nitrogen, phosphorus and potash. High in trace minerals and contains natural growth hormones. Good potassium level of about 3%.
- *SEAWEED (meal)* – One of the best substitutes for general all-purpose fertilizer. Tends to be well balanced and has a slower release of nutrients. High in trace minerals and has an excellent combination of nutrients. Higher priced than most general all-purpose fertilizers. Best applied when the soil is warm. Has nitrogen content of 3% and is high in potassium and low in phosphorus.
- *WOOD ASH* – Excellent source of potassium and phosphorus when limbs and small trigs are shredded, burned and composted into ash. The level of the minerals depends on the materials burned.

ASHES TO ASHES
Remember to save the old ashes from a fireplace, dry them and use them as a fertilizer in the spring to increase the pH (alkalinity) of the soil.

A GOOD SOIL TO GET POTTED IN
An excellent potting soil is one part of vermiculite, two parts of peat moss and one part of perlite. These are required to give the soil body and to aid in water retention and drainage. Perennials need a different type of potting soil composed of two parts of common topsoil, one part peat moss and one-part sand.

THE EARLY PLANT GETS THE FOOD
Most plants produce their food in the early part of the day. Plants have difficulty producing food, as the day gets hotter, especially in the afternoon sun.

DON'T IRRITATE YOUR PLANTS
Watering should never be done at high noon since plants tend to perspire at around this time. The process is called "transpiring." Plants must do this to regulate their temperature from the sun, humidity and wind. If you do water at this time, the majority of the water will be wasted through evaporation.

OUCH! STOP POKING ME
If you poke your index finger into the soil around a plant, the soil should be completely dry before watering. If the soil is the slightest bit moist, the plant does not need water.

PINCH ME, PINCH ME, BUT NOT TOO HARD
Seedlings need to be pinched in their early growth stages to assure that they will have more than one stem. If the seedling is not pinched properly it will not bush out.

IT IS A LITTLE TOO TIGHT IN HERE
If a seedling has yellow leaves at the bottom, it may indicate that the seedling has been in too small a pot for too long a period.

I'M TIED UP IN KNOTS, THIS CAN'T BE HEALTHY
Be sure when purchasing seedlings that the roots are not coming out the pot in all directions. This indicates a root-bound plant and that is not a healthy sign.

HOW BROWN I AM
Seedlings should not show signs of browning or wilting. If browning is evident it has probably been caused by over-watering, or a plant disease.

CUT ME, CUT ME, I'LL GROW MORE
There are flowers that when cut regularly they will produce more flowers. These include roses, antirrhinum, cosmos, verbena, viola, nicotiana and heliotrope.

I NEED MY SUNGLASSES
Some plants prefer shade and will grow better if not in direct sunlight. These include begonias, some varieties of viola and coleus.

MULCHING TIME AGAIN
Mulches are the best method of maintaining even soil temperatures in the summer months. They are important, especially in the heat of the day, keeping the soil an even temperature.

VARIETIES OF MULCH
- *BUCKWHEAT HULLS* – These are lightweight and will not blow away easily. They have the ability to retain moisture very well but are expensive mulch.
- *COCOA SHELLS* – If they become too moist, you may end up with mushrooms. Recommended for flowerbeds. Expensive mulch. Never apply more than one-inch because of its high potash content.
- *LEAVES* – One of the best mulches for adding nutrients and keeping the soil in shape. Keeps the soil moist and cool. Should be shredded for the best results.
- *PINE NEEDLES* – Do not retain moisture very well.
- *SHREDDED BARK* – Comes in different grades. Use the coarser grades for under large shrubs and the finer grades for flowerbeds. Reasonably priced.
- *WOOD CHIPS* – Only use aged wood chips or shavings since wood chips remove nitrogen from the soil. Aged wood chips are best since they will break down and add organic matter to the soil.

NITROGEN BY ANY OTHER NAME
- *NITRATE* – This is the form that is available to the plant.
- *AMMONIACAL* – This is available to plants only when it is converted to nitrates by the action of bacteria. The time of conversion depends on the temperature of the soil. Warm soil promotes faster conversion than cold soil.
- *ORGANIC* – This includes sludge, cottonseed meal, etc. organic matter is slower to breakdown than inorganic matter.
- *UREA* – Synthetic organic matter: that is reduced to inorganic ammonia very rapidly.

STOP! DON'T MOW ME
If the grass is wet or frozen it should not be mowed. A frozen lawn should not even be walked on.

WHEN A LAWN IS NOT A LAWN
Dichondra is not really a grass, but a broad-leafed plant. It is more popular in the warmer southwest climates and needs a lot of watering. If it gets below 25°F it may die out and need to be re-seeded as soon as the weather warms up. Grows best in light-sandy loam so that water can penetrate easily.

FLOWER ARRANGEMENTS

A LITTLE SEASONING FOR YOUR FLOWERS
A few pinches of table salt should be added to the water in a flower arrangement from a flower shop. The salt will slow down the growth of harmful bacteria.

SWEET & SOUR FOR FRESH-CUT FLOWERS
You can prolong the life of fresh-cut flowers by mixing 2 tablespoons of white vinegar with 2 tablespoons of granulated sugar in 1 quart of water.

A LITTLE DIP WILL DO YA
If you dip freshly, cut flowers into a solution of ½ cup of baking soda in 1 quart of water it will extend the life of the flowers.

LAWN CARE

COOL LAWN!
Grass for the most part is a cool weather plant and grows better in cooler climates. If you are going to seed a lawn, remember to seed a lawn in the early spring for the best results. Depending on the area of the country you live in, the fall is also a good time.

SPROUTING TIMES FOR LAWN GRASSES	
	DAYS
Bentgrass	7-12
Chewing's fescue	10-20
Common ryegrass	7-14
Creeping red fescue	10-20
Kentucky bluegrass	20-28
Meadow fescue	7-14
Merion Kentucky bluegrass	20-28
Perennial ryegrass	7-14

HUMIDITY HIGH – DON'T WATER AT NIGHT
If you live in an area of the country that has frequent high humidity, it would be best not to water late at night. Watering just after the sun goes down is ideal in these areas.

THIS WAY AND THAT WAY BUT NEVER THE SAME WAY
It is best to occasionally altering the mowing pattern. Best not to go in the same direction every time you mow. However, altering the direction every time you mow is not the best idea either.

MOWING TIPS TO THE WISE

- Try and mow the grass and keep it at about 3 inches high. High mowing keeps the weeds from getting sunlight.
- Mow as often as the growth requires mowing.
- Never cut more than 1/3 of the length of the grass blade or you will slow down the food production capabilities of the blade.

MIXED GRASSES TO THE RESCUE

To reduce the possibility of diseases attacking your lawn, use a mixture of grasses since diseases attack different varieties. Eventually a turf disease will reach an area of grass that is resistant to the disease and terminates it.

USELESS FACT

In every 100 square feet of lawn you will find about 100,000 turf plants.

SECRETS OF THE PERFECT MOWING

1. *SHARP BLADES* – Dull blades tend to pull and make ragged cuts, which may lead to lawn disease problems.
2. *REGULAR MOWING* – At least once a week is recommended during the height of the growing season.
3. *MOWING DIRECTION* – It is impossible to get a clean cut if you cut your lawn in the same direction every week.
4. *MOWING DURING DROUGHT* – Best not to mow your lawn during a drought period because the lawn is in a stress situation.
5. *WET GRASS* – Mowing wet grass tends to leave wet grass residue, which can damage a healthy lawn.
6. *DRY CLIPPINGS* – Clippings should be raked up within 48 hours of mowing. The lawn disease, thatch is the result of leaving clippings on the lawn for too long a period of time.

TYPES OF GRASSES

GRASSES FOR COOL SEASONS

Bent Grasses
- *ASTORIA* - Has fine leaves and is a dull green color, is not very vigorous and tends to get summer diseases easily. It does not like deep shade and prefers full sun.
- *HIGHLAND* - Has upright leaves and is grayish-green in color. Likes full-sun or part-shade.
- *PENNCROSS* – Has flat, narrow leaves and is bluish-green in color. Prefers sun or part shade. Should be mowed at about ½-inch.
- *SEASIDE* – Has flat, narrow leaves and bluish-green runners. Very susceptible to summer diseases and should be mowed ½-inch.

Fine Fescues
- *CREEPING RED* – A fine-textured, dense turf that mixes well with bluegrass. Works good in shady areas and should be cut 1½ to 2-inches.
- *ILLAHEE* – Has a very fine texture and is bright green. Very susceptible to summer diseases and tends to grow in clumps. Should be cut 1½ to 2-inches.
- *RAINIER* – This is a very delicate, soft grass with a deep green color. Prefers shady locations.
- *CHEWING* – A delicate grass that is soft and gray-green in color. Does well if moisture and food are in short supply. Tends to yellow in winter.

Coarse Fescus
This is a wide-bladed clumping grass that is best suited for a football field or areas that receive very rough treatment. Should be seeded at 6-8 pounds per 1,000 square feet. If you sow at heavy rate the texture will be finer.

- *MEADOW* – A very pliant, medium-coarse grass that is dark green. It grows very quickly and is very strong. Should be mowed 1½-inches.
- *ALTA* – A very sturdy grass that is drought-resistant and has a long lifetime. Needs regular mowing and if neglected will get tough. Should be cut ¾ to 2-inches.

Blue Grass
- *KENTUCKY* – A very dense sod with dark green leaves. The best all-around lawn for the cool-season grass areas. Growth is slow in summer and it tends to grow faster in cool seasons. Does not do well in shade and prefers full sun.
- *MERION KENTUCKY* – A denser grass than the traditional Kentucky Bluegrass. Dark blue color and more resistant to drought conditions. Tendency to be susceptible to rust and should be mowed ¾ to 1-inch.
- *NEWPORT* – Has the same texture as Merion Kentucky, however, it less susceptible to rust. Should be cut no lower than 1½-inches.
- *DELTA* – Similar to Kentucky Bluegrass and there are no advantages over it. Not quite as dense as Kentucky Bluegrass, but is more erect and stiffer.
- *PARK* – Has very strong seedlings and is similar to Kentucky Bluegrass in all other areas.
- *POA TRIVIALIS* – This is a very fine-textured grass that is a reddish-green color. One of the best growing grasses in wet shady areas. May not do well in high summer heat.

Rye Grasses
Does not produce a really tight, knitting grass. Used as a temporary ground cover in the Southwest.

- *PERENNIAL* – A medium course grass with sparsely set leaves. Does well in most climates and is hard to mow in the summer due to its bunchy growth. Mow at 1½-inches.

- *ANNUAL* – This is a coarser grass than perennial rye and used mostly as a cover for winter grass over a Bermuda grass lawn. Usually contains some perennial rye and dies out in about 1 year. Should be mowed at 1½ inches.
- *REDTOP* - Tends to grow in coarse, weedy clumps in the spring, but will turn into a fine, bent-grass in the late summer. Capable of growing in moist or dry soil conditions and is able to grow well in both shade and full sun. Mow at ¾ to 1-inch.
- *CLOVER* - Has the ability to make its own nitrogen, which means that the grass will require fewer feedings. Grows in a dark green color and is very lush.

SUBTROPICAL GRASSES

Zosia Grasses
These are slow-growing grasses that take about 2-3 years to develop a solid turf surface. Work great for shade areas and hold up very well when dormant.

- *Z. JAPONICA* – A coarse tropical grass that is disease resistant. The grass handles drought conditions well but does require 1-2 years to get a solid covering. The grass grows very well in shade and should be cut to 1½-inches.
- *MEYER* – The blades are very broad at the base and tend to taper to a point. Looks similar to a high grade of Kentucky Bluegrass when matured. Handles drought conditions well and is very disease resistant. Good grass for high traffic lawns, especially with children. Only grows fair in shade and the winter color is brown. Should be mowed ½-inch.
- *Z. MATRELLA* – This is a medium to fine-textured grass and very easy to maintain. It is resistant to heavy wear and is capable of growing in shady areas. Mow to ½ inch.

St. Augustine Grass
Very wide blade, rugged tough grass. Does not need a lot of feeding nor watering to survive. Requires a power mower and turns brown in winter months.

HOW SMOOTH I AM
A lawn bed should be as smooth and flat as possible allowing for a slight pitch to accommodate drainage. A grade that is from 6-10 inches in about 100 feet is not too much. Once the roots have reached their saturation level the water should run off easily and not be allowed to form standing puddles.

NUTRITION FIRST
Before starting a new lawn it is always recommended to work a phosphate fertilizer into the soil. This is an important nutrient to have in the soil, especially for a new lawn. Phosphates do not move into the soil well after the lawn has been planted.

YOU WON'T FAIL IN THE FALL
The best time to plant a new lawn is in the fall, allowing at least 6 weeks of temperature around 50^0-70^0F. This is the preferred time and temperature to guarantee success with a newly planted lawn.

309

DON'T BE A HEEL

When working a newly seeded area, be sure and wear shoes that are flat-soled, tennis sneakers or go barefooted. Never wear shoes with heels since they tend to dig in and leave an indentation that is difficult to remove easily.

SATURATION A MUST

Peat moss is commonly used to cover seeds, however, it does not retain water well. If you do use peat moss, be sure and wet it down and saturate it really well. One successful method is to pre-soak the moss before you apply it to the area. Keep mulch dark with adequate moisture.

DON'T BE A DRAG

One of the more common mistakes people make is to drag a hose across the newly planted area. Make sure that you have a hose that is long enough to do the job.

INDOOR PLANTS

YOU'RE KILLING ME WITH KINDNESS

Over-watering is the cause of most plant failures. Leaves will wilt, turn yellow and drop off. It is easier to revive a plant that has had too little water than to try and save a plant that has been killed from over-watering.

HOW CLEAN I AM

Use an old clean, cotton glove and dip into room temperature water then clean both sides of the leaves.

GETTING POTTED? USE FOAM

Small pieces of foam used in the packaging industry works better than pebbles in the bottom of flowerpots. They don't add excess weight to the pots and tend to retain some of the water more efficiently.

SAVE THE EGGSHELLS

Crushed eggshells should be added to the soil of indoor plants to provide better drainage and some needed trace minerals.

OUTDOOR PLANTS

Many outdoor plants are called "annuals." Annuals are plants that flower, set their seeds and die off. They have a short lifespan and most of their energy goes into producing flowers instead of a hearty root system. They usually grow very quickly and produce a flower the first year they are planted. Biennials are plants that take about 2 years to grow and produce flowers. Many of the annuals and biennials will self sow and keep producing flowers. Perennials are just plants that always continue to self sow and have a different lifespan.

> Flower carpets that have been impregnated with seeds and nutrients are an excellent method of growing annuals.

NAIL THOSE AFRICAN VIOLETS TO THE GROUND
If you plant a few very rusty nails around your African violets, the blossoms will be larger. The plants like a little iron in their diet (I wonder if Geritol® would work).

ISOLATION IS A MUST
When you add a new plant to an existing bed of plants, be sure and place the new plant in isolation for 2-3 weeks before you plant it. Be sure and inspect the plant every 3-4 days to be sure that there are no insects or areas of disease forming before planting it. Even new plants from nurseries can pose a problem.

HELP! MY PLANT IS GOING INTO SHOCK
New plants that have been grown in a greenhouse environment often go into "greenhouse shock." The healthy leaves wilt, there is a tendency to over-water and the plant dies. To avoid greenhouse shock, try placing a plastic bag over the plant for 1-2 weeks and gradually open the bag over the 1-2 week period, just a little each day. The plant will acclimate to the different humidity of its new surroundings.

YUCK! TAP WATER AGAIN
Most of the tap water in the United States contains chlorine. The chlorine is not going to kill the plant but might make it ill. If you allow tap water to remain at room temperature for 24 hours the chlorine will dissipate into the air and the water will be safer for the plants. Cold water also has a tendency to shock plants and room temperature water is best.

I'M THIRSTY, MY POT IS POROUS
If you have plants in clay or ceramic pots, they will need more frequent watering since the pots are porous and causes water to evaporate more quickly. Plastic pots tend to work better if you are using the pot as a hanging pot.

HOE, HOE, BUT NOT TOO DEEP
When you hoe to eliminate perky weeds, be sure and never hoe more than 2 inches deep. Hoeing deep may force weed seeds to germinate, surface hoeing is recommended.

HIGH NOON

The best time to water plants in the summer is high noon since the plants will lose more water during the hot afternoons. In the winter water in the early morning since the plant has all day to lose moisture.

STORING CUTTINGS

If you can't plant cuttings immediately, the best way to store them is to place them into a plastic bag and save them in the vegetable drawer in the refrigerator. Spray a small amount of room temperature water into the bag and seal well. The cuttings should last and still be in good shape for up to 5-7 days.

DON'T SOIL THE SOIL

Never work soil that is too wet or you will damage the soil. When you can squeeze a handful of soil and it crumbles then it is OK to work or till.

OUCH, OUCH, THAT HURTS ME

Never walk back and forth on wet or very damp soil. This will damage the soil by compressing it too much. By compacting the soil you can damage the root system of the plants.

NON-MEDICAL STERILIZER

Potting mixes should be sterilized to kill bacteria and weed seeds. One of the simplest ways to do this is to place the potting mix or compost soil mixture in a clean wheelbarrow. Only place a 2-3 inch layer and cover the layer with plastic bags and leave it in full sunlight for about 8 hours. The mixture should be turned 3 times during this period.

HOLEY, HOLEY

To make it easy to start plants and seeds, just purchase a bag of planting mix or peat and poke holes in the top while the bag is lying on its side. Plant small starter plants or seeds in the holes and punch holes in the bottom for drainage. When the seeds or plants are ready to be planted, just plant the entire bag as is.

DON'T TILT YOUR TILLER

There are a number of tips when using and storing your tiller that will increase its effective life.

- Always idle your tiller on a level surface for 1-2 minutes before you shut it down. If the engine cools evenly it will reduce the chance of warping and allow oil to lubricate all parts.
- Change the oil shortly after you use the tiller while the oil is still warm and any dirt or residues are still in suspension. Residues will settle out after the engine cools down.
- When you store the tiller, make sure you close the fuel shutoff valve all the way to stop gas from seeping into the engine or leak on the floor.
- Make sure you always check the tiller for loose nuts and bolts every time you store it.
- Cleaning any residue when putting the tiller away will increase the life of the tiller and reduce the chances of overheating the gear housing and shaft.

PANTYHOSE INSTEAD OF METAL TIES

Old pantyhose can be cut into narrow strips and used to tie up plants. This works better than green metal or plastic ties. The pantyhose expand as the plant grows.

SHAKE 'EM UP

To plant small seeds such as carrot, radish or celery, just use an empty seasoning container with holes that are the right size for the job.

PASS THE POTATOES

Next time you plant rosebush slips, try inserting the slip into the center of a white potato. The rose slips will take root faster.

ROSEBUSH HOLDERS

The old-fashioned clothespins work great to hold onto rosebushes while you are trimming them.

HEAR YE, HEAR YE, FUNGI HATES CINNAMON

Peonies tend to attract fungi, slime mold and mildew. If you sprinkle some cinnamon around the plants fungi will not grow. The active ingredient in cinnamon that stops the fungi growth is called ortho-methoxyannamaldehyde. Research has proven that fungi will not grow on cinnamon.

DON'T BUY FLOWERING ANNUALS
While those flats of annuals in full bloom look great they will not be the best ones to buy. Most of these flats will have yellowing leaves and will not last very long. The best way to buy these flowers is to buy them when the buds are just appearing.

IVY SOUP ANYONE
If you have some small patches of ivy in a location that you don't want to use weed killer on, just pour boiling water on the ivy and that will kill it.

WEED ERRADICATOR
A claw hammer is ideal for removing small tough weeds. Just place the weed in the claw and pull it out.

OUCH, OUCH, YOU'RE KILLING ME
Ground cover should never be planted in an area that has traffic. Almost all ground cover is too delicate to be walked on. Make sure that you make walkways through ground cover area.

MAIL-ORDER BARE ROOT SHRUBS
Be sure and place any mail-order bare root shrubs in a bucket of cool water overnight before you plant them. Be sure and remove any broken or dead branches.

YOUNG ONES ARE BEST
Best to purchase young, small shrubs. They are much easier to grow and will actually grow more rapidly than larger ones, which will be more expensive as well.

WHAT YOU CAN'T SEE
Some plants are pruned before you purchase them to remove dead or diseased branches. If a plant doesn't look right and there is evidence of recent pruning, it would be best not to purchase it.

GET OUT YOUR SPYGLASS
Be sure and check the roots of any plant you are purchasing to be sure that the root system is adequate and not in a stunted condition for that size plant.

COLD CAN BE YOUR FRIEND
Many plants, trees and shrubs have certain chilling requirements. Many trees and plants need a number of hours below 45°F before their buds may be ready to break dormancy. If the buds do not open in time they will drop off before blossoming. Fruit trees are especially susceptible to this problem in California.

FLOWERING PLANTS THAT PROVIDE NECTAR OR POLLEN
FOR BUGS AND PARASITES OF INSECTS & MITES

Carrot Family	Sunflower Family
Caraway	Blanket Flower
Coriander (cilantro)	Coneflower
Dill	Coreopsis
Fennel	Cosmos
Flowering Ammi	Goldenrod
Queen Ann's Lace	Sunflower
Toothpick Ammi	Tansy

Wild Parsnip	Yarrow
Mustard Family	**Miscellaneous Families**
Basket-of-gold Alyssum	Buckwheat
Sweet Alyssum	Cinquefoil
Yellow Rocket	Milkweeds
Wild Mustard	Phacelia

WEEDS

A weed is really just another plant that is unwanted in a specific area. It has similar characteristics as most plants. Some weeds are actually desired in gardens because of their colors. Many people keep certain weeds as part of their gardens.

IT'S A BIRD, IT'S A PLANE, IT'S A WEED CARRIER
Annual weeds can be carried into your yard by birds, animals, wind and even raindrops. They may also exist in the soil and not be activated unless you disturb them by tilling the soil.

BETTER PULL IT OUT BY THE ROOTS
Perennial weeds must be removed by the roots and pulled out completely or they will easily re-root. They normally have underground runners that run horizontally through the soil. The long taproots must be eliminated.

CATCH THAT RUNNER, IF YOU CAN
Weed runners can be as far as 2-3 feet from the plant. It is necessary to dig deep when trying to get rid of some weeds.

KILL THEM WHILE THEY ARE YOUNG
Weeds should be eliminated while they are young. The longer you wait, the harder it will be. Taproots are the weakest when the plant is young and easy to remove. Don't wait too long or they will develop seeds!

THERE GO THE FLOWERS
Herbicides will kill weeds, however, they will also kill all the other plants and flowers if it gets too close to come into contact with them. Herbicides actually cause the plant to die of starvation by interfering with the plant's ability to produce food.

VINEGAR TO THE RESCUE
Before you try and kill weeds with an herbicide, try using white vinegar on them. This method is much easier on the environment.

THE TOP TEN TAP ROOT WEEDS
1. Bindweed
2. Burdock
3. Wild Carrot
4. Chickory
5. Dandelion
6. Dock
7. Horse Nettle
8. Wild Parsnip

9. Pokeberry
10. Swallow-wort

GARDEN PESTS ASSOCIATED WITH WEEDS		
Armyworms	Crickets	Cutworms
Darkling Beetles	Earwigs	Flea Beetles
Grasshoppers	Lygus Beetles	Snails
Slugs	Stink Bugs	Thrips
Aphids	Leafhoppers	Scale

WEEDS THAT WILL RETURN EVERY YEAR
These weeds have seeds that are capable of returning year after year.
1. Beggar's Tick
2. Chickweed
3. Crabgrass
4. Knotweed
5. Lamb's Quarter
6. Pigweed
7. Ragweed
8. Shepard's Purse
9. Wild Mustard
10. Wild Oats

WEEDS THAT WILL GROW WITH RUNNERS
The runners usually run above ground and may root along the way depending on conditions.
1. Creeping Buttercup
2. Devil's Painted Brush
3. Ground Ivy
4. Milkweed
5. Stinging Nettle
6. Plantain
7. Poison Ivy
8. Quack Grass
9. Thistles

PESTICIDES

There are hundreds of pesticides available on the market and most work very well. The following are some of the more common ones. If you have a pest problem in your garden it is always best to bring a sample of the problem to a gardening professional and get advise as to the specific pesticide and its safe use.

ALCOHOL

Use 70% isopropyl alcohol (rubbing alcohol) to control a number of common pests. Works good on scale infestations, but be sure and test an area before spraying. Best to dilute 1-2 cups of alcohol in 1 quart of water.

ALL-PURPOSE INSECT SPRAY

Grind up 1 whole garlic bulb, 1 small white onion and add 1 teaspoon of cayenne pepper and place the mixture in 1 quart of water. Allow the mixture to stand for 1 hour then strain through a piece of cheesecloth and add 1 tablespoon of liquid dish soap and mix well. Spray on plants and be sure and spray the underneath side of the leaves.

AMMONIA

Mix 1 part ammonia with 7 parts tap water and spray the leaves. Try the mixture on a few leaves to see if any damage will occur first. This spray works well on aphids, fleas, beetles, scales, thrips and whiteflies.

BAKING SODA

When used in a spray bottle, baking soda has fungicidal properties. It will protect the plants as well as eliminate a number of pesky critters. Dissolve 1 teaspoon of baking soda in 1 quart of warm tap water, then add 1 teaspoon of liquid dish soap. When sprayed on this solution will last a long time and keep its effectiveness.

BLEACH

Bleach is excellent for disinfecting garden tools. Bleach should always be used in its diluted form since it is very toxic. Best to use 9 parts cool tap water to 1 part bleach.

BORIC ACID

One of the best baits to control ants is with boric acid. Works great when combined with grape jelly to attract them.

CAYENNE DUST

This hot pepper herb can be used as a dust to repel onion maggots, ants and aphids. It will also discourage most animals from damaging your plants.

CITRUS OILS

Citrus oils obtained from the peels of citrus fruits have chemical properties that tend to kill or discourage certain insects. The active ingredient "limonene" will be on the label of certain products. Some of the insects that are susceptible to the effects of limonene are the leaf-eating caterpillar, potato beetle, fire ants, aphids, mites, flies and wasps. One of the best commercial products that contain citrus oil is Aphid-Mite™.

DIATOMACEOUS EARTH (DE)

This abrasive dust has been used for years to kill common pests. It is composed of fossilized silica shells of specific algae. The sharp needle-like projections in DE penetrate the insect outer shell and kill it by dehydrating it. A light dusting of DE is very effective in controlling aphids, caterpillars, leaf-hoppers, snails, slugs and thrips. Best to wear a dust mask when using DE. One of the problems with DE is that it will cause irritation to all animals and will kill the beneficial insects as well.

FUNGICIDE

Two of the most common are copper and sulfur, which are deadly poisons. They will eliminate the growth of fungal spores. Best to follow the directions of a gardening professional before using any products that contain these fungicides.

GARLIC OIL

When sprayed on plants will kill a number of common insect pests, however, it may also kill a number of beneficial insects. If you use garlic oil with soap added to the spray it eliminates even more of the beneficial insects. Garlic has also been known to damage certain foliages so you might want to test a small area before general spraying.

LIME

Has been used for hundreds of years to control a number of insects. If you do use lime, you must wear a mask to avoid inhaling the dust. Needs to be re-applied after every rain to be effective.

MINERAL OIL

For the best results using mineral oil it should be added to garlic oil or a soap mixture. The oil actually traps the insects, coats their bodies and suffocates them. Has been used for many years on ears of corn to eliminate the problem of corn earworms. Just apply 1-2 drops of mineral oil to the tip of each ear of corn after the silks have wilted to solve the problem.

NICOTINE

Nicotine is extracted from tobacco and is very poisonous. Depending on the concentration used it can kill most soft-bodied insects. If mixed with soapy water it is even more effective. It is used to kill aphids, mealy bugs, scales, fungus gnats and spider mites. Be sure and wear gloves when handling nicotine since it can enter the body through the skin. It is also very harmful to all animals.

SALT

One of the best uses for rock salt (NaCl) has been in the growing of asparagus plants. However, table salt that is iodized is not recommended. Rock salt produced from calcium chloride is not recommended only from sodium chloride (NaCl). Rock salt may be sold as pickling salt. If used, apply about 2 pounds of rock salt per 100 square feet of your asparagus bed.

SOAP SPRAYS

This is an oldy but goody. Simmer a pot of water with shavings of Fels Naptha™ soap. After it has simmered for about 20-30 minutes remove the pot and strain the solution. Allow the mixture to cool before using in a sprayer. Best used on aphids, chiggers, whiteflies, earwigs, mites, scales and flies. Always spray the solution on a few leaves to be sure it is safe for the plants. Doesn't do any good to kill the bugs if you end up killing the plant as well.

STARCH SPRAY

This is another old remedy for a variety of garden pests. A number of starches have been effective over the years such as potato starch dextrin and even all-purpose flour. Just mix 2-3 tablespoons of potato starch or flour in 1 quart of water and to make it more effective, add 2-3 drops of liquid dish soap. Mix well and spray covering the leaves on all sides. The all-purpose flour has been used as a dust and gets very sticky when it becomes damp, trapping the insects.

SULFUR

Sulfur is a very effective protective fungicide and is used both on plants and trees. **Best to wear protective clothing when applying sulfur.** The problem with sulfur is that it may kill the beneficial insects as well as the pests and fungus. Use a sprayer with all plastic parts since sulfur may corrode metal. Instructions for its use can be obtained through your local gardening supply store.

PLANTING

TURN ME OVER AND OVER

The day before you plan on planting any plants, be sure and turn the soil over well. Be sure to also water the soil to allow it to settle.

UNDER A SHADE TREE

Plants in containers should be stored out of the sunlight and in the shade. Make sure they have received adequate water.

THE IDEAL DAY

Planting should be done on a cool, cloudy day if possible. Wind is a problem as well and should be avoided. The best times to plant are before 11AM or after 3PM.

I'M GETTING DIZZY

Staging your new plants is important. They should be placed in the proper location and turned in the proper direction. This is even more important for shrubs since they cannot be moved once they take hold.

GETTING RID OF THE LITTLE GUYS
Make sure that you consider thinning out seedlings to allow more room and the growth of healthier plants.

A SLIPPERY SOLUTION
When planting roses, be sure and add some chopped banana skins to the hole. Banana skins will improve the texture of the soil as well as help the soil to retain moisture.

WHAT A TANGLED WEB WE WEAVE
Before planting roses, be sure and place them into a bucket of water for 1 hour or more so that you will be able to untangle the root ball before planting.

HECK OF A HOLE
The hole that you prepare for the root ball should be about twice the size of the root ball for the best results.

MAN THE LIFEBOATS
If you are going to plant roses in a heavy soil, make sure that you do not add any type of organic matter that tends to retain water. Organic matter tends to draw water out of the moist soil and create a very wet area around the roots. This may cause damage to the root system

FIT FOR A KING
Next time you choose a perennial, check the crown (at the base of the plant) for new growth. Be sure that the crown is in good shape and is not damaged.

WELL I'LL BE WILTED
Perennials should be checked well for any wilting condition, which is usually caused by poor watering or drying out too often. These plants will never do well.

GETTING POTTED FOR TOO LONG A PERIOD
If a plant ahs been in its pot for too long a period it may develop algae, moss, a variety of weeds or liverwort. Don't purchase plants before a thorough inspection.

NOT ALL ITS CRACKED UP TO BE
Be sure when purchasing plants that the container or pot is not damaged and cracked. If this has occurred, the roots may have sustained damage.

SEEDS & SEEDLINGS

TIME FOR A DIP
Before you plant seeds, soak them in warm tap water for about 30 hours to soften the seed coat. This will cause the seed to sprout faster. The preferred method is to place the seeds into an insulated bottle, such as a thermos to keep the water warm for a prolonged period of time.

NOT TOO WARM, NOT TOO COLD, JUST RIGHT
If you are starting seedlings indoors, make sure that the water you give them is at room temperature. Cold tap water may slow the growth of seedlings since it tends to chill the roots.

IT'S TEATIME FOR SEEDS

Very hard seeds may need to be soaked in a container of strong tea for about 8-10 hours before planting. The tannic acid in the tea will soften the seed covering allowing for faster sprouting.

LIGHT-UP YOUR BEANS

Bean will sprouts faster if you warm them by placing them near a 75 watt bulb, which will provide just enough heat to help them sprout. Place the beans in a large jar and wrap the jar in a towel allowing one end to remain open for ventilation.

USE A ROLLING PIN, BUT BE GENTLE

Beet seeds will be easier to germinate if you spread the seeds on a piece of wax paper and roll them lightly with a rolling pin. By slightly crushing the outer husk it allows the seeds to germinate faster.

AVOID PASTEURIZATION FUSS

It is recommended that when you start seeds it is done in a sterilized soil mixture, however, you can use a mixture of sphagnum moss, perlite and vermiculite. The seedling should be transplanted as soon as the first leaves appear since there are no nutrients in the mixture.

GENTLY DOES IT, WHEN PLANTING SEEDS

A mistake many people make when planting seeds is planting the seeds too deep with a heavy layer of soil. Most people use a trowel or their hands to cover the seeds resulting in too heavy a layer. Try using a soft bristle paintbrush to brush the soil over the seeds and they will germinate faster.

SAVE THE OLD GRAPEFRUIT HALVES

One of the best seeds holders is half an orange or grapefruit that has been eaten. These make excellent containers to start seeds. Just fill them with soil and plant the seed; then place the holder in the ground when the seeds germinate. The holder will rot away leaving nutrients in the ground around the seed.

JUST ENOUGH HEAT

For fast germination, try placing your seed trays on top of your water heater. There will be just enough heat to speed up germination without harming the seeds.

PREVENTING DRIED OUT SEEDS

Seeds in flats tend to dry out very quickly. To avoid the problem, just place the seed flat into a plastic bag and check it at regular intervals to be sure that there is not too much moisture in the bag, which may cause mold or disease.

PLANT THEM OR SEAL THEM UP

Most vegetable seeds will last for 3-5 years if stored properly. Place them into well-sealed jar with ½ cup of flour or non-fat dry milk to absorb any excess moisture that might still creep in. Pre-packaged silica works well in the jars.

FORGET THE GROW LIGHTS

The new fluorescent light bulbs that have become popular in the last 2-3 years will work just as well. They are less expensive to operate and will last about 10,000 hours. These new lights provide the blue end of the light spectrum, which is what the plants desire.

EASY DOES IT WHEN WATERING

When watering newly planted seeds and seedlings, be sure and water gently so that you will not damage or uproot them.

MINI-SEEDS

If you are planting seeds that are as fine as dust, just broadcast them over a smooth-surfaced bed and then press them gently into the soil with a float. They should not be covered with mulch.

SEEDLINGS NEED TO BE PRICKED-OUT

Transplanting seedlings from a seed flat to a larger flat is called "**pricking out.**" This step is very important in assisting the small seedling to better develop their root and leaf system before being plants in the garden. As soon as the seedling has two sets of leaves they should be pricked out. Make sure when you remove the seedling you do not injure the delicate roots.

WAIT FOR THE CLOUDS

When setting out newly transplanted seedlings the best weather would be cloudy or overcast days. When that is not possible then the late afternoon would suffice. It is best not to place newly transplanted seedlings into the direct sunlight until they have a few hours to recover from the transplanting shock.

WATER IN THE HOLE

When you prepare a hole for a transplanted seedling, be sure and place water in the bottom of the hole, especially if the soil is very dry.

FOLLOW THE INSTRUCTIONS

When planting seeds, it is always best to follow the instructions to the letter. There are many variables when planting seeds and not all seeds should be planted in the same manner.

SOIL PREPARATION

There are only 5 main soil types: these include silt, limestone, clay, sand and peat. They all contain a unique blend of minerals and nutrients. The proportions of these essential elements will vary, however, even in a small area. Managing these various soil types will determine when you cultivate the area as well as the type of plants that will grow there successfully.

SILT
When silt is wet, it tends to pack down turning it into a cold, heavy and badly drained soil, very similar to clay in consistency. Manure tends to help improve the consistency.

SAND
Has the tendency to warm up fast in the spring, which makes it easier to cultivate earlier than most other soils.

CLAY
Very heavy and cold and when compacted it becomes hard. Will not drain easily and is very difficult to work when wet. Usually a very fertile soil that is high in nutrients.

PEAT
Always a dark color and has a high degree of organic matter and nutrients. Must have some type of drainage and usually needs liming.

LIMESTONE
Limestone is a dry soil with a pale color usually with many small stones. Loses nutrients very quickly. Not good for deep-rooted plants.

SALTY SOIL, A REAL PROBLEM
In the west, salty soil can prevent germination or stunt plants that are already growing. This salinity condition; is usually caused by too much salt in the fertilizers used, the water or added chemicals.

PEST PROBLEMS ASSOCIATED WITH SOIL & NUTRIENT CONDITIONS	
SOIL & NUTRIENT CONDITION	PEST
High Organic soil content	Symphylans, springtails, cutworms, wireworms, green fruit beetles
Poor decomposition of garden debris	Squash bugs, symphylans, springtails, cutworms, wireworms, green fruit beeltles
Poor decomposition of manure	Root maggots, green fruit beetles

Dry, dusty soil conditions	Mites
Sandy soil with poor water retention	Root knot nematode
High nitrogen content	Aphids

FRUIT TREES

THE WINTER SECRET IS MULCH
The colder the winter, the tougher it will be on fruit trees, especially if they are very young. The secret to helping the trees through the winter is to place about 4 inches of mulch around the base of the tree in late fall after you have seen the ground freeze up. The addition of mulch will keep the trees from freezing and re-thawing too many times. The mulch also helps retain the loss of soil moisture.

CALLING TOM SAWYER & HUCKLEBERRY FINN
If the sun becomes strong in early spring, the bark of fruit trees will not respond well and bark injury can take place, especially if there is a very cold night after the heat. If you paint the trunk and main limbs with a white exterior latex paint in the fall, the paint will reflect the sunlight and heat just enough to prevent bark damage.

BE KIND TO OLD FRUIT TREES
Fruit trees, especially old apple trees that have had their best days and are in need of extensive pruning to place them back into production can be a problem. If you prune them too heavily it may kill them off. However, if you space the pruning over a 3-year period you will be amazed at the results.

PROTECTION, A MUST
Best to place metal or cement edgings around your trees to protect them from lawnmowers. Best to hand trim around trees. Even a lawn edger with plastic rope is capable of damaging the bark of most trees.

DON'T USE ANTIFREEZE
Newly planted evergreen trees can be severely damaged by winter temperatures. The best method of protecting them is to staple burlap bags to stakes about 6-inches from each tree. Tie them up well or the weight of snow will break them.

STAKE 'EM IN GOOD

When planting bare-rooted trees, be sure and drive a stake about 18 inches into ground. Be sure that the stake is at least twice as thick as the trees stem it should be about 1/3 of the way up the trees trunk. The stake must be solid in the ground.

MOVING IN THE WIND

Newly planted and staked trees should only be anchored at the base. This allows the tree to move with the wind, which results in a stronger and thicker base and root system. Never use wire or a plastic twine that has the tendency to cut into the tree.

WATERING

When talking to a gardening professional, there is one comment regarding watering that I will always remember. When you water, *WATER THOROUGHLY – AND INFREQUENTLY.* Over-watering is one of the biggest problems most plants and gardens face.

NOT TOO SHALLOW

If you want a good deep healthy root system, then you need to water deep. Roots will develop deep if there is adequate water, good soil and nutrients to feed on.

A LITTLE WATER DOES NOT GO A LONG WAY

Many people tend to water just enough to cover the ground. Watering needs to be adequate and allowed to percolate deep enough to do some good.

GOING DOWN

Some plants are capable of developing root systems from 2-10 feet, which requires that the water sit on top of the ground and gradually enter the soil. Grapes and tomato plants can have 10-foot deep root systems if watered properly.

WATER, WATER, EVERYWHERE

A 100 square foot garden will require 125 gallons of water to soak down 2 feet. If there is a loam layer then 190 gallons are required and if you have clay soil you will need 330 gallons to water the same area.

HELP! MY WATER IS RUNNING AWAY

Depending on how dry the soil is you are watering, the water runoff may be significant. If you have heavy soil, the penetration will be very slow and you can lose 50% of the water. One of the ways to overcome the problem is to aerate the soil by spiking.

GETTING GYPED CAN HELP

Adding gypsum to the soil can help with water penetration. You can add as much as 10 pounds per 100 square feet of garden area.

I'M CHOKING TO DEATH

Over-watering can fill the interspaces around the plant roots and actually cut off the plants oxygen supply. If the respiration of the plant is reduced or cut off it will affect the growth of the plant and can even kill the plant.

I'M BEING ATTACKED
When too much watering is done and the soil becomes low in oxygen, certain bacteria and fungus can become active and damage or kill the plant.

TIMING IS EVERYTHING
The days between watering, is dependent on the depth of the root system. Your gardening shop should have a chart telling you the root depth of your plants. The following is a chart on how many days to allow between watering:

	Sandy	Loam	Clay
Shallow-rooted	4-6	7-10	10-12
Medium-rooted	7-10	10-12	15-20
Deep-rooted	15-20	20-28	30+

DIGGING A MOAT
The most effective method of watering trees is to dig a small basin around the tree to hold water and allow it to seep into the ground at its own pace. Some plants will also do better using this basin method of water retention. Make sure that you do not scrape away the plants surface soil to make the basin. Basins around full-grown trees should be at least 9-12 inches deep.

SOIL SOAKERS
One of the best methods of slow watering to achieve the best penetration is to use a soil soaking hose. This hose has small holes and only allows a small amount of water to be released.

FURROW WATERING
Scooping out the soil between rows and leaving a furrow for the water is an excellent method of watering. Your furrows should be wide and narrow for the best results. Make the furrows before the plant roots develop or you may damage the plant.

IT'S RAINING, IT'S POURING
One of the best methods of watering is with an overhead sprinkler system. It will spray water evenly over an area. A fine mist spray is recommended, which allows for gradual water penetration. If you use this method, make sure you only water in the morning so that the leaves are dry before nighttime.

SOFT WATER, NOT THE BEST
In some areas of the country, especially the Southwest, the water is soft and contains chemicals that may affect the growth of certain plants. Discuss this problem with your gardening store if you have soft water coming into your sprinkling system.

LEAF PROBLEMS

Leaves stippled with yellow
This is usually caused by spider mites who feed on the underneath side of the leaf. When they suck sap, the result is a yellow flecking. Spraying the underneath sides of the leaves 2-3 times a day for 2-3 days usually solves the problem.

Leaves yellowed
Usually caused by whiteflies, which feed on the sap from the leaves. They tend to release a "honeydew" substance, which is sticky and encourages a leaf fungus to grow. This fungus looks black and the best cure is to spray the leaves with insecticidal soap every 3 days for about 2 weeks. Spray the underneath side of the leaves well.

Leaves with large ragged holes
These are usually the result of hungry snails and slugs. Sprinkling diatomaceous earth or cinders around the plants will stop them in their slimy tracks. Shallow dishes of beer will also make them drunk and kill the little critters.

Leaves with a black coating
A black mold caused by a fungus, which lives on the sticky substance released by aphids and mealybugs. Best to deal with the pests that produce the sticky, sweet substance that the fungus lives on.

Leaves with powdery white areas
This area is covered with powdery mildew in the form of fungal strands and spores. This is usually an upper leaf problem and causes some yellowing. This problem can spread to other plants if not handled quickly. Thinning out the area and keep the leaves as dry as possible by watering from below.

Leaves that are growing poorly and are greenish-yellow
Leafhoppers carry the disease and spread it through their eating habits. Flowers may be deformed or never bloom. All flowers that do bloom usually turn a yellow-green. Remove any infected plants and see your garden shop for a spray to eradicate them. They tend to flourish in areas that are over-watered.

Leaves spotted and buds turning dark
This problem is caused by plant bugs with red mottling on their wings. They normally prefer the ornamentals and can be controlled by dusting with the chemical rotenone.

Leaves with spots
Usually caused by fungi or bacteria. There are many varieties that cause leaf spots and if not stopped will eventually spread to the entire leaf. The infected leaves need to be discarded and the area thinned as much as possible.

Leaves rolled over
The problem of rolled over leaves is caused by the leafroller caterpillar. One of the best methods of eliminating the problem is to open the leaf and remove the culprit and then escort them out of the garden with extreme prejudice.

PLANTING IN POTS

THE RIGHT POT MAKES ALL THE DIFFERENCE

If the pot will remain outside year round, the pot should not be made out of terracotta or clay, especially if you live an area that freezes.

YOUR POT MAY BE THIRSTY

Many pots are porous and may drink up a lot of the water you are providing for your plants. Be aware that these plants may need more frequent watering. Clay or cement pots are guilty of high water consumption.

GETTING POTTED IN PLASTIC

Plastic pots are inexpensive and very lightweight. They also do not drink water like the clay or cement pots. Fiberglass pots are also becoming very popular.

WOODPECKER CHOW

Wooden planters and boxes are ideal for planters. Be sure, however, that the wood has been pressure treated, if so they will be a better quality and last longer.

GETTING WIRED AND FRAMED

Plant holders made from wire lined with spaghum moss are excellent planters and do not require special watering methods. Best to spray these and not just pour water in. The moss does not absorb the water very fast. The moss will also take water from the plant and you need to be sure that the moss is good and damp.

DON'T GET SOILED

Be sure and use potting mix instead of regular soil when planting in a plant container. The soil from the garden does not drain well and if brought indoors, the warmth may cause different diseases to get a start.

THE MAD SCIENTIST

Make your own potting soil for potted plants by using one part perlite, one part peat moss and one part vermiculite. Always add a fertilizer to a potting soil. Sterilized organic compost is ideal as an additive to potting mix.

ROCK'IN THE POT

A layer of small pebbles or rocks should be placed in the bottom of the pot to allow for drainage and to keep the potting mix in the pot. To avoid making a large pot too heavy, try using Styrofoam peanuts in the bottom.

YOUR POT MUST BE HOLY

Never purchase a pot if it doesn't have a drainage hole in the bottom. When you place a plate under the hole, be sure that the plate does not touch the hole and cover it. There should be a small distance between the hole and the plate.

THE DEEPER, THE BETTER

Perennials should be planted in deep pots for the best results. The root systems need all the room they can get. This will also help them make it through the winter months.

IT'S MOVING DAY

If plants in pots are not doing well in the location you chose for them, don't be afraid to move them around and try different sites.

DRIP PANS NEED CARE

Water in a drip pan cannot be left in the pan or it may damage the root system of the plant. One-inch of water, left for a week can permanently damage the roots. Potted plants should be checked at least 3-4 times a week.

IT'S FEEDING TIME AT THE POT

When feeding potted plants, it is always better to underfeed than to overfeed them. Use either a water-soluble fertilizer (one that dissolves in water) or a quality dry fertilizer. Watering washes away the fertilizer so if you can find a time-release fertilizer it would be the best way to go. Wait at least two to three weeks before feeding a newly planted potted plant.

COMING IN FROM THE COLD

Potted plants should be brought in the house in the fall before the first freeze to keep them safe. If possible place them in a warm, sunny location, especially the annuals and herbs.

BIGGGG OUTSIDE POTS

If you have big pots that can't go in the house, you need to remove the plant and soil and clean them out well. The pots should be covered with plastic and boards to keep the snow out.

APPENDIX A

BACILLUS THURINGIENSIS (Bt)

This is a bacterial pathogen that is used to control pest larvae. Its safety has been proven with humans and animals as well as plants and trees. The names it is marketed under include Dipel™, Thuricide™ Biotrol™. You can purchase it as a wettable dust or as an emulsion. While it is stable when stored it will lose potency in sunlight. It is available in most garden supply stores or through mail order. Pellet bait is also available and marketed under the names Soilserv™ and Bacillus Bait™. It is approved for use in California and is widely used on an assortment of vegetables and fruits.

GARDEN PESTS CONTROLLED BY Bt

CROP	GARDEN PEST
Almond	Peachtree Borer
Alfalfa	Alfalfa Caterpillar
Apple Tree	Codling Moth Worm, Tent Caterpillar Fall Webworm, Eyespotted Bud Moth, Apple rust mite, Tentiform Leafminer, Winter Moth and Redbanded Leafroller
Artichoke	Artichoke Plume Moth
Castor Bean	Castor Semi-Looper
Celery	Celery Looper, Cabbage Looper
Citrus	Anise Swallowtail
Corn	Corn Earworm, European Corn Borer
Cotton	Cotton Leafworm, Cotton Leaf, Perforator, Bollworm
Crucifers	Cabbageworm, Diamondback Moth, Cabbage Looper
Grape	Grape Leafroller, Western Grapeleaf Skeletonizer
Lettuce	Corn Earworm, Tobacco Budworm
Orange	Fruit Tree Leafroller, Orangedog
Peach	Peachtree Borer
Stored Grain Crops	Variety of Insects
Tomatoes	Tomato Hornworm, Tobacco Hornworm, Cabbage Looper, Tomato Fruitworm
Trees (General)	Fall Cankerworm, Spring Cankerworm, California Oakworm, Fruit Tree Leafroller, Gypsy Moth, Linden Loopers, Spruce Budworm, Winter Moth. Etc.

GENERAL INFORMATION REGARDING
PREPARATION OF PLANT SPRAYS

- Almost all sprays should be re-applied after it rains.

- Soap is often recommended to help the spray stick to the plants or the insects.

- The majority of plant oil extracts will act as a contact poison on all insects, however, the insects must be covered by the spray.

- When preparing the sprays be sure that direct sunlight does not hit the liquid since sunlight will break down the spray and reduce its effectiveness.

- Be sure and test a small area of any plant you are going to spray to be sure that the spray will not damage the plant.

- The preferred time of day to spray is the evening hours, the later the better.

APPENDIX C

PLANTS THAT REPEL PESTS

PEST	PLANT
Ants & Aphids	Pennyroyal, spearmint, tansy, southernwood
Aphids	All of the above as well as garlic, chives, onions, coriander, anise,
Armyworm	Bear hops, mescal, coral bean Nasturtium, petunia
Asparagus Beetle	Tomato
Bean leafroller	Larkspur, Spanish dagger
Borer	Garlic, tansy, onion
Cabbage Maggot	Mint, tomato, rosemary, hemp, sage
Cabbage Moth	Mint, hyssop, rosemary, thyme, sage southernwood, hemp, wormwood, celery, catnip, nasturtium
Cabbageworms	Turkey mullein
Carrot Fly	Rosemary, sage, wormwood, black salsify, alliums, coriander
Chinch Bug	Soy beans, false indigo
Codling Moth	American wisteria, common oleander
Codling Moth (larvae)	Black Indian hemp
Colorado Potato Beetle	Green beans, horseradish, dead nettle, flax, catnip, coriander, nasturtium, tansy
Corn Borer (larvae)	Manroot, wild cucumber
Cucumber Beetle (spotted or striped)	Tansy, radish, buffalo gourd, false indigo
Cutworm	Tansy
Diamondback Moth	Rayless chamomile
Flea Beetle	Wormwood, mint, catnip
Fruit Tree Moth	Southernwood
Gopher	Castor bean
Grasshoppers	Chinaberry tea
Japanese Beetle	Garlic, larkspur, tansy, rue, Germanium, dwarf or red buckeye
Leafhopper	Petunia, geranium
Melonworm	Canadian fleabane

Mexican Bean Beetle	Marigold, potato, rosemary, petunia, summer savory, California buckeye Chinese wingnut
Mice	Mint
Mites	Onion, garlic, chives
Mole	Spurge, castor bean, mole plant, squill
Nematode (eelworm)	Marigold (African & French), salvis, dahlia, calendula, asparagus
Pea Aphids	Balsamroot, Sour sop
Plum Curculio	Garlic
Rabbit	Allium family
Rose Chafer	Geranium, petunia, onion
Slug (snail)	Prostrate rosemary, wormwood
Squash Bug	Tansy, nasturtium, catnip
Striped Pumpkin Beetle	Nasturtium
Tomato Hornworm	Borage, marigold, opal basil
Whitefly	Nasturtium, marigold, nicandra
Wireworm	White mustard, buckwheat, woard
Woolly Aphid	Tung-oil tree

SUPPLIERS OF BENEFICIAL INSECTS
AND MICROBIALS

Ringer Corporation
9959 Valley View Rd.
Minneapolis, MN 55344
(800) 654-1047
Full line of products

Natural Pest Control Co.
8864 Little Creek Rd.
Orangevale, CA 95662
Mosquito fish

ARBICO
P.O. Box 4247
Tucson, AZ 85738
(800) 505-BUGS

Pest Management Supply
P.O. Box 938
Amherst, MA 01004
Pheromones

BioChem Products
Box 4090
Kansas City, MO 64101
Bt and Bti

Jungle Rain
(619) 436-6605

Deer Off
(800) Deer-Off

Beneficial Insectary
14751 Oak Run Rd.
Oak Run, CA 96069
(916) 472-3715
Beneficial insects

BioLogic
P.O. Box 1
Willow Hill, PA 17271
(717) 349-2749
Nematodes

Beneficial Insects, Inc.
P.O. Box 40634
Memphis, TN
Beneficial insects

Abbott Laboratories
1400 Sheridan Rd.
N. Chicago, IL 60064
Bt for mosquitoes

Bronner's Pure CastileSoap
Box 28
Escondido, CA 92025
Peppermint soap

RINCON-VITOVA
P. O. Box 1555
Ventura, CA 93002
(800) 643-5407
Insects of all types

Tanglefoot Co.
314 Straight Ave.
Grand Rapids, MI 49504

CATALOGS OF PEST CONTROL PRODUCTS

Gardener's Supply
128 Intervale Road
Burlington, VT 05401

Harmony Farm Supply
3244 Gravenstein Hwy North
Sebastopol, CA 95472
9731

Natural Gardening Co.
17 San Anselmo Ave.
San Anselmo, CA 94960

Solutions
P.O. Box 6878
Portland, OR 97228-6878

Maag Agrochemicals Inc.
5699 Kings Hwy.
Vero Beach, FL 32961-6430
Fire ant baits

GOPHER TRAPS

Guardian Trap Co.
P.O. Box 1935
San Leandro, CA 94577

PLANT NETTING

Orchard Supply Co.
P.O. Box 956
Sacramento, CA 95805

SLUG & SNAIL TRAPS

Cedar Pete Inc.
P.O. Box 969
Mt. Shasta, CA 96067

Gurney's
110 Capital St.
Yankton, SD 57079

Mellinger's
2310 W. South Range Rd.
North Lima, OH 44452-

Walt Nick's Garden Talk
P.O. Box 433
Topsfield, MA 01983

Unique Insect Control
5504 Sperry Dr.
Citrus Heights, CA 95621

Bat Conservation Intern.
P.O. Box 162603
Austin, TX 78716-2603
Bat house plans

Joseph B. Cook
11508 Keith Dr.
Whittier, CA 90606

Animal Repellants Inc.
P.O. Box 999
Griffin, GA 30224

Brucker Snail Barrier Co.
9369 Wilshire Blvd.
Beverly Hills, CA 90210

SCARY BALLOONS

Rid-A-Bird Inc.
P.O. Box 436
Wilton, IA 52778

FERRET SCENT

Bio-Pest Control
Box 401347
Brooklyn, NY 11240

ULTRASOUND

The Monadnock Co.
P.O. Box 189
Dedham, MA 02026

GLUE BOARDS

J.T. Eaton & Co.
1393 Highland Rd.
Twinsburg, OH 44087

MOLE TRAPS

Nash Mole Trap Co.
5716 East "S" Ave.
Vicksburg, MI 49097-9990

SECRET BUG REPELLANT

When you are out-of-doors and the bugs are sure to bother you there is an herb that works to repel insects and even some animals. This herb solution has been around for hundreds of years and is easy to use.

The herb is anise, which you have probably heard about when making licorice. However, anise has chemical properties that make it one of the best natural bug deterrents that anyone has found.

Anise oil is available in all health food stores and you may also be able to purchase it through your local pharmacy, agricultural or garden supply house. Fisherman and hunters swear by anise oil and those in the know will not go on a hunting or camping trip without it.

One of the best ways to use the anise oil is to add a small amount to the clothes you will be wearing on the camping trip. Place the oil into the wash cycle so that it mixes with the soapsuds. This will place the oil into the clothing.

Anise will repel almost all bugs, especially houseflies, gnats, mosquitoes, green bottle flies and black blowflies.

To make a commercial bug repellant more effective and make it last longer: just add a few drops to the bottle and shake it up. Many people prefer this since many of the bug repellants have a more pleasant scent.

If anise seed is given to dogs it will make them more affectionate and may be used by breeding kennels. Anise is a love potion for dogs. If you encounter a dog and the dog licks your clothing that has been washed in anise oil, they will not be aggressive and be very affectionate.

GLOSSARY

Bacillus Thuringiensis (Bt)
The most widely used bacterial pesticide. *Bacillus thuringiensis* is a microbe that will infect most species of caterpillar. May be purchased under the names of Biotrol™, Dipel™ or Thuricide™. Bt will not harm plants, animals or humans and most beneficial insects. Bt is very selective and for the most part only affects the bad bugs.

Bti
This is a special strain of Bt that only affects the larvae of mosquitoes and black flies.

BORIC ACID
Formulated from boron and is similar to borax. Boric Acid is one of the safest methods of killing cockroaches and other insect pests. **Poisonous if ingested by humans.**

COMPOST
Composed of decaying plant matter, which has decomposed sufficiently to be a good source of plant food and may be used as a fertilizer. It is also a major component of forest soil. Other names may be humus or leaf mold.

DIATOMACEOUS EARTH (DE)
A mined mineral product; consisting of fossilized one-celled diatoms. Its sharp silica edges puncture the bugs outer shell and cause death by dehydration. The product will not affect birds when they eat the insects. DE will not kill earthworms.

HERBICIDE
These are usually petroleum-based products that stop plant growth and are used for weed and grass abatement. There is a new group of herbicides that are plant specific.

LARVAE
Stage in the life cycle of some insects that occurs between the egg and pupae stages. Normally, it takes the form of a soft-bodied caterpillar, grub or maggot and sometimes referred to as the worm stage.

LIME
Substance: that can supply calcium to the soil and plants while neutralizing acidic conditions. Very effective in sprays to control or kill many pests. Can be used to change the pH of the soil to make it more alkaline. Other forms include quicklime or hydrated lime. Lime draws water out of insects and causes them to dehydrate.

MICROBIALS
These are natural occurring microscopic organisms that can be found in the environment and can be produced on a large scale.

MILKY SPORE DISEASE
This is the common name for B*acillus popilliae,* which is a naturally occurring bacterium that kills the Japanese beetles and other beetle pests. It is placed into the soil and the grubs eat the bacterium, which turns their clear blood milky and kills them. May be harmful to fish so it would be best to keep it away from fish ponds and lakes.

Nc NEMATODE
An organism: that lives in the soil and is microscopic in size. It is worm-like and comes in several strains. They will feed and reproduce inside insects and eventually kill them. There are bad nematodes that attack and kill plants.

NEEM
Neem™ is produced from the margosa tree, which is an evergreen tropical tree that has insecticidal properties.In the United States the tree only grows in Florida and California. This is one wood termites will not eat. There are about 150 insects that are repelled by the extracts of this tree. It can be purchased under the name Margosan-O™ in most garden shops.

NICOTINE
Can be purchased and used as a dust or a spray can be made from the tobacco plant instead of using cigarettes. This is the most toxic pesticide that is sold for home use. The least toxic form is the nicotine sulfate form. Best to forget about using nicotine since if not used properly may poison many beneficial insects and even an animal or two.

NPV
Nuclear polyhedrosis virus is an insect pathogen that has been registered for a limited number of pests and causes a disease process to occur. It is a microscopic organism or microbe.

NYMPH
This is a stage in the life cycle of a number of insects between the egg stage and adult. The life cycle of insects with a nymph stage is called incomplete metamorphosis since there is no pupae or cocoon stage.

ORGANIC
The most natural method of insect control: utilizing the least dangerous methods or chemicals to control insects. This method may employ many homemade sprays and remedies.

PUPAE
This is a stage in the life cycle of a number of insects between the larvae and adult stages. It is usually inactive in the cocoon or a hard shell found in the soil.

PYRETHRUM
Produced from the dried flowers of the daisy plant *Chrysanthemum cinerariifolium*, which is mainly grown in Africa and is the only chrysanthemum plant with the effective pest control affects. Was used against body lice for hundreds of years. Do not purchase pyrethrum if it is combined with any other pesticide. The plant has been known to cause allergic reactions in susceptible individuals.

This is a potent stomach poison that affects insects and is prepared from the extracts of the tropical plants derris and cube.

ROTENONE
Produced from the root of the Derris Tree or the cube root. Has a low toxicity level for humans and animals and shown to be very effective against all soft-bodied insects, leaf rollers, spiders, snails, ticks and mites. Do not use around ponds or lakes since it may affect fish. Wear a mask and goggles. When using against bees it is best to apply after the sun goes down when bees are the least active. Do not mix with alkaline water for the best results.

RYANIA
A natural insecticide that is safe to use around humans and pets. Produced from the ryania plant that is native to Trinidad and is a relative of the tobacco plant. Has the effect of incapacitating the insect's ability to eat and they starve to death. Best used on caterpillars, codling moths, spiders Japanese beetles, thrips, moths and fleas.

Ryania is available as Triple-Plus™, which is a formulation that contains ryania, rotenone and pyrethrum. It is applied as either a dust or wettable powder. The other product that is available is R-50™, which contains 50% ryania and surfactants with clay.

SABADILLA
Produced from the South American lily it is an organic pesticide dust that has been in use since the sixteenth century. The plant has also been used to lower blood pressure. It does kill a wide range of pests, however, it is toxic to toads and bees. **This is the most toxic pesticide to humans and animals.** It is effective against grasshoppers, codling moth larvae, armyworms, European corn borer, silkworms, aphids, cabbage loopers, melonworm, chinch bugs, webworm, greenhouse leaftier and the harlequin bug.

SILICA AEROGEL
Has the ability to dehydrate the bugs by absorbing moisture from the bug's outer surface. The particles in the gel have the ability to absorb hundreds of times their weight in moisture.

SULFUR

This is one of the oldest known pesticides: even the Egyptians used it to fumigate their granaries. Should be used when the temperature is over 70°F and under 90°F for the best results. A powder form is now available for dusting plants. Should not be used within 2 months of spraying horticultural oils.

TANGLFOOT

Sticky substance produced from castor oil gum residues and vegetable waxes.

TRICHOGRAMMA

This is a very small insect that lays its eggs inside other insect's eggs and causing the host egg to die.